Letters from Kabul

1966–1968

A MEMOIR

BY

JANICE MINOTT

Order this book online at www.trafford.com/06-3108 or email orders@trafford.com

Most Trafford titles are also available at major online book retailers.

The epigraph from Jalaluddin Rūmī is from Coleman Barks, *The Illuminated Rumi*, copyright 1997 by Coleman Barks and Michael Green, published by Broadway Books, a division of Bantam Doubleday Dell Publishing Group, Inc.

The teaching story described in Chapter Seventeen has also been recounted by Gurumayi Chidvilasananda. See "Blaze the Trail of Equipoise and Enter the Heart, the Divine Splendor: Siddha Yoga Message for the Year 1995," in *Sādhanā of the Heart: A Collection of Talks on Spiritual Life by Gurumayi Chidvilasananda. Siddha Yoga Messages for the Year Volume I: 1995–1999*, pp. 19–20. South Fallsburg, NY: SYDA Foundation, copyright 2006.

Front-cover photo of the author by Walter P. Blass.
Frontispiece photo of Kuchi nomads on the move was a gift to the author while in Afghanistan, original photographer unknown.
Photo on page 362, The ancient arch at Qalah Bist, by Walter P. Blass.
Back-cover photo on the author by Susan Abeloff.
Cover design by Cheryl Crawford.
Book design by Cheryl Crawford and Denton Lesslie.

Note for Librarians: A cataloguing record for this book is available from Library and Archives Canada at www.collectionscanada.ca/amicus/index-e.html

Printed in Victoria, BC, Canada.

ISBN: 978-1-4251-1349-0

 **Trafford** PUBLISHING™ www.trafford.com

North America & international
toll-free: 1 888 232 4444 (USA & Canada)
phone: 250 383 6864 ♦ fax: 250 383 6804 ♦ email: info@trafford.com

The United Kingdom & Europe
phone: +44 (0)1865 722 113 ♦ local rate: 0845 230 9601
facsimile: +44 (0)1865 722 868 ♦ email: info.uk@trafford.com

10 9 8 7 6 5 4 3 2 1

Out Beyond Ideas of
Wrong-Doing & Right-Doing
There is a field
I'll meet you there

— JALALUDDIN RŪMĪ,
born 1207 in Balkh, Afghanistan

For Christopher, Gregory, and Kathryn,
and to all my guides and teachers who have illumined the way.

With special gratitude to the two great luminaries,
Baba Muktananda and Gurumayi Chidvilasananda,
whose presence in my later years has made all the difference.

ACKNOWLEDGMENTS

First of all, I wish to acknowledge that I don't believe I would have been able to live my story but for the strength and courage I derive from my Maine upbringing. Having grown up as I did before World War II in that northeast largely undeveloped corner of the country, I found much about the Afghan character strangely familiar: rugged independence, initial suspicion of outsiders, and finally an acceptance and friendship as firm as our rock-ribbed coast or their rugged mountains. I discovered there is a strength rooted in my soul as deep as that of the century oak under which I grew up. Likewise, there was an endurance I recognized in the people I met in Afghanistan born of almost unbelievable hardships and isolation.

This book has been gestating a long time. The letters only began to reappear thirty-seven years after I wrote the first ones, many of them having been lovingly saved by my dear friend and former neighbor, Phyllis Crowe, who moved back to Canada many years ago.

I began to polish my writing skills long before that. In 1998 I was seventy-three and increasingly aware of so many stories from my past wanting to take shape. During my annual summer visit back to Maine that year, I began to work with Joan Hunter, an extraordinary writing teacher. She had an unusual approach of having us write to baroque music — since it has the power to awaken our alpha state.

During my first workshop, an image of my great-grandmother, Octavia Minott, surfaced. She was a sea captain's wife, and I saw her standing at the railing of her husband's ship. He took her on only one voyage before leaving her ashore for long years at a time. I had ever been curious about her reason for taking her own life. I also felt a connection. I inherited her gold jewelry and a certain physical likeness, but I made an early determination not to be left ashore, as she had been, when it came time to embark on adventures.

Joan encouraged me, saying she felt Octavia wanted me to tell her story. When Phyllis Crowe returned my Kabul letters in 2002, Joan was the first person I showed the initial manuscript to. "This is your voice," she said, and affirmed that my story was the story Octavia had not been able to live.

My family has been there from the beginning: ex-husband Walter and three children, Kathryn, Christopher, and Gregory Blass. We lived the story told in the letters together, and they have supported me with their interest in sharing it and their willingness to coach me in producing the manuscript on the computer. Since Chris lives nearby, he is the one most frequently called upon and has earned the title of "tech support." Walter has supplied many photographs, as well as letters I wrote to his family, to Dr. Gloria, our children's pediatrician, and to a Quaker friend whom I have called Isabelle.

There have been many helpers with the book. Early on there was Tasa Faronii, proprietor of the no-longer-with-us Oracle Bookstore in Liberty, New York — who initially suggested that I write additional pieces from the person I am today to fill in some gaps in my story. These appear with the dateline *Upstate New York*.

In 2004 I rode the train to New Mexico to attend a writer's workshop with Martin Prechtel, author of several books including *Secrets of the Talking Jaguar* and *Long Life Honey in the Heart*, which I have read more than once. During my last night there, I dreamed I was nursing a baby. When I shared the dream, Martin said, "Oh, you're writing a little book." It has turned out to be rather larger, but I have striven to keep in mind his oft-emphasized instruction to "break the rocks of literalism."

And then, miraculously, there was the appearance over the horizon of my editor, Ellen Porter, and her team: Cheryl Crawford, designer, and Cynthia Briggs, copy editor. All these ladies I refer to as "The Goddesses." They bring with them the years of experience needed to bring this project to closure.

Ellen first went on a rampage to eliminate my parenthetic remarks, saying, "It's as if you're whispering." What a difference that has made in me and in my writing. Her suggestion of having my children write their own experiences added another dimension to the book, one that gladdened this mother's heart. As someone outside the experience I lived, she has been instrumental in opening my eyes to how transforming it truly was for all of us.

My appreciation to others who have read, made suggestions, and encouraged me along the way: Susan Corkey, Christine Downing, Jo Anne Garreffa, Christel Henning, Camille Marevegas, Jacqueline Remlinger, Priscilla Webster, Efrem Weitzman, and Carolyn Zeiger.

Some of the photos in the following pages were taken by the United States embassy photographer; the pictures of the Istalif chest and of me today are the work of Susan Abeloff. Finally, hats off to Denton Lesslie, who came to our rescue when the project had become stalled and completed it so beautifully.

Finally, I thank Walter Blass, whose dream it was that brought us to Afghanistan, for the excellent family photos he took from our time there, and for the entire adventure.

— JANICE MINOTT
Hurleyville, New York
December 2006

CONTENTS

FOREWORDS

INTRODUCTION
by Gregory Blass

 Even now I can't recall the precise moment my parents told me we were going to live in Afghanistan for two years. Looking back, I'm sure I didn't fully appreciate just what this meant — in terms of the passage of real time or distance.

Only five at the time, I do recall much of the fuss surrounding our departure. The uncomfortable feel of the very sensible, stiff leather shoes my mother bought for me before leaving; then trying the same shoe in the next three sizes as she and the salesman speculated about the growth of my feet and likelihood of finding good shoes in Kabul.

Very clear is the memory of watching my brother, dressed in his best clothes, fall out from a speeding red wagon into a muddy puddle on the street — only moments before a reporter and photographer arrived to interview us for the local newspaper. I remember the smell of my grandmother as she hugged me goodbye at the airport, and the sound of the voice of the cheerful woman who sat beside us on the airplane. In later years, my mother told me that the woman was drunk before the in-flight meal was served and passed out until we landed at Heathrow. I just thought she was a happy person.

My memory of our arrival in Afghanistan was a disconnected jumble of the sounds and sensations that will stick in the mind of a five-year-old. There was the uneven whine and strain of jet engines finding their way along an unseen flight path between mountains to an airfield somewhere below, standing in line amidst a sea of knees for what seemed forever, the jumble of voices in a language that sounded like someone constantly clearing their throat. But with the rapid-fire *thump-wump thump-wump thump-wump* of the customs agent's stamp in our passports, I knew our journey had at last come to an end. No matter which country you travel to, passport stamps speak the same language.

Forty years later, I now have two daughters of my own — one fourteen and one almost eight — whom my wife and I have yet to take further abroad than Canada. I can't help but compare my parents' decision to bring their family halfway around the globe to the choices my wife and I have made that have settled our family into a very safe and frustratingly busy American suburban life. My mother and father chose to uproot my siblings and me from what was becoming that same western lifestyle and take us halfway around the world on this venture.

As my own children have grown, I've become increasingly proud of my mother and father for making the journey my mother describes in the pages that follow, and grateful to them for including me in the life-changing endeavor of two years in Afghanistan. The world in the sixties was a much larger place than it is now, and at the time, the urgency to see all the different peoples of the world as one community must have felt as great as it does today.

I'm particularly grateful to have had that experience at such a young age. Somehow I think that we see the world very clearly when we are young, before we cloud our vision of events with all the stuff we pack into our heads as adults.

As a six-year-old, I did understand that it was only the accident of birth that placed me atop my bicycle riding past the boys collecting the dried manure left in the street for fuel, and not barefoot beside them. I also understood that it is the same heart-pounding excitement that both sets of boys feel holding onto a kite made from five cents' worth of tissue paper and spit.

Looking back, I can remember having more freedom as a six-year-old in mid-sixties Kabul than we gave our older daughter in Arlington, Massachusetts, when she was twelve. Riding my bike after school to my friends' homes alone was fine — just as long as they lived on the same side of the river that divides Kabul. I guess having to remind a kid to watch out for traffic wasn't such a worry for a parent. On my journeys, I was just as likely to have to watch out for oncoming camels, donkeys, or carts pulled by horses as the cars driven by unlicensed drivers. All that and working my way between the road apples left by the many animals.

My older brother Chris had a real knack for making friends with the sons of visiting dignitaries. The Egyptian ambassador's son was one of these boys. This youngster led us on a thrilling adventure placing cherry bombs under the tires of parked cars in the street below his Kabul apartment balcony. When we returned to the safety of his balcony to await the result of our mischief, this ten-year-old from Egypt introduced us, two wide-eyed American boys, to the Beatles by playing "I Want to Hold Your Hand" at top volume through his doorway into the Kabul street air. He topped off this lesson in western culture with a performance of air guitar on his tennis racket. He was far too cosmopolitan — and much more sure of himself than two brothers from Scotch Plains, New Jersey, could ever be. We just couldn't keep up with this guy. I had to hide my secret relief behind a veil of disappointment when all of our cherry bombs failed to explode.

For many years, I held a memory of visiting a local *naan* shop in Kabul with my father. I vividly remembered the earthen building and the crowd hungry for the afternoon's bread to be baked and sold for their evening meal. I felt safe, hooking my fingers in at the top of the pants pocket of the man standing beside me. For forty years I assumed it was my father Walter because of how safe I felt while the crowd pressed in around us. Clutching at his trousers I knew I wouldn't lose him and I had no fear. In reading through these letters, I've come to realize I was with Bhaktari, the young Afghan man hired to help in our household, on the back of whose bicycle I had ridden to the shop.

The day we left for Kabul forty years ago, there wasn't a single kid, and maybe less than a handful of adults, on my street in Scotch Plains that had heard of Afghanistan — let alone able to place it on a map. Today on my street in Arlington, Massachusetts, that situation is very different. Even the home of my mother's youth, tiny Peaks Island, Maine, has sent a soldier to Afghanistan. Unfortunately, "boots on the ground" has become many American small-town residents' only firsthand experience with Afghanistan.

In reading my mother's letters it is clear to me that both Janice and Walter came away from their experiences in Afghanistan with much more than they arrived with. Our time in Kabul not only became the opportunity for my parents to create and follow their own dream, but paved the way for us children to formulate and pursue our own dreams — no matter how far-fetched they may have seemed. Truly speaking, my family's life is defined by our time in Kabul. The short time we spent there went a long way in launching us three children into the adults we have become.

Kabul has now become a household word. What was home for two years now appears daily in the world headlines. Granted, life in Kabul was a world apart from the way it is today. The mid-sixties was a different time for the region, as it was for our own nation. The letters in the pages that follow tell a timeless as well as a timely story. By giving ourselves to new life experience, we do grow and change. I can attest to this. My life was irrevocably altered, as were the lives of my siblings and parents.

It is a universal truth that despite our common human threads, or because of them, when people from different parts of this earth come together, they inevitably learn from one another. Reading Janice's letters will give you her rendering of this melding experience forty years ago: a glimpse into what one woman's journey felt like as it happened — a woman who didn't know where this endeavor would lead her, let alone what it would leave with her in the years to come.

Packing for Kabul

PREFACE
by Janice Minott

We were five — myself, my husband Walter Blass, and our three children: Kathryn, ten; Christopher, sixteen months younger; and Gregory, almost six. Walter had been appointed Peace Corps country director for a rapidly expanding program of two hundred volunteers — mainly teachers, nurses, and vaccinators — in Afghanistan's major towns and some provincial villages. In the villages, life had changed little if at all since the fifteenth century.

The fifty letters in *Letters from Kabul* cover twenty-two months that my family spent in Kabul, Afghanistan, from June 1966 through March 1968. During that time, we lived in a spacious mud-brick house inside a walled compound in Sherpur, one of the older sections of the city.

My story is a familiar one. For ages women have been packing up their children along with pots, pans and other essentials, and following in the wake of their men's dreams. Although I knew no wife and mother in 1965 suburban New Jersey who organized to move her family so far afield, we were all excited about experiencing life in a country so remote that few people could even locate it on a map. At the time, most people thought that we were headed for somewhere in Africa!

How come we were so psyched up for this assignment? The answer is rooted in who Walter and I were — and where we came from. I came from the coast of Maine, the descendant of several generations of sea captains and the first girl born to the line in 109 years. I sailed my own boat in Casco Bay and dreamed of visiting South America, China and India, and other points to which my great-grandfather, Captain Jabez Minott, had sailed. I told myself that I would not be like Octavia, Jabez's wife, and settle for remaining on shore. These were my dreams in an age when girls were expected to get married and, if not that, to become teachers, nurses, or librarians. The advent of World War II changed my world completely.

Walter was born in Germany in 1930 and grew up in Belgium until he was ten years old. I was born in Pennsylvania in 1925 and grew up in Portland, Bangor, and Peaks Island, Maine. Both of us were only children. When the Nazis invaded Belgium overnight in the spring of 1940, the Blasses became refugees. They were at first separated, then interned, and finally released and reunited in unoccupied France. After making it safely to Marseilles, they were assisted by Quaker relief workers in immigrating to the United States in 1941. They settled in New Jersey and became active in the local Friends Meeting.

The Quakers became our connecting link. I knew Quakers only from quaint pictures in history books until one day when I rode the train from Bangor, Maine, to Boston in 1949 during my junior year at the state university. The gentleman who sat beside me — a look-alike for our dean of the College of Arts and Sciences — was a dean from a small college in Massachusetts and vastly more approachable than ours. He obviously enjoyed mentoring young students and soon had me sharing my hopes and dreams. As the train sped along the river, the rhythmic sound of the wheels created a magical background for an unforgettable moment out of time.

During that period of my life, I was without a spiritual home, but was longing for one — having severed the connection with my childhood spiritual roots some years before in a fit of ado-lescent pique. I was also without a partner. I had graduated from high school in 1942 at sixteen, little more than six months after Pearl Harbor. By the following December, the fellows who graduated high school with me were all in military service. Barely seventeen at the time, I refused to make a wartime marriage.

When the money ran out after sophomore year I worked as a secretary first in Portland and then in New York City. While in New York, I became buddies with my bachelor uncle, Olin Minott, a kindred spirit who had run away from home and become a merchant seaman. During the war, he had made his bundle as a skipper of supply ships to the Pacific war zone. As the very much younger brother to my dad, he had previously written offering to finance my education. My father was too proud to accept the gift, saying, "You'll probably just get married anyway."

In the fall of 1948, Olin Minott met me during my lunch hour at his Wall Street bank, where he deposited three thousand dollars for the final two years of my college education. Leaving me speechless, Olin walked away before I could thank him. I returned to the University of Maine and became the only twenty-four-year-old woman on campus. My male peers were the few vets on campus, a psychology professor, and the foreign students.

All this formed the backdrop for what I shared with my train companion. Toward the end of our journey, this angel in disguise, as I think of him today, said, "As I see it, there are two things you might become. One is a Catholic and the other, a Quaker."

Back at the university, I met the sole Quaker enrolled there when I was put into the infirmary's isolation room with a case of pneumonia. He was the resident night guard. Since I couldn't have visitors, he would sit in the hallway and talk to me. In answer to my question about Quakerism, he gave me a thirty-second answer. "To be a Quaker," he said, "the only thing you have to believe is that there is that of God in every man."

Now I was very interested, but still felt at a dead end. Then in the spring of my senior year, the Quakers (also known as Friends) entered my life in the form of a visiting college secretary from their American Friends Service Committee. She offered me a job as her assistant, recruiting students for international work camps and seminars from their office in Cambridge, Massachusetts.

Thus the stage was set for a young man from "over there," as we in Maine referred to persons born in Europe, and a young woman from Down East to eventually meet. It was a whirlwind courtship since he was in training at Newport, Rhode Island, to become a naval ensign — after which he would likely be assigned to sea duty.

Through the years, I would learn that Walter always operated in a whirlwind. I once told him he "knocked my socks off." One weekend as we walked beside the banks of the Charles River, Walter shared his dream of working in economic development. It was a field he felt held great promise for creating world peace. Since this would involve going to the "undeveloped world," he wanted to know, "How would you feel about living in a Third World country?"

I couldn't help laughing and told him that I already had, that I'd spent one summer with a Quaker project in Jamaica. I had experience working with people of other cultures, had learned to cook on a wood stove and bargain in an open-air market. I also cherished fond personal memories of melding into Jamaica's multiracial society. When my Jamaican coworker took me to visit relatives one evening, the children ran to their grandmother calling out, "The half-Chinese girl from the newspaper is here." The interracial American team's arrival had made the front page in Kingston. My schoolmates in Portland, Maine, had always teased me that my mother must have had a Chinese iceman, but in Jamaica I discovered that, indeed, I could pass as Eurasian. It did help me on at least one occasion in Afghanistan, a country where many people had Asian features.

I felt that my Maine background was another one of my credentials. Having come so recently from "over there," Walter might not realize that many Americans considered Maine to be something of a Third World country itself. While he had grown up in Brussels, I was spending my summers on an island without electricity or indoor plumbing. Some of my fondest memories are illumined by the glow of a kerosene lamp as my father read bedtime stories — once all night long when I had the chickenpox.

From the Jamaica project, I'd also learned what it is to surrender the fruits of our efforts. The small structure that we built that summer in a squatter village, completed hours before a world-class hurricane struck, was ripped out of its foundation by the force of the storm. The emotional bonds forged with some of my coworkers there are still intact.

Before Walter and I asked George Selleck, clerk of the Quaker Meeting in Cambridge, for permission to be married in the meetinghouse, we felt anxious he might caution us to be less hasty. On the contrary, George beamed as he told us, "When you give a mathematician points, he can project lines and tell whether they are going to intersect or not." It was obvious to him that our lives were intersecting. As I see it today, our lines intersected flying into Afghanistan, and like two planets coming into conjunction, blazed brightly and then continued along their own ever-widening trajectories.

We had a definite schedule — and initially everything went "according to plan." Walter completed his military service, but not before Kathryn was born in the Newport Naval Hospital. We moved to Washington, D.C., to serve with the predecessor to USAID. Walter was assigned to the Vietnam/Cambodia desk and we were scheduled to go to Phnom Penh. The temples of Angkor Wat were on a short list of ancient ruins I had always wanted to visit, but again there was a higher power in charge here.

After I became pregnant with Christopher, we were advised to wait until the baby was six months old before going overseas. That space of time was what we needed to become aware that this assignment was not for us. It was the Cold War, and much of the aid was being siphoned into military buildup in the area. Disheartened, we resigned and moved to New Jersey and bought a house one hour from Walter's parents. Through a contact in the Friends Meeting, Walter got a job with AT&T doing long-range economic planning. We settled into a typical suburban life and had a third child in 1960 — Gregory.

President Kennedy's inaugural address and his challenge, "Ask not what your country can do for you. Ask what you can do for your country," inspired us. The Peace Corps sounded great and not unlike the Quaker projects we were familiar with, but with three children, we assumed we were not eligible.

Then out of the blue in the fall of 1965, we received a letter that Walter's name had been submitted twice to a talent search for Peace Corps staff. He called at the end of a day of interviews in Washington to say, "They are talking about Afghanistan. How does that sound to you?"

It rang a bell for me, and I answered, "It sounds fine." Then I went out and bought a copy of James Michener's *Caravans* and shared it with the grandparents. It is a romantic adventure story but it painted a picture that those of us who went to Afghanistan at that time could relate to. We loved that book.

After Walter's Peace Corps supervisor in Washington wrote, "When we hire a married man, we feel we get two for the price of one," I wanted to retort, "Make that five for one in our case!" I knew that our children would be excellent emissaries. And as for me, like most of my peers in New Jersey, I was a stay-at-home mom who was used to unpaid community service.

Once in Afghanistan, we became VIPs overnight. I attended many official functions with Walter and went to them alone during his several month-long absences. As Peace Corps, we were the new kids on the block — or as we say in Maine, a "horse of a different color" compared with the official Foreign Service types.

The embassy doctor scoffed at our lifestyle. He insisted that we would all get amoebas eating from the bazaars rather than the commissary. Sure enough, "Kabul trots" became a fact of life. Dysentery eventually even helped defeat the Russian army during the decade after we left. It's one of the great challenges for western-ers to adjust to life in Kabul.

The truth was that the Peace Corps with a handful of dedi-cated people in country had succeeded beyond anyone's wildest dreams. With LBJ, the pressure grew to expand. During our tour, Walter often found himself, as the regional director in Washington put it, "tested in the fires of adversity," having to serve two hundred people now located increasingly in the provinces outside Kabul.

As the United States escalated its war in Vietnam in 1967, young men who flunked out of the Peace Corps became eligible overnight for the draft. We were getting new staff constantly, and one of my jobs was to help them get settled. It was always hard to predict how long it would take for the new arrivals to adjust. After a series of inner and outer trials, most did come to love the country. To be sure, arriving in Kabul was to enter an undeniable time and culture warp.

After our tour was over, Walter confided in me that if he had needed to worry about the family, he felt he would have drowned. "I knew you could look after them," he said. At the time he said this, it was a revelation to me: I hadn't realized, during those twenty-two months, that we had been occupying separate parallel universes.

Walter is an outstanding figure in the letters, but the story I tell is from my own perspective. I operated in several different arenas, so my time was taken up with the children, running the house, and continuing my language lessons so I could supervise the household staff in Farsi and bargain in the bazaars. I also taught an ESL (English as a Second Language) class for Afghan women.

The three tribal men who worked for us were from distant villages in an area known as the Hazarajat. This is where the people settled whom the Mongol invaders had left behind centuries ago. By the sixties the more adventurous Hazaras were moving into Kabul. Many worked as porters, and there were men like our excellent cook, Anwar, who was literate in his own language. He was also the only one of our three servants who could speak some English. It was a novel experience for me to supervise these three men, and novel also for them to accept a woman as their boss. Interacting with them gave me many glimpses into Afghan culture that were not easy to come by in those days when contact with westerners was not encouraged.

I have often wondered about their fate during the years of fierce fighting later around Kabul. Like many Afghans, they had only one name. To positively identify someone, you had to know his village and father's name. On top of that, there were no street signs or house numbers, and few working telephones. To get in touch with someone, you had to send a messenger. It was all person-to-person. I have sent out many prayers that they have survived the harsh years since our departure.

While in Afghanistan, I made it a priority to write frequent and voluminous letters to my folks back home. It was exciting to share what I considered to be my extraordinary good fortune at being able to experience life in such an ancient and vastly different culture. I felt then as now that once we become modernized, something gets lost along the way. At first living the adventure was just one exotic day after another. But by the end of a year, things like camel caravans passing the house became commonplace.

As I felt more at home in Afghanistan, gradually the tone of my letters changed. I began marveling at the resourcefulness of the people and questioning what we were really doing there.

During our second Fourth of July celebration held in the garden of the American ambassador, I had an encounter that reinforced my questioning. Since I had begun to have some hearing problems, I tended to stay on the fringes of any group. I noticed a small group of people in the far corner of the garden. I was drawn to them. The center of attention was an Afghan man from the Agricultural Ministry who was talking about his work with the farmers. He said that he was rarely in Kabul, preferring to be with the farmers whom he loved. Smiling and indicating a suit that could have dated from his college days in the States, he said, "This is the only suit I own." Out in the villages, he wore only traditional Afghan attire, long shirt and baggy pants. I sensed his genuine warmth and empathy and decided enthusiastically that the country was in good hands with men like this — particularly since the majority of the Afghan people earned their living from the land.

In the days before instant messaging and e-mail, my letters became a lifeline to the familiar world that I had left behind. Now, forty years later, they have taken on a life all their own.

There were several categories of letters. First were the woman-to-woman ones that I wrote to my best friend and neighbor in Scotch Plains, New Jersey. Phyllis, from Nova Scotia, Canada, had a daughter Kathryn's age and likewise two younger boys. Phyllis and I shared an earthy humor about love and marriage.

I often typed eight- to ten-page letters addressed "Dear Folks," mailed them to my mother in Maine, and asked her to send copies to Phyllis. Sometimes I also wrote to Walter's parents. These are the letters addressed to Richard and Malvi. They had welcomed me into the family with open arms, and their more open, friendly style was a balance for my austere New England background.

My mother didn't save her letters. I suspect she must have thought I was truly a maniac to have left the state of Maine, which she considered the safest place on earth. As a growing girl, she'd spent her summers on her grandfather's fishing vessel and felt competent and confident to handle my father's motorboat alone with a girlfriend in Maine's coastal waters. But she had no interest in what lay beyond. She was content with her life.

On the other hand, I was completely restless in suburbia. I had loved working and living in New York City and Cambridge, Massachusetts, as a young single woman, but suburbia felt like a cramped environment in which to raise a family.

I believed that life in a Third World country would expand all our horizons and I was prepared to cope with whatever our term in the Peace Corps required. Ironically, the challenges turned out to be quite different from what I imagined. I thought my life might require me to live more as a typical Peace Corps volunteer — cooking on a kerosene stove, at least, as I'd seen my mother do. I had not expected that I'd have three servants and be housed in a residence large enough to hold our whole Scotch Plains house inside it with space to spare. That house enabled us to hold countless official functions with as many as one hundred people in our sixty-foot living room.

All this and more is contained in the letters that I dashed off in the moment — and forgot. Back home, the children grew up. Walter and I separated, then divorced. Over the years, I traveled six times to India, lived in an ashram, and settled in upstate New York. My untold story remained somewhere in the back of my mind, buried deep within my heart.

After Afghanistan became a hot media topic, a serendipitous event presented me with a rare opportunity to share my experiences of the Afghanistan I had known. This was an Afghan world that was not dominated by competing warlords or Taliban. It was a simpler and less complicated country and culture — with the seeds of controversy just beginning to surface.

In August 2002 I walked up to my mailbox one morning, beside the little-traveled road where I now live, to discover it was stuffed with two bulging manila envelopes. Phyllis had returned to Canada many years before, but we continued to correspond. Her husband had passed away that spring, and in downsizing her possessions, she rediscovered my letters. "I have reread them," she wrote, "and thought that you — and maybe even your children — might enjoy reliving your time there."

Until now, my family and I had shared memories of our time in Afghanistan only with one another. Now we have collaborated in telling our story to the world.

The first letter was written to my parents before I left New Jersey. Luckily I recorded it in my journal. It reveals that despite all my brave assertions of readiness for the adventure, there was some genuine apprehension.

May 18, 1966
Scotch Plains, New Jersey

Dear Mother and Dad,

I just learned they will move us out of the house on May 26. What a feeling to be cast adrift in this universe! Phyllis said the other day, "We've been talking about your leaving since

September, but how can you just walk out? I hope you leave in the middle of the night."

Life is such a mixed bag! We never know the value of things unless we have to give them up. Somehow, we avoid thinking about the eternal questions in day-to-day life.

We will fly over Portland, Maine, six miles up. Just think of that! And I'm scared for you of the trips you two take in your little boat in Casco Bay.

Hope you are well.
Janice

Thus ended the months of preparation during which Walter wound up his work with AT&T and traveled to Washington for weeks of orientation. All the while, I shopped from long lists that I received from my predecessor in Kabul. I discarded many items, organized our sea freight, packed other belongings for storage, set aside what was to go by air, supervised the children packing their suitcases, and readied the house for sale.

My orientation consisted of weekly tutoring sessions in Farsi from an Afghan grad student who was employed by the Peace Corps to come to the house. In addition, I was required to be judged by a psychiatrist as stable and fit for a hardship post.

The family had to make frequent trips to the Department of Health in New York City for a variety of shots — familiar and unfamiliar — such as yellow fever. On one of those trips, the family accompanied me to the psychiatrist and waited while I sat for my interview in his private office. He admitted he had never had such an assignment, and floundered at first when he asked if I had any fear of bridges or tunnels. I pointed out that I frequently made the trip into the city from New Jersey. Then he got a gleam in his eye and asked, "You're not being dragged by the hair of your head, are you?" He may have picked up on Walter's intense and forceful energy. Greg used to say that it sometimes seemed his father entered any room bursting through the wall rather than the door.

I emphatically retorted, "I feel this is my destiny." Whereupon the doctor's mouth dropped open and his eyes registered disbelief and alarm. "Don't tell me you believe in kismet, Mrs. Blass."

I quickly recovered and related to him the story of our commitment on the banks of the Charles River and our years of association with the Quakers' Peace Testimony, and he was placated. He must not have realized that I was going to be living in a culture where all plans were prefaced with *enshallah* ("if God wills it"). My answer surely revealed some underlying compatibility with that philosophy.

I looked forward to the four days we were to spend en route to Kabul in Copenhagen with my best friend from college. From there we flew to hot, steamy Teheran, arriving after midnight on a wild ride from the airport with a driver who ran all the red lights and only put his headlights on when he saw another car approaching the intersection. We spent a full day and night in that modern city.

During the last lap to Kabul, we left at dawn for our flight over the desert. I had grown up on an ocean. I was moving to an ocean of sand and remember the distinct feeling of awe at this sight. Beneath the plane lay mile after mile of undulating desert. The only man-made thing I could detect below looked like a series of oversized pothole covers. I would learn they were an access to the *karezes* — a centuries-old network of underground water channels. Where there was water in the valleys below, I could see slivers of green. Those valleys, I would discover, were little Shangri-las.

Finally we landed in a valley with the nomads' black goat-skin tents pitched near the runway.

As we stepped out of the plane onto the airfield, I felt as if I was standing atop a roof. I could see for miles to a horizon lined with the black, snow-capped Hindu Kush mountains. Whereas it had been hard to breathe in the stuffy Teheran air, there was a fresh breeze blowing here. The many colored flags on the terminal were waving. On the balcony sat a line of women, each one covered from head to toe in a pale blue, red, or green *chadri*. This scene provided an enigmatic welcome to our arrival in Kabul on our daughter's tenth birthday — June 9, 1966.

* Author's Note: In the original letters that follow, I use the Afghan Farsi (Dari) expressions we learned. I also refer to the *burqa* as a *chadri* and use the local expression *enshallah* instead of the more formal Arabic *insha'allah*.

GETTING SETTLED

JUNE–JULY 1966

The greenhorns en route

Beside the airport road

CHAPTER ONE

Walking These Streets
Evokes Bible Times

I LOVE THESE PEOPLE

June 13, 1966
Kabul, Afghanistan

Dear Folks:

Naturally we have received no mail from home since we've been here barely five days. So much has happened, so many new people met and new sights seen. To us novices, it feels as though five years have already elapsed.

Everything is very different and we must adopt a completely new lifestyle. Being the Peace Corps rep's wife doesn't involve as much protocol as being in the regular Foreign Service, but it's not exactly like being a Peace Corps volunteer or staff wife either.

There is far more responsibility than I could ever have imagined. For example, while my cook is preparing dinner, the *baacha* (house helper) cleaning, and the *dhobi* doing the wash squatting at a floor-height pan, it seems I will be attending official functions, chauffeuring new staff members around, and arranging entertainment for other officials, their wives, and the increasing number of volunteers.

During the last year, the program has expanded. At our welcome party, one of the volunteers told me, "Congratulations. You now have two hundred children, Mrs. Blass." And this is just the tip of the iceberg!

Being a housewife in Kabul is multidimensional, too! When the cook is off on Friday for his Sabbath, it's going to take me all day to shop for and prepare three meals. Simply everything is done from scratch and all fruits must be soaked in a solution of iodine.

They taste delicious, even so. There are so many kinds in the bazaar just now — many I've never seen before. However, they do help to bring on the "Kabul trots," which we've all had and keep having from time to time.

This morning I had to attend a coffee at the ambassador's residence. I secretly stowed away a small bottle of Kaopectate in my purse. Still, had I needed to rush out (which I didn't), no one would have batted an eye. Folks really do sit around and discuss the subject like nowhere else in the world. It's a fact of life here, and no matter how careful a person is, not a single man, woman or child escapes.

We have been living with one of the other staff families and are being well cared for. Come Thursday when we move into our new quarters, I'll be on my own. I've been busy borrowing or buying emergency items to use until our airfreight arrives.

The Peace Corps is a real "do-it-yourself" outfit. As a result, there is a tremendous camaraderie among the staff. We are a heterogeneous bunch of people who pull together in marvelous ways. We're already seeing that the new replacements are all much younger, as the former rep and doctor leave. So Walter, with his ageless face, will have to convince the volunteers he is one up on them. Thus far, he's doing well.

Mother, I wish you would send a copy of this letter to Phyllis Crowe — who can share it around. My friends on the street are eager to know what I would do with three servants. Even households with servants here still don't function as speedily as our system at home. One gets involved with their problems too.

I really love these people. The sights outside our compound walls are fantastic and it's impossible to do them justice in this first brief letter. At 8:30 PM as I write this, the city is very quiet — no Jersey Central freight trains running through the night or jets roaring overhead.

In Kabul planes only arrive and depart on Thursday and Sunday. I have yet to hear one, but at midnight when I am still wakeful due to jet lag, the donkeys are braying, the cocks crowing and the packs of street dogs racing around barking. You hear and see animals absolutely everywhere. I don't hear any camel, goat, sheep or water-buffalo noises that I can identify; however, I've decided that animals are like young babies — they retire early, have a wakeful midnight until 2:00 AM and then get up early. The pace of life here is from another time.

We hope to hear soon from stateside and learn that you who receive this letter are well. I would prefer to have written separate letters, but arrivals, like departures, are very busy times.

In my heart, I know that this assignment we're on is very worthwhile. Very. Nonetheless, I think of you all often and am amazed at how different life becomes by simply changing locales overnight.

I'm eager for home news — not to lose touch with my real life, as it were.

Jan

TRYING MY LIMITED FARSI VOCABULARY ON THE DARK-EYED CHILDREN

June 19, 1966
Kabul, Afghanistan

Dear Phyllis, Peggy, Karen, Faye, and Selma,

I'm envisioning you all sitting together reading this. We're still living out of suitcases, although now staying in the previous Peace Corps director family's house since the day they departed. Their staff is looking after us as nicely as possible given the few items we've managed to accumulate from the Peace Corps emergency kit, embassy thrift shop, and other staff.

Yesterday we got the disappointing news that our air-freight with the most basic items has not yet left the States since it was overweight by 178 pounds. Since overweight costs $2.50 per pound, we gave instructions to ship the 178 pounds with our sea freight. Who knows what will arrive when?

We will have a great time experiencing other parts of the world, and I believe we'll arrive home in 1968 flat broke — with a few very lovely carpets to sit on! Actually much is available in even the tiniest bazaars. Notably, although Walter is cosmopolitan in many ways, he's miserable without his Gulden's mustard. When you transport your body to completely new regions, it's amazing to observe where the "missing" shows through. I priced the smallest-size jar today for 15 *afghanis* — close to a dollar.

Life here is full of surprising contrasts. I spend minutes looking for a pen and paper to write to you while our wonderful cook is busy concocting homemade soup for lunch. For breakfast, he served pancakes and syrup — both from scratch — and as delicious as I've ever eaten.

The children are behaving really well while sitting at the long table being served. We've insisted upon great courtesy and politeness toward these men who work for us.

Like most mountain folk, they are very reserved. Our servants are mostly Hazaras, descendants of the Mongol invasion centuries ago. Within the culture, they are discriminated against but are very industrious people who pool their resources.

I'm finding that now I can sleep when I am supposed to. The "donkey singsong" no longer keeps me awake half the night. I can only think the manger must have been a pretty noisy nursery. One feels very close to Bible times walking these streets among the low mud-walled dwellings — those, and passing occasional northern tribesman in their long, colorful robes. I'm told that when one gets out of Kabul, with its newer buildings, the feeling is even more ancient.

On the other hand, driving a car in the city is perilous. Few people in Afghanistan have been conditioned from childhood and so are not used to automobiles. The result is that both adults and children unexpectedly step out in front of moving cars. If you hit someone, and there's no policeman in sight, we've been instructed to head straight for the embassy.

I don't yet have an Afghan license or a vehicle to drive, so I've been walking and trying my limited Farsi vocabulary on the little dark-eyed children who are cute and friendly as children the world over.

Kathryn, Christopher, and Gregory restlessly await the beginning of the American International School summer enrichment program — though they always refused to attend these types of programs at home. There they'll get some Farsi instruction, a swimming lesson and some arts and crafts. For the time being, they come with me on errands and play together.

Yesterday while at an outdoor vegetable and fruit bazaar, we met an old man (known as a *babeh* here). He had a parrot on his arm that spoke fluent Farsi. Gregory had five afghanis in his hand and wanted to buy him. Suddenly, the area was filled with the sounds of cocks crowing and bird songs—a young chap on a bicycle, the best ventriloquist you've ever heard, was responsible.

We had to get up bright and early this morning to go to the airport to meet six men who have been reassigned from Turkey where they were idle for nearly a year. We spend our time making such people feel at home—or will when the dishes arrive. Imagine keeping house when every drop of water you drink, brush your teeth with, wash fruits and rinse dishes with has to be carried from the embassy's deep well.

The kids are drinking lots of Cokes—something I only allowed at parties at home. Coke is a worldwide addiction but at this point, I'd rather have them get cavities than amoebic dysentery. Even the Peace Corps doctors get it. Everyone is resigned and jokes about this. It permeates the whole country. You only need one fly to alight in the right places.

So far, we have had no letters from the States. HINT.

Jan

P.S. The children really miss their home gang. In this interim period with no school or car, it's hard for them to meet other children. It turns out that the Afghan children go to school all summer and take off in the winter when the unheated school buildings are closed. Meanwhile mine are making up all sorts of games, and since there is no TV in this country, they even pantomime shows for me to guess.

LIFE CHANGES WHEN FAUCET WATER
IS NOT FOR DRINKING

June 24, 1966
Kabul, Afghanistan

Dear Phyllis,

I guess that a fly lit in all the right places. The next day after writing to you, I came down with dysentery. What an experience! I wanted to die!

I had recovered enough by yesterday, Friday, the Muslim Sabbath and cook's day off, to tear into the kitchen and try my hand. This new region is still pretty confusing and I'm tormented by doubts. Do I wash the food in Tide and regular water and then cook it, or do I wash it in embassy well water only? Or is it better to soak it first with iodine tablets? You see, even in exotic places, it's really all about the basics of living.

Right now I'm feeling that it will take me the longest of all five Blasses to adjust. These first few weeks will not be easy. Kathryn's already made a bosom friend on the street — a very nice child in her same school grade who is physically beginning to swell a little in the bust. She has lived abroad before but doesn't seem overly sophisticated.

I've spent most of my time these past days trying to get myself on my feet and amuse first Greg with his sore throat, and now Chris with dysentery. What germs do you have on Whittier Avenue this week? I understand it has been cold. When I was sick here, I longed to hear a gentle rainfall. Even Gregory asked if it would rain, and I had to tell him not until next spring.

.

When we arrived, we had marvelous views from certain points of the Hindu Kush — the great black jagged peaks etched with snow. Now whole scenes are blocked out with dust, and so there's one more kind of pill I have to take. Walter, who looks simply grand by the way and is loving his role, keeps claiming that there's nothing allergy producing in desert dust, but I disagree. Of course, when a little rain falls, many things grow out of that dust. Perhaps it's just that I'm allergic to the donkeys that we don't have at home.

You know, I'm finding out how much more rigid I am now than when I was twenty-four. It appears these first few weeks won't be easy. Life is so very different. But then I remind myself that it's only for two years and I did sign up for this. Then we go back. On a positive note, I just love the house we are going to live in. I'll describe it to you sometime soon.

UPSTATE NEW YORK, 2006

It was discouraging to be the one to get sick, particularly after I'd been so confident about my ability to cope with life overseas. Walter was so engrossed that he dismissed it saying, "Everyone gets these little things out here." It became clear during the night that it was not a "little thing." At one point, I collapsed on the bed and gasped, "If I could crawl to the airport, I would leave in the morning." He asked the Peace Corps doctor to come look at me first thing.

Dr. de Maine discovered that before leaving the States I'd been given one of the new steroids for my allergies. He told me that if I didn't stop using it, I would catch everything going because it was depressing my entire immune system. Then he gave me medicine for the dysentery and advised me to eat anything that I wanted as soon as I felt up to it.

"Your system will eventually get used to the local bugs," he reassured me. He also sent his lovely wife and nurse, Lourdes, to comfort me. She arrived bearing tempting goodies all the while singing, "Welcome to Kabul, Janice!"

That afternoon, I was awakened from a nap by the sound of rain on the parched earth. This was an answer to my prayer, for I had found the combination of fever and hot dusty weather hard to bear. The unseasonable rain confirmed that I was going to cope with anything Afghanistan had to offer.

Gregory also had his epiphany. He clung to me a lot at first. The older two, now nine and ten, went out exploring every afternoon. But he would stay home and play by himself always close by me. Finally he asked in a very small voice, "When are we going home?" "When Daddy's job is finished," I replied.

"When will that be?" he asked. He had heard the details about our moving to Afghanistan many times in the past few months, but to his six-year-old mind, the words had no meaning until now. "In two years," I reminded him. "Oh," he said and then was thoughtful for a while — after which he added very quietly, "I believe I could be happy if I could just have a kitten."

Kathryn had already made friends with the other American family on the block. They adopted a street cat that lived in their compound and were hoping her kittens, now six weeks old and not yet streetwise, would make good house pets. It was a long shot since Afghans did not domesticate the street dogs and cats. But Greg had a magic way with animals and having a kitten at this time eased his way into his new home.

AROUND TEN O'CLOCK, THE REFRIGERATOR BEGINS TO DANCE

Sunday, June 25, 1966
Kabul, Afghanistan

Phyllis,

I've been blinding myself writing letters in the dining room's dim overhead light. Then Walter — who is sick tonight — went to the bathroom, passed the transformer and turned it up to 110 volts. Now suddenly, I can see!

Most households cook on small electric hot plates in the sections of the city where there is electricity. In the evening when everyone is making a meal, the electricity gets dim. There is a transformer in our front hall with a wheel and a dial to adjust the voltage. Then later around ten o'clock, the refrigerator begins to dance, a signal that it's time to turn the juice back down.

The kids spent about three hours today on a ladder up in our dozen or so cherry trees picking the abundant ripe cherries. If I had some pectin and jars, I'd make jam. As it is, we washed, sorted and bagged them in miscellaneous plastic bags we could find and put them in the Steiners' freezer that we just purchased.

I was just contemplating how life changes when you can only go to the faucet to wash your body. Walter needed some ice cubes. Sometimes the servants set the tray on a warm stove burner to loosen them. The stove has been on and off all day, so I settled for pouring water from the ever-present teakettle over the tray. My first purchase in this country has been a large red enamel teakettle.

What's new with your little family? Kathryn says she has written to Becky and is pining for an answer. The mail arrives twice in a week.

Love,
Janice

Neighboorhood boy

WE WILL LIVE IN A ONE-STORY
AFGHAN HOUSE

Tuesday, June 27, 1966
Kabul, Afghanistan

Dear Phyllis,

Just received your first letter. You don't know how much it meant to get some news from Whittier Avenue. How I have missed you all. This is about the eighth day I have either been sick or had someone else to pamper back to health.

I'm really worried about Chris. He just won't eat or drink any more because he says it only makes him sick all over again — and that's not right. We will get the Peace Corps doctor to see him as soon as he checks the stool sample. What a pain! Hope we will all be in good health for the celebration on the Fourth of July at the embassy. I understand there will be lots of things for kids to do.

Soon we would also like to take a picnic to Paghman, one of the nice gardens about twenty miles outside of Kabul. I'm eagerly awaiting my Afghan license. I'm even ready to tackle this unpredictable mixture of cyclists, donkeys, jeeps, taxis and children who constantly dart at you. Dr. Morgan loaned us a VW while he's away for the summer. That's about as large a car as I want to maneuver here.

Many of the little shops sit on very narrow streets. The other day, I went shopping by myself for the first time to get a can of tuna. What a laugh. First salmon, then tunny (which is a sardine, isn't it?) were offered to me. He kept trying hard to sell me canned ham or pork and beans that he pulled out from under the counter.

16

Since it's not allowed on the Muslim diet, all were most likely stolen from some embassy household.

The school is on the other side of town, so our children will have to take a bus — it's the side of town where the new homes are being built for the increasing number of USAID families. The streets are not paved there yet, nor any lawns growing — just dust, dust and more dust everywhere.

We will live in a one-story Afghan house of sun-baked bricks. They are so cool in the hot weather but hold the heat well in the winter. The house is very charming. That much I am very happy with. Adjustments continue!

Much love,

Janice

Garden of Kabul house

PICNIC AT PAGHMAN GARDENS: WHAT'S THE DIFFERENCE BETWEEN AN OX AND A BULL?

July 2, 1966
Kabul, Afghanistan

Dear Folks,

Someone is leaving for the States tomorrow, a chance for us to send some stateside letters. We are more or less living out of suitcases. There's still no word of the whereabouts of any of our things. This is par for the situation, I hear. Then finally one day, some men arrive at your door with an elephant-sized crate.

I love the Steiners' house and wish we could remain here. There are so many trees in this and the surrounding yards that we see lots of birds. I can't tell you their names, but they're unusual. The compound wall cuts very close to the dining room, and while sitting at the table, we often see birds hopping along the top of the wall. In the evening, I could also hear chanting coming from the garden on the other side.

Probably when our things arrive and we get into our own place, I'll finally feel "This is my home." So far, I still feel more or less a visitor. The children also talk a lot about their friends at home because they don't yet have new playmates to take their place. We've been spending lots of time together. The Chinese-checkers board that we brought with us has been used constantly—also the badminton rackets we got in Denmark. I hope the worst is over. Next week they will go to the international summer-school program and finally meet some playmates of their own sizes.

We're due to move into our own quarters on July 13, the

house with the big living room. Vice President Humphrey, one of the founding fathers of the Peace Corps, is due here on July 18th. If he decides to meet the Peace Corps volunteers, our new house has room for everyone to stand around at once. So before my household goods even arrive, I may be learning to receive the vice president of the United States. What a strange new life I have plunged into!

Each day I gain confidence in running this new household. Today I hired a cab again and went to our little supermarket run by an Afghan graduate of the University of California. It is small and stocks very few items but probably has the best meat available.

It's amazing how quickly one learns in a new country the essentials like giving directions to a taxi driver. He didn't even make off with the $15 worth of stuff from the supermarket when I asked him to stop at an open-air fruit bazaar and was out of sight for a few minutes. Old-timers tell me I ran a 50-percent risk. I'm terribly innocent in some ways and feel I have yet to be initiated into my new life.

Gradually we are expanding our diet. We had the new office secretary plus John Wicklund, an old-time staff member, for lunch today. The cook makes a very good spaghetti sauce, from scratch of course, including the stewing of the tomatoes for the paste. I spent about an hour making the salad, first washing lettuce from a friend's garden in Tide and water to get rid of the ever-present dust, and then rinsing with embassy well water. The cucumbers were soaked in an iodine solution — the same jazz with the bunch of grapes given to Greg by the market man. He treasured them all the way home without eating a single one until they had been through the works.

The amazing thing is what wonderful flavor fruits and vegetables have even after all the scrubbing, soaking, and/or cooking — always twenty minutes to kill the amoebas. Organic fertilizer really produces flavor, I have to admit.

Yesterday, we had the first day in three weeks more or less to ourselves. Now I know why an old-timer told me during our first week that I would have to get my husband out of the country for his yearly vacation to preserve his sanity.

There is no getting away from this job. Before we could depart for our picnic up in the foothills at Paghman, he had to take a young lady who is terminating under distressed circumstances to her plane. This once incident has kept both Walter and the doctor occupied for days.

He could hardly wait for the green light to speed the jeep out of town; however, we sort of leapt from the frying pan into the fire. We managed to find a secluded spot in which to eat our cold chicken, cucumbers, cookies and Cokes. Then we packed the gear into the jeep and started to walk up the road ever farther into the foothills — always following a stream from the melting snows up above.

Whenever we stopped to rest, we collected a crowd of young men dying to try out their English on Walter. Their cultural pattern is to show respect by not focusing on women. Even at this picnic spot, we saw mostly men.

I did see some westernized families with unveiled women at the little town near the arch where one enters the gardens. Farther up I saw only one other group of women, mostly hidden from view by a curtain made of blankets tied between trees. One of the men-folk shook his fist at me for trying to peek at the women.

So many of those young men invited us to come with them to their groups for tea and naan. We could not have accepted all those invitations, and I wondered if Kathryn and I would have been the only women if we had. The contrast between these friendly young people and the conservative older man who shook his fist is amazing to me. Thus it is all over the world. The thirst for knowledge for an expanding universe lies with the young.

As we wound our way up the trail between these brown hills of Afghanistan, we passed many donkeys laden with great blocks of snow wrapped in burlap for the bazaars in Kabul. It makes me chuckle to remember that one of the cargoes my great-grandfather carried from Maine to Brazil was ice.

There is a snow bazaar where you can go to buy snow to pack your ice-cream freezer. Someone hikes up into the Hindu Kush, carves it out and transports it out to the road, where it's trucked to market. The truck chassis are purchased abroad, but the bodies are built here. They are very high sided and gaily painted with intricate designs. Even bicycles are decorated with real and artificial flowers. You should see how the trucks sway down the road at top speed with Afghans hanging off at all angles. They have a fatalistic approach to their driving. *Enshallah*. God willing, they won't find a car coming the other way when they pass you on a curve.

By the way, getting out of Paghman was as bad as getting away from the Jersey shore on a Sunday. I've only been out of Kabul once, but the camel is definitely a backwoods item. I didn't realize at the time that the nomads were in the far north for the summer. So far, I've seen only four camels but every type of automobile imaginable, and they too are often loaded down with a whole clan of people.

One evening we took a drive after dark. The greatest hazard was the stalled cars sitting on the road with no lights to betray them. Also there was one lone motorcyclist trying to start a cranky vehicle in the middle of the road.

On our guided tour — you might call it that since we were unable to shake off the hard core of our young men — we saw some marvelous examples of why I'd hate to be condemned to be stoned à la ancient tradition by an Afghan mob. Every so often one of the fellows would spot a large lizard sitting on a rock. Neither Katie nor Christopher nor Greg could see them, since they are the same color as the rocks and perfectly motionless. These lads would pitch stones from some distance with unerring aim, landing them one inch from the lizard to show the kids where to look. Their marksmanship was very impressive, and later I was grateful they had remained with us.

On the open trail, it was very bright and sunny, but because of the altitude, not unbearably hot. When we wanted shade, we would go and sit under the willows that grow beside the streams. I was delighted, at last, to be near the sound of a bubbling brook. It is so dry and dusty everywhere in Kabul. Only now can I appreciate the many references in the Bible to the importance of water. As I wrote earlier, I often feel very close to the Bible times here in spite of the building boom in Kabul and the many vehicles.

When we got too hot and dry, we bent over the stream and splashed ourselves with the cold water — then drank the lukewarm water in our canteens while our Afghan hosts laughed and drank directly from the stream. With so many donkey drivers going uphill for the snow and little kids driving sheep and cows across the stream every so often, we didn't feel secure to drink from it ourselves.

Besides, on the way up where the stream crossed the road, we had to wait for an old man with his pants down washing his nether regions. (Much later, I realized he was performing a ritual before prayers, but his western trousers did not provide the same privacy and cover as the traditional baggy pants with the drawstring waist.) He was an awfully clean-looking old gentleman, but whatever water is around is used for everything. As one of the Peace Corps nurses said to me, "You can get these germs out by boiling and filtering, which you can't do with the industrial wastes at home." So who is worse off?

We exchanged language lessons on our hike, our asking the boys the Persian words for things and vice versa. I lagged

behind on the way down and was not watching ahead very carefully when I heard Walter call back, "What's the difference between
an ox and a bull?"

I didn't take the time to answer because among the cattle
coming up the trail was definitely a bull. When he caught sight of
me, the only female in sight and wearing a red shirt to boot, he put
his head down and started in my direction. This was when I was
grateful for the quick reflex action of the Afghans with their rocks
and stones. I stayed amidst the men the rest of the way back to the
jeep. Then we joined the four o'clock exodus of families trying to
get their cars back to Kabul. As John Wicklund had commented to
us earlier, "The covered-wagon days are over in Kabul."

Walter is dying to cross the desert in his jeep. Afghanistan
is still a very manly place to be, and he is glorying in it.

We seem to be over the series of little upsets we had and
are enjoying good health again.

Lots of love to all of you from all of us,

Janice

SHOPPING THE BAZAARS
FOR MY EXPERIMENTS IN COOKING

July 5, 1966
Kabul, Afghanistan

Dear Phyllis,

Your two pages of delightful news and chitchat arrived today — the whole fifty cents' worth. If you keep sending us wonderful letters like that, don't mention anything else. Tell Becky we will bring her back an Afghanistan doll complete with chadri or what Kathryn calls "spook dress," but shipping halfway around the world is problematical.

Shopping these bazaars is to shop the world. There are labels in every language. Still no tuna fish, but I've been offered sardines, shrimps, salmon and clams.

I'm sometimes surprised at what one can find and not find in these little shops. When one sees a can or a box or two of something, it's been stolen from some *godown* (someone's pantry) or elsewhere, and they have no idea how to price it. Some guy has a few jars of Dutch peanut butter that look good for a mere $2.50. No sir. On the other hand, a jar of English Meltonian shoe polish cost me 15 *afs*.

Chris's new American sneakers were stolen at the International Club pool, so we went to one of the big bazaar areas, called the Green Bazaar because the shops all have green doors. We went down the line stopping at about ten shops and finally found a pair of sneakers that fit, made in Pakistan, for about a dollar.

The stench in some of these back alleys is getting stronger now that summer is here. There are lots of alleys between compounds that seem designated as places to defecate. I may take to wearing the veil because as a woman you don't count, so the men who use these alleys ignore you. I find dark glasses hide my embarrassment. I might as well take advantage of the local dress code! As Greg and I were walking to a friend's house today, we passed a truck with soldiers shoveling up the alleys. That was encouraging.

Your faith in my ability to learn this country, its people and the language is uplifting. Sometimes I feel pretty discouraged because it's like nothing I've ever known or done before. The kids started Farsi today in a rather large class, and I'm having private tutoring beginning tomorrow. We shall see.

My travels within the country will have to be confined to winter and spring. I can't take the dusty dirt roads without my allergies kicking in. Sometimes there are real dust storms. Luckily, the high walls cut it down inside the garden, but I now stay indoors like a real Afghan woman when the dust is blowing. It's a very strange culture to get accustomed to.

On the other hand, I've gotten used to having the men around the house, and I no longer feel guilty about letting them do the chores. Just learning to get around town and shop is my project at the moment. I also haven't felt ship-shape every day.

Every so often, I make little experiments in cooking. One day, the children picked cherries because our trees were loaded. I boiled them up, took the juice to make Jell-O desserts and with the pulp made a jar of jam. We used an empty instant-coffee jar and an old candle for wax. We froze some too in old plastic bags found in drawers around the house.

Here nothing is wasted. The servants sell the tin cans, the farmers collect the garbage, and we use old bottles to store water. A gin bottle, because it's square, is the best to sit on the bathroom sink for toothbrushing water. Think of us the next time you throw out an old bottle.

Have I mentioned the climate yet? I do not miss the New Jersey humidity. There is none of that here. Many places go up to 110 and even 120 degrees in the summer, but Kabul is so high that the heat is only in midday. Evenings are already cool, even chilly. I nearly froze the other day in a sleeveless dress at a baseball game at 4:00–5:00 PM.

Thanks again for your letters. You are the only one outside of family who has written us. Your letters are wonderful.

By the way, Walter is glorying in his job. It makes it all seem worthwhile when I have a bellyache or a roach crawls on me in the middle of the night!

Love,

Jan

SALANG PASS DAY TRIP:
GIVING A DISCARDED TIN CAN,
WE FEEL LIKE PHILANTHROPISTS

July 19, 1966
Kabul, Afghanistan

Dear Folks at Home,

An unseasonable thing happened last week. It rained both Friday and Saturday — rather substantial showers. Never have I seen Afghanistan look as beautiful as when we rode out to the countryside early Sunday morning. Every leaf sparkled because it had been washed free of dust. This was a great relief for my allergies. Lambs and other animals were gamboling and people seemed gayer perhaps because of the lovely fresh smell of the earth and the coolness.

Walter, who is always worried about which direction the cows, herds of goats and sheep and so forth are going to bolt, eyed a pair of mules who were tearing along on the other side of the *juie* (all-purpose drainage ditch). He exclaimed, "Now what are they going to do?" Except for the fact that Walter has tougher insides and is less frequently off his food than I am, my Maine background seems to have prepared me for many aspects of a preindustrial society more than his urban European upbringing. So I suggested, "He thinks it's spring again, but she's not interested."

We were glad we made plans to do our traveling on Sunday this week, not only because we benefited from the rain, but because we avoided Friday, the Muslim Sabbath. Very little business is done on that day, but we are frequently so tired Friday mornings that we can't get started early enough to go very far. Also, the cook is off, so I have to return to cope with preparing an Afghanistan meal for the five of us at the end of a long ride.

Walter worked hard all day and late into the evening on Saturday so we could get an early start on Sunday when our embassy is closed. We were hoping to reach the mile-long tunnel that the Russians constructed at the Salang Pass — 12,000 or so feet up in the Hindu Kush. It was well worth the time it took to get there — about three hours. The Russians also built the approach road.

I would have been terrified to negotiate that approach on the old dirt road. We always go in a Peace Corps Scout (a jeep with windows). Even though it has no springs, it feels good to be in a tough vehicle under mountain conditions, and when we drive off the road to find a spot to picnic or sightsee, the four-wheel drive becomes necessary. If we come to grief in Afghanistan, it won't be due to unfriendly natives or microscopic enemies, but some hare-brained driver. We are eager to learn the appropriate phrases to holler at the fools, packed seven or eight in a sedan, who pass on a blind mountain curve.

On the way up, we saw many trucks with their engine blocks beside the road or their rear axles being removed. When we returned in the late afternoon, most of the car parts that had been beside the road in the morning were being put back into place.

Since Sunday is a big market and workday here, we are not mobbed whenever we stop as we are on Fridays. On Sunday the adults are working and the children are in school. Our three have gotten used to being surrounded by Afghan men and children two and three deep whenever we stop in a village on a Friday when folks have lots of time to just stop and chat. It's only Walter who gets fidgety.

When I worked in Jamaica years ago, the women would gather around wanting to touch my skin and hair. Of course I have not yet met a crowd of Afghan women. I'm looking forward to accepting one of these invitations to go into a village for tea and naan, but we will have to be sure we can politely ask that the tea water be boiled for ten minutes.

I met a volunteer Monday morning who was on his way home to bed. He had tea in a village on Sunday and said that he either had — or his mind was convincing him he should have — the trots. By the way, naan is the unleavened whole-wheat bread that represents the staple diet here. Poor people eat naan and drink very sweet tea three times a day. Even our servants, who are not the poorest of the poor, seem to work all day on tea and naan. Then, as Kathryn, who is such an observant child, said, "It logically follows that *naan* is also the word for a meal." *Naan taiores* is approximately how one pronounces that a meal is ready.

We ate our lunch on this side of the tunnel, crossing a small branch of the Salang River by skipping over some rocks to a field we shared with a herd of sheep. Walter cut himself on his jack-knife opening a can of Coke. As the youngest, Gregory was given the smallest bundle, containing our cookies and a can opener, but had left it behind on my bureau. When we crossed back over the river, Walter slipped and got a bad bone bruise and a star-shaped cut on his knee.

Our audience consisted of one soldier who was on his lunch break. Six others later joined him as we were leaving. He watched these strange people shaking his head sadly at Walter's performance. Afghans negotiate the most hair-raising footpaths and never seem to slip. For newcomers, however, the altitude can produce some lightheadedness. What's more, Walter was balancing a plastic pan with our lunch leftovers as well as the Cokes as he crossed the river.

But we all felt it was worth it. One gets such a feeling of being in a remote place looking out at the view, and yet we never seem to be far from a shepherd and his flock or a man far away on a snowfield chopping blocks of snow for the snow bazaars. Our first installment of things arrived this week. We now have an ice-cream freezer, so I guess I will learn where the snow bazaar is when it comes time to turn the crank.

One striking thing to see are the gangs of men still finishing the highway and tunnel by hand labor. We had to turn our brights up every few yards in the tunnel to spot the crews. We saw some men finishing an embankment with mortar and hand trowels.

I'm always asking my economist husband what comes after the consumer society. Here there's a preindustrial society with its inefficient methods, but keeping hordes of people busy and utilizing every scrap of material. By contrast there are the advantages of our industrial society and its concomitant disadvantages of unwanted leftovers piling up all over the landscape and refuse being pumped into the air and water. Should we be so cocksure of the direction we are taking and trying to lead every one else?

As one volunteer said to me recently, "Here, one can feel like a philanthropist simply by giving someone a discarded tin can."

Our *dhobi* (laundryman) was most delighted when Walter said that he could have the steel bands that had held our airfreight cartons together. Afghans are very proud, and there has been very little begging until recently, when more and more foreigners abound. Many little children try their luck, not too seriously, by selling a few flowers or simply asking for *paiseh* (coins). It reminds me of Christopher wanting to find a way to sell somebody something that's not needed. Maybe the penchant for selling is inherent in some little boys.

I finally found out where our kitchen garbage goes. Our baacha (literally "boy" but in fact a house helper, who can be any age) goes out with the pail every evening around the corner to an alley, which serves as an outdoor toilet as well, and adds it to the heap. The first time I walked that way, I was wondering about the source of the odor when I saw a truck and a crew of soldiers with shovels stop and start shoveling out the alleyway. Fertilizer for those delicious fruits and vegetables we get at the bazaar. We cook everything at a rolling boil twenty minutes, and still I have to admit that the flavor is very, very good.

Of course no Americans except the Peace Corps seem to eat from the bazaars. Everyone is convinced that 100 percent of the Peace Corps eventually come down with amoebas, but so do other people. Our Peace Corps doctor saw a servant using his dirty hand to swish out the water cans he was filling from the embassy's deep well supply. He was most likely working for a family who felt they were safe by eating only commissary food.

We have a marvelous Peace Corps cookbook that tells how to wash and prepare everything, including instructions for testing oven temperature on a kerosene stove by seeing how many minutes it takes for flour to turn brown. I'm getting a hankering for cottage cheese, so I will soon try to make some as they suggest by straining yogurt through cheesecloth.

Our cook makes wonderful yogurt — nice and thick every time. He brings the powdered whole milk made with embassy deep-well water to the boil and adds the starter when it has cooled somewhat. I asked him how he knew when to add the starter. He can't keep a straight face for two minutes. Grinning sheepishly, he held his little finger pointed downward, as if being in the yogurt, and counted "*Yak, du, sey, chor*" and so on up to seven. And so it goes! As Dr. de Maine says, "It's like playing Russian roulette with a loaded pistol to eat in Afghanistan." Sooner or later, your number comes up.

We have been excited and delighted by the many answers to letters we have gotten from friends. It's a toss-up whether it means more to us to get a letter or that the folks stateside receive ours. I only know that people must really love to read my inaccurate typing and still say they get something out of it.

We understand that the heat at home is extreme. Here the daily cooling breeze is coming up right on schedule, at four o'clock. My Farsi teacher will be here any minute.

The last two mornings were very hot, hitting 100 degrees in the sun and probably more, but the shade was only 80, with absolutely no humidity. This is desert climate. In the bright, unprotected areas, it's burning hot. A few feet away in the shade of a tree, pleasant — and every night, very pleasant. The brightness forces even me to wear sunglasses all the time. I forgot them yesterday when running errands and suffered for it. There's blinding sun. Many Afghans are carrying umbrellas for sun protection this week.

I'm grateful that Ramadan does not fall in the summer these days. Never a water guzzler at home, I certainly am here, and I cannot imagine the horrors of going for a month without food or drink from sunup (before five) until sundown (after seven). I just don't think I could ask our helpers to prepare me anything. This year, it starts on December 13. Most folks give servants their holidays during the last days when they are getting prepared for the big celebration that ends it all — and when tempers are about ready to snap.

My girlfriends in New Jersey were all wondering how I would spend my time with three men to do my chores instead of machines to operate myself. Actually, I got more done by myself. One chore I didn't have back home was standing up at obligatory official functions at least eight hours a week.

The photographer for the United States Information Service took a really funny picture of me looking sidewise at the man next in line to me. We actually have to "toe the line" so our formation was more military than that of the conscript Afghan army troops lined up on the other side of the blazing hot Kabul airport.

I simply refuse to wear a "Pepsodent smile" all the time, so I was looking sidewise trying to figure out who the new person next to me was. Later when the photos were available at the embassy, Walter was checking them out when that very chap asked him, "What does your wife have against me?" The photographer answered for Walter, "Perhaps she knows who you really are." Apparently he is what we call a "spook" for the CIA, posing as something else.

The occasion was the arrival of Secretary of Agriculture Freeman to dedicate the new Kabul–Kandahar highway — our competition to the Salang tunnel. Maybe camels kick up less dust than mechanical vehicles, but I can't imagine anything worse than dirt roads in a country where it usually doesn't rain at all for six months. When the wind comes up strong, as it sometimes does after four o'clock, we all wish we could wear a chadri to keep out the dust. Last week two of our windowpanes were broken during a sandstorm. All the windows in the house are European windows — that is, what we would call French doors. In rooms that have a cold exposure, they are double. All are loosely set in because of earthquakes.

We have not experienced one yet; however, they are supposedly frequent but light. There was a big one in Tashkent, USSR, to the north of us at the end of May, before we arrived. Kabul had two minutes of shakes, and my neighbor's sun porch fell down.

In most countries, you are told to stand inside a doorway during a quake. Here, we are told to get out fast. The reasoning is that our houses are of mud-and-straw-brick construction. Sometimes one can see the sag in someone's living-room ceiling. The beams are all young poplar saplings that are farmed for the purpose. You can tell the old-timers by who gets to the street first. I'm told that half the Peace Corps staff seemed to have been taking a bath during the May quake.

I now have my ten-page Afghan driver's license, complete with a picture of me and text in Arabic script — which my tutor says he will teach me. Phyllis asked me, "When you take the wheel, do you say three Hail Marys, close your eyes, and count the bumps?"

The advice I got when I first came was to keep one hand on the horn, one on the wheel and, if I could manage it, one on my heart. I worry for the women wearing chadri. I can see how a chadri provides some protection from the dust and male stares, but I find it alarming to observe an Afghan woman caught in the middle of a Kabul street with the free-for-all of buses, cyclists, donkeys, and porters drawing two-wheel moving platforms — when I know they are trying to see out of two inches of netting.

I travel far and wide now, looking for some item we need, and I walk miles in bazaars along unpaved streets, usually narrow, lined with tiny shops. Recently it was tall glasses and an eggbeater I was searching for. This is why everyone told me to bring so much. It is a personal triumph to track down what you need and not get skinned alive on the price.

I am beginning to put Farsi sentences together, but don't always understand the replies. I find some of the young fellows who work in the bazaars amazingly friendly. No one has spit at me yet for being an unveiled woman and a foreigner.

The other day when I was buying tomatoes from a young

donkey vendor, his donkey didn't want to stand still while I made my selection, and he (the boy, not the donkey) wanted to know several English words for things. Many of the young people are as eager to learn English as I am to learn Farsi.

Walter really loves his job, and the kids are having fun learning Farsi. They have a much better accent but smaller vocabulary than Walter and I. The children are also swimming at the International Club, which is the only place the Peace Corps swim because it is truly international and not strictly American. Afghans can and do belong, as well as many Germans and French.

At times, I envy the single volunteers their involvement in the life of the people. Then I remember that Saint Thérèse said married people must be content to proceed "at the pace of a hen." Peace Corps nurses really see the more ghastly side of life, and some of them will tell you stories with tears in their eyes. Because of the low level of calcium in the diet, just a little *makse* (yogurt), and the practice of veiling the women, many a young wife's pelvis collapses and makes childbirth well-nigh impossible. Even the modern schoolgirls without veils wear long black stockings and long-sleeved black uniforms in this summer weather, so they also receive no Vitamin D.

One Peace Corps couple told me Afghan women besieged the wife with questions about pills to help you have babies and pills to help you not. The latter are sold cheaply on the bazaar in Kabul. Even though the volunteer's language lessons had not included these kinds of words, the questions came with such regularity that she soon learned them.

Her husband taught a class of teenage boys, all of whom were married; they had a total of nineteen children, none of which were living. I'm told there is a saying in the villages, "The first one is for the wolves and jackals," from the need to cast the bodies outside the compound wall during hard winters when no graves can be dug. The student's wives were twelve and thirteen. In the villages if a girl is single at fourteen, she has already been passed by.

Some days are discouraging. Chris and I have the weakest systems, but he is cheerful about it and packs a piece of burned toast in his pocket when needed to help with the symptoms of dysentery. Greg and Katie seem to have Walter's toughness, but Greg tells us of one six-year-old friend who "has it all the time" standing on a post at the school hollering to the world at large, "I am the King of Diarrhea."

Just when I feel most low with symptoms, we drive out into the countryside. Pastoral Afghanistan is truly lovely. One has to get out of the compound and out of the city to experience it. Now the wheat fields are golden, and the other crops and trees still green. Wherever there is water, there are green, little havens of shade and fertility that people have wrested out of the tired earth.

The predominating color of Afghanistan is brown, as in the hills that divide Kabul into two sections and the homes made from the same brown earth and set into or on top of those hills. Riding north behind those hills one sees the black giants of the Hindu Kush rising high in the sky.

This was where we were headed on Sunday, to go back to the beginning of this letter. The scenery made you want to stretch out your legs, like the heroine in Michener's book *Caravans*, and take off with the nomads. The altitude may give you visions but also shortness of breath if you try to hike very far.

We sometimes see Kuchi camps in the fields. We're told these are "little" Kuchis, nomads who wander around within a small area. "Big" Kuchis traditionally traveled north into Russia and south into Pakistan, but modern states try to prevent the nomads from crossing their borders. Some Kuchis now travel on trucks and are becoming the entrepreneurs of Afghanistan.

The truck bodies are always added in country so that they can be made wider than normal and hand painted in intricate and colorful patterns. Sometimes the hood and front bumpers are removed and a sort of side platform is constructed. Thus it is not unusual to see a man sitting on either side of the block. Buses have roof passengers and always one or two men hanging on the rear, seemingly by their fingernails and toes.

Once, on a mountain road, I saw a roof passenger climb down the side of the bus, open the rear door and get inside, all while the bus was tearing along at the usual breakneck speed. When there is a breakdown, the passengers get out and pray.

Industrialization must create havoc with the five daily prayer times. One sees no general stoppage of work, but many men carry prayer beads in their hands as they walk about. One evening at sundown, we were very touched to hear the family on the other side of our compound wall chanting their evening prayers.

Today I realize that although we lived very near the Sherpur mosque, I never heard the call to prayers nor saw large numbers of people going in and out. Perhaps Afghans practice their faith more in solitude.

Being in a strange country makes you cling to what is uniquely you. Now the children insist on our Quaker silence before meals. We sometimes wonder what we will do about religious education since we don't fit into any of the groups that meet here in the various embassies. Anything that can be taken as proselytizing is forbidden in Afghanistan, so foreigners conduct their religious observances privately.

On any drive into the countryside, one has a strong sense of being plunged back in time, albeit in a four-wheel drive, to the days of the Old Testament. The villages and the clothing resemble illustrations in a Bible textbook for youngsters. Sometimes when I see a man leading a donkey with a woman riding and holding a small child, I catch my breath thinking of the holy family escaping to Egypt.

So in spite of the fleas that bite Walter at night, the roaches that sometimes share our bed, and the absence of a good piece of meat, we feel privileged to be here, part of the world as it was for countless ages, before this way is completely gone. Perhaps it will never be entirely gone. Perhaps, indeed, it should not completely change, but change it inevitably will, and our presence in the Peace Corps jeep is part of the change.

We've been here about six weeks now.

Lots of love from all of us,

Jan

Man with his wife riding a donkey in the backcountry

Tent-pegging contestant

CHAPTER TWO

The Whole Country Gets a Bit Wild during August

IN OUR OWN HOUSE NOW
THAT I CALL A SMALL HOTEL

August 10, 1966
Kabul

Dear Phyllis.

I find that I have a couple days a week over here when I feel ghastly physically. The kids too have their bad moments, but they pass. The Peace Corps doctor just tells me that with cooler weather and the passage of time, our systems will get accustomed to the local bugs. The servants also get more darn things, particularly accidents. They seem immune to the bugs that get us, but unused to machinery. One hurt his eye badly when we moved in by running into the corner of a heavy armoire.

Another, who is supposed to be sleeping here and waiting for the former tenant to come back from home leave, dropped something on his toe when they moved out. It looks positively gangrenous today. They don't trust their own doctors and always prefer us to take them to the Peace Corps doctor, who is flat out at this time of the year treating about thirty-five cases of amoebic dysentery. Finally, Walter intervened today at the local hospital and got an American CARE Medico doctor to look at him. I've given up trying to explain to the fellow that he infected a toe that was only bruised by soaking it in a cracked pottery bowl that once had plants in it that had been watered from the all-purpose ditch. If it looks clean to them, it's clean. He even insists that he washed the bowl.

The worst problem is they do think we have some kind of magic and can help them after they've neglected something for so long. The chap with the oozy toe came to me two different days always at a time when my stomach was about ready to give way anyway. The Afghan hospitals are sad looking. Last week, I took the chap with the injured eye. A policeman, probably to keep out all the relatives who are literally camping on the grounds, always guards the hospital door.

As we passed the wards, I saw mostly old people. The CARE Medico nurse told me they just don't come in time. Every week someone comes to me for the day off because someone for him is *mord* (dead). They seem to grieve more if it's a male child or friend, but not if it's a daughter. I have just learned that the grief period for a mother is three days. There are some very old-looking people around — probably tough as nails.

Well, I really didn't mean to go on like this. Usually, we are all quite gay. Even the Afghans grieve at one moment and in the next are laughing. Even when they try to get more money and are turned down, because you aren't dumb enough to fall for it, they will smile.

We go after lunch to the embassy to sign the papers selling our house. Apparently, the same family that looked at it before we left finally sold theirs and bought ours "as is."

We are also in our own house here now — a small hotel, I call it. There is a main living-dining room about the size of our first floor on Whittier, a reception room that I call the lobby, with a small private office off to the side for those very personal interviews Walter sometimes has to have. We already have enough stories about volunteers' problems and adventures and misadventures to fill a book, but they are too personal to circulate. Then there is a family wing which looks like a hotel corridor: three small bedrooms all in a row, each big enough for a bed, chest, and bookcase.

Our bedroom at the end is quite spacious, a little larger than our living room at home, which as you know was admittedly small. All the windows in the house face the garden with a row of tall pines near the back wall. They sigh in the wind just like the pines on the island in Maine and keep me from being homesick. An apple tree in the middle is now loaded with apples. Outside the bedroom window is a garden of dahlias, another reminder of Maine and my favorite.

Our Quaker Meeting friends are laying bets that we will become subverted by foreign assignments and never come home for good. I believe we would not want to be a foreigner for the rest of our lives. "How can we sing the Lord's song in a strange land" is the dedication to our Peace Corps cookbook that gives us recipes for the delicious local dishes.

I'm gradually getting to know the volunteers. The group I enjoy the most, so far, is made up of three couples. All the husbands and one of the wives are doctors. They are now in Kabul for the summer because their post in Jalalabad was too hot. They are part of a medical-school program to train local doctors. The man in one couple must be seventy-two and she about seventy. They ride their bicycles like all volunteers to their jobs. I just got my bike out by the way, but I ventured no further than the Blue Mosque Bazaar three blocks away. My wheels are unbalanced, so I need to get them fixed. There is a shop that can repair bikes and other things right at the end of our block.

Some days I do very well with my language skills and negotiate most of the day with what Farsi I know in the bazaars and around the house. I'd like to get to the point where I can talk with an educated Afghan woman about subjects of mutual interest, not just vegetables and how to get housework done; the truth is that many of them know some English.

My life is really crazy and split up. We will soon have to give a reception for our new deputy and doctor to be presented to the official community — about one hundred persons. I'm still trying to figure how you do this without commissary privileges. It all comes out of our own pocket as well, but at least we don't have to pay rent. The Peace Corps rented this larger house so that we wouldn't have to rent outside facilities anymore for this kind of thing.

I've decided to get the International Club to cater it. Anwar and I can get together a meal for twelve or twenty or thirty very nicely. I surely appreciate that man's abilities even though we've had one big fight during which he threatened to quit over the issue of wearing clean clothes. He's been building his own house and was cooking for thirty volunteer nurses in town for a conference in those same clothes.

I insisted he change. When he threatened to quit, I simply walked away and left him alone and trusted to his pride to finish the meal. By the time next morning rolled around and no one had mentioned his threat, he was a teary-eyed man (in his early thirties, I think) telling Walter that we were really like a mother and father to him.

Walter let him know that he was not the one to come to with problems and questions, that he should bring them all to me. This is our division of labor. He already has his hands full. Still, sometimes it does seem like having six children, and that just isn't right. They are all grown men and are paid well to do their jobs. I refuse to mother them, but perhaps with their attitude toward women, it's the safest role to adopt.

Our new doctor is Chinese American, a twenty-two-year-old genius with a redheaded wife, twenty-eight (a greater age difference than Walter and I). They arrived last week. I've been shepherding her around the bazaars and helping her get settled. She's already buying rugs, something I'll have time to do about next Christmas when it gets cold.

In thirteen days our deputy director arrives. His wife believes she can live in the hotel (there is no Intercontinental Hilton here yet) and look for her own house with no car, no Afghan license and less Farsi than I had when I arrived. She just feels that no one can pick out a house for her even though the Peace Corps has an empty one for which it must pay rent until December anyway. I've been corresponding with her and humorously giving her some of the facts about life in Afghanistan and how none of us goes it alone. The embassy housing officer, who must okay everything, is a stinker who started a new leaf by being agreeable with us. We are all holding our breath about his reaction to this.

So I will next have to teach someone how to survive in Kabul, and I've only been here eight weeks myself! I was sick the day our embassy had its orientation for newcomers, but other Americans never do have to get out into the environment the way Peace Corps does. Some friends of mine said that Walter gave the best speech of the whole day. He was a speaker but he also received the usual obligatory invitation to attend his own orientation. Ha! Ha! George Carter, the area coordinator in Washington, told him he was the best-oriented Peace Corps rep ever to leave Washington, having been here for two weeks in the spring.

I'm just waiting to catch our new arrival when she faints dead away from surprise. They were in Jamaica with the Peace Corps and feel they know all about foreign living. Ha! Ha! Kingston has clean tap water, an agreeable, one-season climate, no altitude and no time differential, so one doesn't arrive with jet lag. Do you realize we are always getting up when you are going to bed?

Just wait until she's flown for several hours over that desert and lands in a narrow valley of green surrounded by high mountains. Driving into town from the airport, she will pass mud-walled villages, men threshing wheat now as they did in the Bible times, sheep being herded across the road, and little children and market men washing vegetables in the ditch, the same vegetables she will have to eat. Delicious they are, but dangerous if not handled correctly.

She says she'll have fun living in the hotel and looking for her own house. Walter started looking in March when he was here alone. We moved in August first after about two months in the former rep's house, a very comfortable one and still available. Can you see living in a hotel all that time with six- and thirteen-year-olds while there is an available house? There is a Yiddish expression for this that I can't spell.

Honestly, Phyllis, your letters are just wonderful. By the way, Kathryn has one German girlfriend, and they get by somehow with a little Farsi, a little English, and a little German. Walter watched a bridge game at the International Club going on in French, German, and English. Each person exclaimed in his own language, and the others understood. He said, "I swear this is the New World!"

We now live surrounded by Afghans. Some lovely little girls run up to me on the street. The level of living is so different, I don't know if our kids will make these contacts stick. Some Afghan boys ganged up on Chris when he was riding a friend's bike, but an Afghan man rescued him. You see, no Afghan child has a bicycle. Their fathers do. The boys ride on donkeys. It's the old story. You come in with all your different gadgets and ideas and start changing a culture, and you get new and different problems.

Two nights ago a British volunteer was badly treated by six young Afghans in western clothes while walking from one house to another at 11:00 PM. They probably figured she was looking for some excitement. Our girls usually go in pairs and on bikes. If it's real late, some of the fellows accompany them home. Some sections are poorly lit.

I've adapted the westernized Afghan style of wearing a thin scarf around my head and over my nose after dark. It helps keep out the dust and is the symbol of modesty. That was what the chadri was all about — protection of women. Too bad men can't conduct themselves without this, but perhaps we are fighting nature if we feel women can always protect themselves.

I do wish I could find your letter because you asked so many questions. Since you went away, our sea and airfreight arrived within ten days of each other. So what was all the flap about? I should have sent it all by sea. After unpacking our boxes, I felt that my home is here now, and I should write to you on one of those days when my spirit is high. It's on those days, however, that I can most go out and cope with learning Afghanistan. Then I get a couple days of bad digestion and low morale and I stay inside to write letters.

I've a good bit of shopping to do for this house. We are entitled to new drapes for the large living-dining room and reception rooms. There are five large French doors about eight feet high and five feet wide to be covered in the large room and two in the smaller. I imagine the windows rattle some in an earthquake.

The Afghan air-force jets were practicing for Jeshen, a national weeklong holiday at the end of August, and the sonic boom reverberated along all that glass. Otherwise this place is peaceful, and when I read the *Times* with all the race riots and mass murders, I shiver and shake. Our doctor's wife recently accompanied a pregnant volunteer to the States and says, "Never again." It was too much in too short a time, and she was glad to get back. Isn't that something!

Phyllis, I hope you and Karen had nice vacations. If I haven't answered all your questions, I will eventually. I read your letter four times, so I should remember. Sorry I have no decent paper.

By the way, Walter comes to the States on September 6 for a week. He will pass through Westfield, I think. I will try to find one of the Afghan dolls dressed in chadri so you can get a picture of style in this country. If you are still intent on sending us something, why don't you save a heap of money on postage and let Walter pick it up. He only has forty-four pounds of luggage on the flight, but what is really most appreciated here are little packages of dehydrated things like sour cream, mushroom gravy, spaghetti sauce or soups. It takes so long to concoct anything here that such things are very helpful on the days the cook is away.

I'm sorry for the horrible writing. My penmanship is even worse than my typing. When I have an Afghan stomachache, I'm lightheaded and find it more comfortable to sit in a chair with paper and pen than at a typewriter. The doctor has a picture in his office, composed by a volunteer, of all the assorted bottles and vials that come in our Peace Corps medicine kit, entitled "No matter what you do, you are sick half the time anyway."

It is certainly true of me, but when I feel good, I feel very, very good and eat and do everything. What else can one do? It's only unfortunate that today when I'd rather not have to cope with cooking, it's the cook's day off and the houseboy is at a three-day funeral for his mother. The only one left to help is the fellow hobbling on his bad foot. You see, it is like having an extended family. One gets as much problem as help sometimes.

Lots of love,

Jan

STRAIGHT OUT OF A CECIL B. DEMILLE MOVIE: HORSEBACK TENT-PEGGING CONTEST IN JESHEN

August, 1966
Independence Week, Kabul

Dear Phyllis:

Yesterday was quite a day for me. It seems I've been here just long enough that I'm entering the four-month depression crisis that all the volunteers go through. As we sat at the breakfast table, Walter talked of renewing our exit visas so that we would always be able to leave should an emergency arise at home. Having just dealt with our latest servant crisis, I leaned on my elbow and said, "Yes, you keep that exit visa in shape. I just might want to leave on a moment's notice."

The crisis involved our dhobi (laundryman). Abdul Ahmed would not be coming in for a few days because, we were told, he had been stabbed while coming home late from a wedding. We visited his compound later to find out how he was doing. He came to greet us happily cradling his infant son and wearing one of the elegant long purple-and-green striped robes common for men from the north. This took place in a large compound that housed several families. Before we left, one of the Indian neighbors took us aside and told us that Abdul Ahmed had really gotten high on hashish. When his father-in-law tried to restrain him from leaving the compound, they struggled with a knife. That was how he got injured.

The whole country goes a bit wild during August. This week is the official Independence celebration, Jeshen. There are only two official days of school closings, but a whole week of parades and athletic events. People pour into Kabul from all over the country.

We've been strongly warned to double-guard everything. Yesterday afternoon we visited the Jeshen grounds. The police were very protective of foreigners. Our foreign faces just assured they would usher us through the crush. Our servant, who was on duty yesterday, couldn't get in to work until ten o'clock because of the early-morning opening-parade crowd. "Not so good for Afghans," he explained, "but okay for Americans" to get through the traffic.

So I cooked breakfast, which does not sound like much. But I can never find anything because the fellows put everything in different places. I have to open every drawer before I find what I'm looking for. Later I tried to make some of your cooked mayonnaise. I have discovered that the cook makes his with raw eggs. The doctor says this is "*Khub na'ez*," not good.

It is discouraging to cook in Afghanistan. There are so many things you can't use raw, and there are so many things you just can't get. Then too, I had just received my mother's letter evoking all the fresh smells of the Maine seacoast and a picnic they had out in the boat. I was very near to tears in reading the letter and trying to make the mayonnaise.

The summer has been unusually hot. Every day when I step outside the compound, the feces odor hits me. The men squat anywhere, particularly now with so many country folk in town. Fortunately since the climate is hot and dry, everything dries out pretty fast.

Finally we took off after lunch to witness one of the Jeshen events. I had no idea what to expect. This was an experience one could only have in Afghanistan. It was straight out of a Cecil B. de Mille movie!

Walter got us into the grounds and left us in the shade of a canopy, sitting on a thick dark red carpet with the boxy black designs called *filpoy* or elephant feet.

This is how it works. There was a very narrow ditch between us and the field where the horsemen were going to compete. They race down the field with an outstretched forked lance and pull up a wooden tent peg. It's called a tent-pegging contest — a skill needed for surprising the enemy in his tents. This would be performed at breakneck speed on a field about a quarter of a mile long. It was obvious that the event was not quite ready to begin, so ever-restless Walter left to go to the post office.

Just before he appeared back on the scene, we heard the tribal drums sounding. Above the heads of the crowd (all men) on the opposite side of the field, we saw the colorful flags of the horsemen waving. Suddenly across the field thirty of them emerged in their brightest and finest clothes. They were wearing gorgeous velvet vests trimmed with gold braid — and their horses were adorned with colorful bridles ornamented with silver.

The crowd got so excited they charged with them. This is when I didn't know what was part of the script. The kids and I just sat there on the red carpet and stared in complete fascination. I had an image of a thousand years ago of the horsemen and tribesmen of Tamerlane crossing the Asian steppes. Surely, those tribesmen were dressed exactly the same with their turban tails flying out behind.

The horses were the greatest horseflesh I have ever seen. They stopped on cue directly in front of the ditch at the edge of the carpet for anyone who had a camera to take their photo. Sadly, we didn't have ours. The ragtag crowd, yelling with excitement, leapt the ditch hoping to settle down with us in the shade. It seemed, however, that the canopied section was reserved for government officials, foreigners, and guests of the royal family. So far only the children and I were sitting there.

At this point, every policeman in sight started beating the people on their heads with billy clubs and shooed them all back. The crowd was mostly laughing and appeared to be resigned to going back across the field. It had been a good try, but it was rather sad in a way. I think it would not endear foreigners to Afghans at large.

The whole sequence took place in front of and all around us. After twelve years of marriage, I am used to being abandoned in public places by my husband, who simply cannot bear to sit still for two minutes. But you can imagine that when those horses, drummers, and hundreds of shade seekers started charging toward the children and me, I was not thinking the most complimentary thoughts about him. It turns out he saw the whole thing as he was coming in the gate, but the effect could not possibly have been as startling and impressive for him as it was for us.

The tent-pegging contest was marvelous to behold. The Afghans are certainly dashing horsemen. Their verve is more admirable on a horse than charging down the highway in an overloaded Ford sedan. They rarely missed scooping the peg out of the ground — but we did wonder how they managed to raise the lance in time to prevent breaking an arm at the speeds they were traveling.

Only one horse was not perfectly trained, and charged the crowd on the opposite side of the field instead of the peg. The umpire, who blew a whistle to signal the next rider to take off, first stood next to the peg as the men started off, so they could tell more or less where it was. After all, there was no tent to mark the spot!

One rider actually wore glasses, something I have not seen on any other Afghan. A few of the men had dyed red beards — a sign that they have been to Mecca. I wondered where these dashing horsemen and fiery horses hide all year?

Halfway through the contest, the prime minister, dressed in a western suit, crossed the field. He looked quite drab beside the contestants in their colorful vests and turbans. They all ran forward to kneel and kiss his hand, an act he seemed to accept with a mixture of annoyance and resignation.

By now there were others under the canopies, including three women all wearing the Nuristani garment for Jeshen: baggy pants of bright colors under a black, full-skirted dress sewn with many bangles, bright green filmy head scarves and, of course, a lot of silver jewelry.

One of the girls was Afghan; the other two were American. The blonde posed for a photo holding the bridle of one of the horses. We were all speculating.

An American girl arrived recently wanting to become the second wife of an Afghan. The embassy is in a tizzy. Walter asked a chap from the embassy who he thought the blonde was. He had a quick answer. "Oh, that's Ellen Jaspers." If you read Michener's *Caravans*, you'll get the joke.

And now, to answer your question about Vice President Humphrey . . . he did not come. Secretary of Agriculture Freeman came in his place. He stayed with the king about forty-eight hours and asked us to bring the Minnesota PCVs to the palace annex, a long narrow room with lots of carpets and a few couches against the wall for western seating. Next Tuesday, however, we give a reception for about one hundred people to meet the new deputy and Peace Corps doctor. About 160 Afghan, UN, CARE and other agency officials are invited. About one hundred come because those Afghans who do come do not bring their wives.

No, Phyllis, I never wear shorts or slacks inside or outside the compound. The servants seem to look upon me as a sort of mother figure. It's a better relationship than stirring up other feelings in this most puritanical of people. Walter has been warning all our girls to walk in groups if they have to go out after dark.

One British Peace Corps volunteer was recently picked up at about 11:00 PM by six semi-westernized Afghans and driven about fifty miles. No Afghan woman, even in chadri, is seen out after dark without her husband, brother, or son. So they interpreted this girl's actions as that of a lady drumming up business. After they undressed her, she fainted and they fled.

Only at the International Club do I peel down to a bathing suit. The Afghans who work there must be shockproof by now because you should see the bikinis the German women wear.

A few weeks ago Walter arrived for a quick dip after work in time to pull a three-year-old German child, who had drowned, out of the pool. All other adults were packing up to leave so he started her breathing again by mouth-to-mouth resuscitation. When I asked him who she was, he said, "I don't know, but her mother is one of the bikini girls. I know them all by sight." Her daddy has since been to the office to thank Walter, so we now know their name.

Some months later, the family invited Walter to dinner and presented him with a beautiful lapis and gold ring the father had made for him. He saw the child asleep in her bed and could tell she had grown. As he showed me the ring, he shared what came to him seeing her again: "Well, at least, I saved one of yours." It seemed to bring him some of the peace he was seeking and release from a feeling of guilt for having survived the Nazis when so many others did not.

Life may have its heartaches over here, but at least it is never dull. By the way, we had our first earthquake last week, a few hours after one in Tashkent, which is the usual pattern.

Before we could get our feet out of bed, however, it stopped. It was about 7:00 AM, and we were just waking up when the bed began to rock. There was a grinding sound, sort of like the big oil trucks changing gear out on North Avenue at the end of our block at home. But there are no trucks that big here to jar a bed. When I realized where I really was and opened my eyes, I could see the chandelier swaying. Still half asleep, Walter moaned, "Janice, stop shaking the bed."

Walter comes to the States on September 6 and returns on the 21st. Save yourself some postage and mail your most welcome dehydrated packets to him at 108 Runyon Avenue, Deal, New Jersey. He is bringing Becky one of the cloth dolls made by Afghan women. It is dressed, complete with chadri, with its many pleats that are put in when the material is wet.

I would like a glass of fresh milk so much I can taste it. Powdered whole milk is available in quantity but tastes awful straight. It's fine for cooking. Finally, after three months, I couldn't bear it, so I asked someone going to Kandahar to bring back some powdered skim where they openly sell CARE and UNICEF milk on the bazaars.

Don't be disillusioned. This is the way of the world. Afghan adults and children alike will only drink tea, so until they learn new habits, we will gladly buy back the milk that generous people send over. We do crave something other than the gallons of tea that all five of us consume.

Dr. de Maine and his wife Lourdes recently drove across the desert in a jeep to visit volunteers in some of the remote areas. These are the volunteers that really make the Peace Corps great. They do a terrific job, often with very little help from anyone because they are so isolated.

They are usually healthier because the small towns are cleaner than Kabul. Kabul is simply filthy. The de Maines had to drink the water from the irrigation ditches, with the addition of iodine tablets, and they always ate the naan, tea and kebabs in the little roadside stopping places. Someday I will go with Walter, but I gather I should take an inflated pillow because you do not drive on a four-lane highway, but rather straight across the desert, guided by the Afghan driver's memory.

Thank you so much for your wonderful letters. They do evoke strong and heartwarming memories.

Jan

A street in Kabul

Balahisar Citadel, Old Kabul

Janice on high mountain pass

Walter on a solo trip to the interior

CHAPTER THREE

Lessons and Boundaries

PASHTUNWALI
HAS ITS LIMITS FOR ME
September 2, 1966
Kabul

Dear Phyllis,

Your letters seem to arrive when I need therapy the most. You asked if the new deputy director and his family had arrived. The answer is yes, and we obeyed their wishes of not fixing a house for them — albeit with some misgivings. They were visibly shaken when they got off the plane, so naturally we brought them home and put them up. There was no more talk of going to the Kabul Hotel.

Of all the new staff, they are the only ones who have had a previous Peace Corps assignment. Some newcomers were looking forward to their modeling ways for us to cope. Unfortunately, there is no resemblance between Kingston, Jamaica and Kabul! The husband is a perfect Southern gentleman and very protective of his wife. She has a saccharine voice — meant to hide hostility to her husband, I suspect. I've discovered that even Southerners can be puritans, and I'm so damn glad I'm married to a non-puritan.

Kabul has been a culture shock for all of us, but then it really grows on you. There is something special about being a part of the Peace Corps mission in this remote and starkly beautiful ancient world.

The Afghans have a traditional practice of hospitality called *pashtunwali*: you must give hospitality to the traveler, even if he is your worst enemy, for three days. (A bit like our saying that after three days relatives and fish . . .) This is the tenth day for us with five extra beings in the house (four humans and one cat), and I told Walter one hour ago that when he leaves in three days' time for his next trip back to the States, if our new arrivals aren't out on their own — I am.

It may look easy to manage a household with three servants, but it's a job of another kind — much like being an executive. I must learn to supervise in a foreign language. They need explicit directions and also come to you with all their troubles. But we are settling down to a dull roar now. When the Binghams arrived, I had underfoot, besides them and their culture-shocked black cat, five bearers from the embassy digging a drainage pit for the new servant washroom, three tailors doing drapes, and two extra servants that the previous tenants wanted us to keep employed until they returned from home leave. We have since fired them. At the same time, I was preparing a reception for one hundred people to introduce the Binghams to Afghan and official society, including the UN, CARE Medico, and the rest. The event was a roaring success despite the tailors clearing out barely one hour before the first guest arrived.

You won't be surprised to learn that the other drapes in the house are made of a heavy white Pakistani material with tiny flecks of black. I've sewn bedspreads for all the kids from Afghan textiles. Their bedrooms all have a window onto the garden.

The garden is a great blessing because a compound can be claustrophobic even though I appreciate that the walls do cut down on the dust. My allergies have cleared up, and we now have a kitten and are soon to get a puppy. For Easter, I've said that I'd like chickens and a baby lamb. The kids keep talking about a horse, but the mares are all kept in the countryside. There are only strong-willed stallions in Kabul, I'm told. Since we are not great horse people, I think we'll pass for the time being.

You are a dear, sweet friend to collect goodies for us. We will be ecstatic. Yes, we now have the peanut butter, tuna, and cans of bacon we brought and are rationing ourselves for the duration. It's good for people from the affluent West to have to do this. I agree with you that modern civilization may be due for a downfall. The news from the U.S. surely makes grim reading from this distance.

After tramping to the Old City to find *gur*, brown raw-sugar hunks the Kuchi nomads trade and which one can boil down to molasses, I discovered I still lack ginger to make molasses cookies. Perhaps I could take a slow boat to China for that.

Love and kisses to all
(especially that cute little boy in sunglasses and cap),

Jan

P.S. Our long-lost boxes arrive in Beirut September 10!

UPSTATE NEW YORK, 2006

A SEARCH FOR GUR: WOMEN SHOULD NEVER GO
TO THE OLD CITY ALONE

Anwar's previous employer told me he knew how to make pancake syrup, so I was surprised when he told me that there was no more. He said to make more he needed something called gur, but he didn't seem to know where to get it.

We had not yet established our communication lines. He was getting used to the fact that he must deal with the woman of the house but was still quite guarded. His former employer also spoke fluent Farsi. I saved all questions for my weekly Farsi class with an Afghan instructor who worked for the Peace Corps.

He explained that gur was an item the Kuchis traded and it could only be found in the Old City. Then he gave me clear instructions how to go to the Old City, some distance away from our house. He said I would need to leave my car at the post office because the streets in the Old City were very narrow. Gur is a form of raw sugar from the sap of certain palms, and I was told I would find it next to the raisin bazaar. Anwar looked blank when I asked him if he could get it, so I decided it must be too far for him to peddle on a bicycle.

What an adventure I had! The Old City was definitely an ancient world. No signs of any modernity in those winding streets flanked with tiny wooden stalls on either side. I was the only woman in sight, but was modestly dressed, according to our standards. My high-necked dress fell well below my knees. However, I remembered, after I had gone some distance, that sleeveless dresses were frowned upon. Mine had only a ruffle at the shoulders. I was sorry I'd left my cardigan in the car, but I kept going, asking people for the *kishmish* bazaar and was always told *ruberu*, meaning "straight ahead." Everyone I approached looked at me as if I might have dropped down from another planet.

Finally a street vendor who sold used sweaters stopped in front of me. He had ingeniously draped an array of sweaters for sale on several interlocking hangers over his shoulders. We were standing opposite a *chai khana* (teahouse) where the balcony that jutted over the street was crowded with men — even though it was midafternoon.

When did they work? I told him what I was looking for, and he indicated to follow him. Almost immediately we turned into an even narrower side alley where the buildings were so close together that sunlight barely penetrated.

For a second I held my breath. "Where is he taking me?" I wondered. Then he stopped and pointed to a small shelf cut into the wall of a nearby building. There were three piles resembling stone cairns marking a hiking trail. While he went to look for the shop-keeper, several small children literally came tumbling down the steep alleyway, all shouting, "*Horaji, horaji!*" which means "foreigner."

After I paid the merchant what seemed like a pittance for a large bag of the brown rocks, the sweater vendor and I reemerged into the sunlit main alley opposite the teahouse. Our foray had obviously not gone unnoticed by some of the men on the balcony.

They did not whistle like New York City construction workers at a passing female, but they loudly guffawed and called to my guide in a suggestive tone of voice. It was clear to me they were putting a sexual connotation on our venture into the dark alley. However, the vendor turned to me, bowed gallantly, and went on his way.

My grandmother, with whom I lived as a child, conditioned me to expect only the best from people. She never went anywhere but what she didn't return saying, "The nicest man helped me with my bags." For this reason, my mother refused to let her take me to the New York World's Fair when I was ten years old because "she'd let you talk with strangers."

I didn't write about this adventure to my mother. Why? A matron on post, who frequently imagined illicit sexual dramas, admonished several of us new wives saying, "You must never go to the Old City alone."

I said nothing. My supply of gur appeared adequate for the duration. I would not need to return again, but it was an open window on a world I'd never seen before. It made me wonder what the mothers of the little children who ran after me were doing behind their walls and if I'd ever make an Afghan woman friend.

KATHRYN'S CLASS PERFORMS
THE NATIONAL DANCE: *ATTAN* WITH AFGHAN
CHILDREN AT GHAZNI STADIUM

September 30, 1966
Kabul

Dear Folks at Home,

I am sitting here in the sunny garden hidden partially in the shade of the apple tree. The overhead sun is still very strong at midday. We planned to go to Bamian, or Bamiyan, this weekend because we sorely need to get away. Then Group IX we've been waiting for began to straggle in from the States in dribs and drabs due to governmental red tape. They had trouble getting everyone's clearance finished so that they could travel together.

We had about thirty of them plus staff for dinner on Wednesday, and I was very impressed with the several young married couples in this new group — all of them slated for the toughest assignments in the provinces. In some ways, these are the most satisfying, for the provinces are very beautiful and society still traditional. They will be the only westerners there.

I often wonder. Do we really want the whole world to become westernized? What does it really mean? I am often frustrated with traditional Afghans — namely our servants and the difficulties I encounter with their pride where the burden is on me as the foreigner to learn their language and ways. I suppose they find me puzzling, too. Whenever I lapse into English with the cook, he pretends he understands English very well. The results are sometimes disappointing, but he insists later, when I'm unhappy with the results, "You say! You say!" I told him that Walter and I would be late for dinner the other night, so he didn't save anything for us. We accompanied the new Group IX to the chargé d'affaires' at five o'clock that night for apple juice, popcorn and doughnuts — not a substitute for a hot meal.

It is good that we are staying in town for the weekend, for our little daughter has been chosen to dance at the children's Jeshen (Afghan Independence celebration) on Sunday with some others from the AISK (American International School of Kabul) and Afghan school children. She has been practicing for several weeks, but with her usual modesty didn't give us the full details.

Yesterday they went to the big Ghazni stadium to rehearse the entrance with the Afghan children and to learn the *attan*, a national dance performed by Afghan children — quite different from the square dances that the children from her school will put on. She has a real gift for dance even at this awkward age. Without any embarrassment, she volunteered to show us the attan. She described how well the little Afghans do it, even the ones smaller than Gregory, and how the members of the royal family were out to watch the rehearsal. Did you ever think, any of you grandparents, that your granddaughter would dance before the king of Afghanistan!

It's true that in many ways the children are getting so much more out of this country and its people than we can ever hope to achieve. The father who drove Kathryn home from the stadium just before supper last week was reluctant to let her off with the others a couple blocks from here. She told him, "I'm picked up and let off every day by the school bus in front of my door, and now I want to walk. Besides, everyone around here knows me." It startled me to hear her say this, but it does seem to be true. Every time she goes out onto the street, the neighborhood children surround her. They seem to just wait for her to appear. She has a quiet modesty about her and understands enough of what they are saying. They are always pressing something on her — a bunch of grapes that she quietly gives to a smaller child, or a bracelet like the thin bangles all the little girls here wear.

Chris, too, is more adjusted and happier than I have ever seen him. He has a very special relationship with some of the volunteer fellows and even more contact here than in New Jersey with his very busy father. Then too, he loves all the animals. The other day he came home with yet another street puppy. This one was a male and looked like a beagle, and this scared the rather subdued female Afghan hound mix he brought home a few weeks ago.

When I told Chris that I thought we have enough animals for the present, he said, "But I like this one too!" I felt sad about it because it was a darling puppy. It could get poisoned this winter. When the street dogs become so hungry they become dangerous, the government lays out poisoned meat. If it survives it would most likely become sullen and distant, as dogs are not made into pets here.

If you adopt a street dog as a puppy, you get a good dog. One family even has a Kuchi nomad dog that they adopted as a puppy, and it certainly is startling to have this enormous animal, with a tremendous head and square jaw, slobbering all over you. We passed a Kuchi dog once in the Salang pass. It was tied underneath a truck and was so fierce that we were scared, even inside the Scout.

The children sang the song they learned in French class to finish the tape Walter made for you today. Kathryn says that their French teacher has tears in her eyes when they sing "The Clock in the Castle" song. I can imagine that Nani Blass will too. Their accent is so much better than mine will ever be, in either French or Farsi, although I now know far more Farsi words than they do.

Gregory told one of the volunteer girls that he was going to learn German, and she asked him why. "I think it's because he has a German girlfriend," I confided. There are lots and lots of German families in this section of town. It may be where Chris learned the goose step and the "Heil Hitler!"

As soon as he started it, I called him to me and asked him if he knew who Hitler was. He said that he didn't, so I briefly said that it was because of Hitler that Daddy and Nani and Grampi left Europe. I told him that Hitler was a very wicked ruler, rather like Nebuchadnezzar in the Bible. He, too, built a big furnace and tried to burn all the Jews he could find. I never had to say anything more, and there has been no more "Heil Hitler!" or any nightmares. I didn't lay it on with a heavy hand, but only added that it took a good part of the world several years to stop this man and that most grownups had to give up a piece of their lives to do it. I have always found that children can handle the truth.

Our friends who went to Bamiyan with their four children last weekend say we will be sorry if we don't take them, even if they do miss school. Apparently, there is something to see all the way. One goes through a pass 10,000 feet high to get there and passes so many beautiful valleys where it looks tempting to pitch a tent.

In fact, now that fall is here, the Kuchis are on the move south. Our friends passed many caravans of up to forty camels. Even going to Paghman when Walter was away, I saw my first real Kuchis. They are a marked contrast to the filthy bunch that we see in the general area most of the time. The real Kuchis are the healthiest and wealthiest people in Afghanistan. Even their camels are gaily decorated with scarlet fringes and bells. Their clothes are very colorful too; the women all dressed in scarlet and loaded down with heavy silver bracelets and collars, as well as wearing ear and nose rings.

One Kuchi chief apparently has a big house in Kabul where he lives when he has business to conduct. Then when the tribe is on the move with all their animals, off he goes. I certainly hope that such people never become a thing of the past. In some ways, they are so much more fit for survival than the rest of us who need an array of gadgets and so much equipment to lead our lives.

You know, even on our little back street, we had become aware of this movement of people south. For several days now, when we open the gate, there is a family with at least three camels moving out of town. It is always startling to suddenly see these large animals at arm's length. Their huge feet are so padded that they pass with hardly a sound.

We did see one camel outside town one afternoon whose master was trying to load him. That beast was making a racket like I've never heard before from an animal. At the same time, he was streaking off on his long legs. The man had one hand on the bridle and another on the strap with which he was trying to tighten the load. Afghans are very agile, which is lucky because the camel was covering so much ground that it took the man ten minutes to bring him to a standstill and accept the load.

Life is never dull here for us. In fact, Walter said something telling today. Although he realizes there are Americans with pretty soft berths who have been here ten years and whom, as the saying goes, you couldn't "blast out," he doubts that a Peace Corps rep could stand much more than two years with the program the size it is now.

We must say that the official community has been swell to us. We are on a first-name basis now with everyone from the chargé d'affaires, who's in charge with the absence of an ambassador, right on down. In fact, I dreamed last night about the wife of the chargé d'affaires — a very warm and perceptive woman who is just about my age. She was helping me plant a flowering crab tree that I couldn't find a spot for in our yard. This little gesture was very symbolic, as they had just hosted the staff and the entire new group of volunteers in their home.

During that same evening, I was talking to one of the other women about the decision that our vacation, which will be in January due to the schedule of new groups arriving and departing, will be full of sun and sand — and little else. Even my very active husband has agreed. She suggested that the cheapest, most beautiful and relaxing thing we could do was to take the British service ship from Bombay to a group of islands three hundred miles off the coast of Africa, where there is a British tracking station, a couple of hotels and otherwise just beautiful scenery, sand and water. She said we would have a hard time spending a hundred dollars on the five of us during the seven days until the sister ship would take us back to Bombay.

Walter's comment was that he felt about five days more of his life is all he could bear to spend on the sea, after two years on a destroyer escort. Since his boys have made him promise that we will go home by boat, he thinks we had better explore Ceylon. I hope he reconsiders because I have never been on a cruise, and I don't think I consider the North Atlantic a cruise. I know I would never get him on one any other time.

I hope he's just tired enough that all we would do is sit on deck with a stack of books or listen to the radio for the weather reports. Amateur weather forecasting is one of the only things Walter has as a hobby, and I should think that a tracking station would provide this for him. One sure thing, it's easier to go east from here for a vacation than west. One really gets a sense of being off the beaten track when one sees the few planes that come and go to this capital. We are not on the way to anywhere.

I remember that the lady who wrote about us in the *Scotch Plains Times* quoted me as saying that I felt our children would be one of our greatest assets in this job. How true that has turned out to be! I often think of Kahlil Gibran's words to the effect that you may seek to be like your children, but you may not seek to make then like you — "for they live in the house of tomorrow which you cannot visit, not even in your dreams." They are such a part of this strange and wonderful new world that is being born, accepting life in Afghanistan much as I would have accepted a visit to my grandmother down on the coast of Maine.

Kathryn, or one of the boys, sometimes comes home from school with a story about how the children from foreign families treat their lunches. Since it's not hard for them to get food and supplies, they treat them with the disdain of affluent Americans, throwing sandwiches around the bus or hard-boiled eggs over the school wall at Afghans.

There are only six Peace Corps staff children at the school. The oldest comments on how these kids throw out their Baggies. We won't see a Baggie for two years and we manage to use any wax paper over and over. Then too, the Peace Corps children can appreciate an egg because we have to travel so far to find a good one. The harvest will soon be in, and again the farmers will come to market with eggs.

One day last week I got so frustrated with trying to find a decent piece of meat and get it well prepared that I sat down on the couch and bawled. Kathryn said never a word. They don't complain really even about the horrible powdered whole milk. They sometimes make jokes about how they are going to drink a whole cow when they get home, and they laugh at their friends' mothers who complain because they find weevils in their commissary flour that has been shipped from the U.S. We get all our flour (whole wheat) on the bazaar from an open barrel.

Our boys have developed quite a taste for naan, and Gregory just loves to ride to the naan shop on the back of Bhaktari's bike — Bhaktari in his red sweater with hearts and jitterbug couples outlined in white from the old clothes bazaar. They ride out just before dusk when all the Afghans are going for their fresh-baked naan. I have never been there, but my children can describe to you just what the clay oven looks like and how they bake great sheets of brown, flat bread, the size of snowshoes.

UPSTATE NEW YORK, 2006

Anwar knew how to make pizza from the whole-wheat naan dough, and since we did not have commissary privileges, he volunteered to make it for us. It was delicious, and we all loved it. Kathryn took some to a class party but could not get a single schoolmate to even taste it. "I kept telling them how good it was, and they just looked at it and made a face," she said.

Since I described how Bhaktari dressed, let me describe Anwar's attire. He wore a wool jacket from the old clothes bazaar over tan work shirts and trousers whereas Abdul Ahmed, the dhobi or washerman, dressed in the traditional white baggy pants and long shirt. On his head he wore a turban, whereas Anwar always put on his gray karakul cap before he went outside — a style everyone now knows from the photos of Karzai, the new leader of post-Taliban Afghanistan. It seemed to me to indicate that Anwar had adopted some western culture as befitted his new rank as a cook for western families but kept the best, most prestigious from his own culture, the karakul cap.

Walter greated by students at Tegori

Threshing grain at Bamiyan

CHAPTER FOUR

Bamiyan, *Buzkashi*, and the Caravan Road

SOMETHING HITS ALL STAFF AND VOLUNTEERS IN THE SOLAR PLEXUS

October 3, 1966
Kabul

Dear Phyllis,

Today was mail day. Our "catch" was your birthday card. What timing, what perfect sentiment. Also your nice long letter came. How much you evoke home to us — the sight of a foot of rain tearing along Whittier Avenue!

What a feeling of panic you had when not finding Dave at home! Even though the phones here are few and far between and erratic in operation, it is usually possible in a town this size to find someone rather quickly. We had the weird experience this morning at 5:00 AM of having the cook's nephew, who lives in the house in order to handle the gate, come into the bedroom to wake us up.

So startling, as it was pitch black! We were awake between midnight and 3:00 AM and had just lapsed into sound sleep. Since he knows no English, we have worked out with him the Farsi words for fire, thief, and earthquake. This time he said, "*Nefari amsaye*," "A person from the neighborhood." It was the Marine guard from the embassy with a cable regarding the sudden death of a volunteer's father.

This is something that hits all staff and volunteers in the solar plexus, because then begins a tussle of how to get them out of here. There are planes only two days a week. Walter broke all sorts of rules as usual to get her to London for an earlier connection to Detroit.

There is simply no lull when you have over two hundred adopted children and relatives. Come hell or high water, we are driving out of this town Wednesday morning over the Hazarajat Pass for a couple of days' breather. One can take just so much, and then needs to go to the desert to contemplate.

Remember how I used to say that I felt every home should be equipped with a padded cell where one could go when no longer able to stand the noise and confusion? It is totally dead quiet here in the evening, but the press of our responsibilities to people is great. Although we love it, we know that we will be burned out at the end of the two years. Walter has decided to seriously consider the Bombay boat to the Seychelles Islands for our vacation.

Phyllis, reading your letters and remembering life in New Jersey makes me realize I will have a terrific readjustment, after two years of this lifestyle. This morning in our godown (store-room), I arranged the little packets of goodies you sent — like Midas handling his gold. I never knew I'd be so ecstatic over a package of Dream Whip or sour-cream mix. It's this heightening of appreciation for small things that is the best aspect of this experience, I find.

Walter covered lots of ground when he was home last, but not all. He felt folks at Quaker Meeting didn't quite know what to do about him. They are passing around a horrible thermofaxed copy of the four-page letter I wrote about our Salang trip. I believe it must have ruined the old folks' eyesight, so next time, I'm burdening you with the copying task, honey.

Writing home has become a complete therapy for me; it helps me to work out my emotions. The emotional impact of this whole thing is so intense and constant, but as I have said, the children are my saving grace. They take everything in stride.

7:00 AM, OCTOBER 4

I am finishing this in front of the living-room fire. First thing in the morning, Bhaktari lights a few logs in the small living-room fireplace that really throws off quite a bit of heat. By the time it is burned down, the sun will be hitting the windows.

We will start the *bokaris* (wood-burning stoves) and space heater, like Afghans do, the first of November. Luckily, we brought our electric heater from the porch back home. It can quickly warm the bathroom. This country has so much marble that the window-sills, terraces, and front outside entryway and bathroom are all made of marble. It's easy to clean but a great conductor of cold.

These days, Walter's emotional energy is drained off in so many directions. The problems they come to him with! He also gets long letters from a girl he sent home for psychological counseling and another who was deselected after the training in Texas. She wants him to fight her case and get reinstated.

You spoke of husbands' needing some form of recreation. Most don't seem to get any, do they? It makes it all the more important that they have a job they really love and that makes life meaningful. I can see how people in our generation are now the parents who run the main show. People lean on us from both ends — the older generation because they are getting less sure of themselves and the children reaching adolescence and requiring more guidance and real listening-to. It's a great life — if you don't weaken. I say that advisedly. I've been on my feet every day since Walter came back — a real record. That's all for now.

Much love, Jan

THE BAMIYAN BUDDHAS:
WE STOP FOR CAMELS PLODDING
ALONG THE WAY

October 7, 1966
Kabul

Dear Folks at Home,

Well, our three-day trip to Bamiyan, home of the tallest standing Buddha in the world, turned out to be a two-day trip: one day in over the Unsi and Najigak passes, both over 10,000 feet, and one day back out over the lower Shibar pass. However, on the last stretch home we rode almost 200 kilometers of washboard to reach 62 kilometers of superhighway.

Sadly, we had to forgo a planned one-day campout at the pristine, remote Banda Amir Lakes. It's no time of year to be stuck at 8,000 feet in Central Asia, and we surely would have been. We ruined one tire on the way up which the local bazaar seemed unable to fix. We forgot to check the repair kit and had no pump ourselves. A second tire developed a split and held together just long enough to get to our front door, where it immediately proceeded to slowly sink. The Peace Corps Scout sits awaiting the end of Jimma (Sabbath) and the arrival of a truck to tow it to the USAID compound for the necessary repairs. Still, we saw a lot of Afghanistan on our circle route.

We took the higher route going in, which is avoided by all the tourist buses because the steep grade really requires a four-wheel-drive vehicle. One truly passes over the roof of the world. It was about 3:30 PM when we hit the highest point on our route. We could see nothing in the wide view but 25,000-foot peaks of the Hindu Kush already etched with a dusting of snow.

I remembered the story of two young male Peace Corps volunteers who were on a bus that broke down on this pass about this time of night. Afghan vehicles do traverse it and volunteers travel on them. All hands on board worked feverishly to repair the bus, but the minute the sun reached the horizon, everyone stopped and dashed down the road to the nearest shelter. These two fellows, recent arrivals from the States on their way to post, spent the night crammed into a small room with the other passengers. Every so often, one of them would push his way to the door for a breath of fresh, albeit freezing, outside air.

There is a strange paradox about Afghanistan. As long as one is following the dirt tracks, one can seem to be in the most barren, remote piece of the planet imaginable, yet seldom is it more than a ten-minute walk from some habitation.

The nomads are all moving south to Jalalabad for the winter. They used to go down into India for the winter and even into Russia for the summer, but they are not allowed to cross international boundaries now for fear they might spread smallpox.

On our little-traveled route, we passed one truck going in our direction and the Afghan post on its way out. That was all the vehicle traffic, but there were many Kuchi families with their black tents camped almost on the road. The children would try to jump up and hang onto the back of the Scout. One little girl raced for some distance after us; I can't imagine a little Afghan girl doing that. The Kuchis seem to be a whole lot freer. The higher road is much shorter, but we made about the same time traveling it as we did on the longer route we took coming out. Mostly, we had to stop for camels plodding along the way.

On one high windy stretch, we encountered a freezing fellow who blocked the road with the two camels he was leading.

He made the motions of smoking a cigarette. Luckily, I am at the moment enjoying a cigarette now and then and was able to give him a Chesterfield King that Walter had just brought from America. Most American cigarettes in the bazaar are two years old. It is hard to keep a match burning in that thin air, so Walter pushed in the battery-operated cigarette lighter on the dashboard while the chap leaned on the doorjamb and stared in fascination. Then he went happily on his way, smoking with his mittened hand. It was a small thing, but very human and heartwarming for us all.

We are besieged by requests here and have become almost callous to them. Servants think it is a big game to see how many hard-luck stories you will subsidize. For us now, it is nil, since we know that they are receiving an inflated wage by Afghan standards as it is, albeit they may be supporting untold numbers of people on it.

The newly built section of the small hotel at Bamiyan was closed down because the generator was broken. When we arrived just at six o'clock, we found everyone in the old building in their overcoats huddled together eating supper by the light of one dim bulb hanging from the ceiling. I was surprised to see three elderly English women whom I'd met in Kabul. Their previous stop was China, which we cannot visit. I believe they stay healthy drinking their innumerable cups of tea. The waiters were rushing around lighting kerosene lanterns and chopping a few sticks of wood for the little stoves called bokaris that heat the water in the bathrooms.

We quickly got ourselves moved from the corner room with a broken windowpane and cross ventilation to an inside room with one whole window and a bathroom with a bokari where a few sticks of wood kept the chill off the room all night. We ate a supper of greasy lamb soup, greasier lamb meatballs, potatoes and cooked apricots. I love apricots and discovered they nicely cut the grease of the lamb. As it was, Walter traveled to that warm bathroom many times during the night. If it wasn't for the excellent new medication that our New Jersey doctor sent back with him, I would have been driving the jeep for seven hours instead of only two on the way home.

Bamiyan is the home of all our servants, and now that I have seen it, remote, cold and breathtakingly beautiful, I may understand them better. The cook Anwar is a moody man, as one who has grown up cut off by snow and impassable mountain terrain six months of the year might well be. Growing up as I have on the rugged coast of Maine, I feel some sort of empathy with him.

As I stood out on the hotel terrace after breakfast and gazed at this scene of indescribable beauty, I couldn't help wondering if people who must become inured to cold to survive also become inured to beauty. The valley is wide and long, as valleys go in this country. I could hear the laughter of frolicking children in the first warming sun of the morning and the lowing of cows, numerous here, and most touching of all, the sweet tones of a shepherd's flute, a fitting backdrop for the great Buddha. All these sounds were crystal clear: as if right next to me, even though they came from the far side of the valley, near the feet of the tallest Buddha.

I looked forward to climbing up to the head of the Buddha and exploring some of the caves cut into the cliff, caves occupied for centuries by monks, shepherds, and passersby. Perhaps even soldiers, for Muslim warriors in some past generation used the Buddha for target practice. You can see in the photo how portions of the face and body have been mutilated; however, the force the statue exudes is still very strong. Unfortunately, we could not linger.

After our arrival dinner, when we went out onto the hotel terrace to gaze at the most stars we have ever seen, stars running right down to the horizon, I didn't see the drainage ditch in the dark. It was cut into the cement terrace and my foot was an almost perfect fit, except I got a deep cut in my heel just above my shoe line.

This misstep cut short our visit in Bamiyan. Walter wanted me to get a tetanus shot ASAP even though I received one before we left the States. He pacified me by taking my picture at Buddha's feet. He had to stand so far away to get us both in that you will most likely need a magnifying glass to see there is a person also standing there.

So we packed up to leave the delicious fresh air of Bamiyan and the natural beauty of the landscape, the village and the fields tucked in between the high cliff walls with the deep insets for the Buddhas. The poplar trees were half golden and still half green.

It is amazing how they keep any of their trees. They have to go far into the mountains now to collect a kind of mesquite-looking brush to burn for the winter. Everywhere in the fields, bare now because the grain was all cut, were piles of the stuff waiting to be burned sparingly during the winter.

I must say that the people we saw up there did not look weak. The children were still running on the bare ground with unshod feet. Some of the littlest ones, being carried by older siblings, had that familiar dried mucus under their noses that all mothers know so well. Of course, one doesn't see the women, but they must be healthier than our Kabul women because of the cows. Bhaktari, the cook's nephew who lives with us as night guard and house helper, says they drink much makse — yogurt or dehydrated milk — up there.

Women always get the leavings in this culture, so it could mean stronger men but not necessarily stronger women. How nice it would be, if one day they realized the connection between stronger mothers and stronger babies. More girl children die because they take better care of the boys. There must be so many more men than women in this country.

While I was sitting in the Scout in the bazaar when the tire was being fixed, or rather not fixed, I didn't see a single woman, even in chadri. Perhaps, unlike townspeople, they do not have to shop for foodstuffs. There was very little to be seen except some dry goods and small cans of kerosene. Directly opposite me was an old clothes shop of used overcoats and suit jackets.

Used winter clothing imported from New York City is a thriving business. They prefer their own baggy trousers for squatting but enjoy being able to buy sweaters, jackets, and topcoats that provide a welcome layer of insulation against the cold. We kept seeing some dandy-looking fellows in obvious military jackets from World War II, none of whose insignia we could identify until we passed one arm that read NYPD (New York Police Department).

On this trip I discovered that riding a washboard road is more bearable behind the wheel than as a passenger. After about three hours, I was slaphappy from all the bouncing. I said that I couldn't stand it another minute. I needed to drive. By that time, Walter was happy to be relieved, and was convinced that I was not lying when I maintained that the cut in my heel was closing nicely, unlike the damaged tire that was splitting wider at every mile.

I have always felt I should spare the Afghan villagers' sensibilities about proper behavior for women by not driving out in the countryside. When it became a question of being dizzy and sick to my stomach from bouncing on the high seat of the Scout, where I have to stretch one arm behind Walter's seat to hang on and cling with the other to the rod that holds the sun visor, I chose to become "Exhibit A."

And that I was! Men would stop to stare, laugh and point at the immodest female, much as an American might look at a Russian lady railroad engineer. Walter, being heavier and taller than I, can balance better as a passenger. He sat with his long legs crossed, looking peacefully out at the countryside.

Our friends who had been over the Shibar two weeks ago passed many large Kuchi caravans on the move, but all those we saw were resting or visiting between campsites. We passed close to a stunningly dressed group of women, striding along the road. Their dark red long skirts and blouses were obviously their finest, with lots of embroidery. As they wear no veils, we could see all their silver jewelry, some bracelets four or five inches wide. One of them was carrying a large decorated drum shaped like a tambourine. I felt very excited, like they were going to be singing and dancing soon.

We speculated on what we could offer for a night's hospitality should our car break down. Walter had in his toolbox, although no jack, a nice cutting tool and a file. I had a jar of sugar, which we had not used because we did not get to cook out. I also had a red blouse, their favorite color.

Unfortunately, when you are the Peace Corps country director, you must turn your prayers toward getting back for your appointments and not for being holed up in a Kuchi camp while a camel takes your tire back for repair to the nearest station. I'm afraid I'm just old enough to want some adventure again, but it was adventurous enough and fun to be traveling without the children on my birthday. They stayed with other staff families after school, and a Peace Corps volunteer stayed with them at night.

Walter has finally stopped singing the lyrics from *The Sound of Music* on these trips. These hills are alive not with the sound of music, but rather the sounds of silence — wind moving through great space or through the leaves of a few poplars that have managed to take hold near a spring that bubbles out of the earth and gurgles as it rolls down the rocky hillside.

We ate our lunch near such a spot, and it wasn't more than ten minutes before a shepherd, leading two donkeys loaded with brush, came into view. We could hear him before we saw him, singing for all he was worth, in that high, minor mode of the East. It seems fitting to the surroundings of high brown barren hills and space, space, space. Except for the usual animal and other droppings, the country out here is so clean — no papers, discarded cans or rusting machinery.

When we finally got out of the long canyon, before hitting the paved road at Charikar, we must have both been thinking the same thing that Walter voiced: "Doesn't this remind you of coming home from an outing in New Jersey?" It's dark at six now so we traveled with lights, tense because of the traffic. Many trucks and Afghan buses use this highway and some have no lights.

They stop to let off passengers who fan out in all directions and are not seen until the last possible moment. Everywhere is the smell of exhaust fumes. Although there are fewer vehicles, of course, than on the Garden State Parkway, the Russian diesel oil is smellier and smokier than American fuel. It all but blocked the memory of the wonderful smell of the air at 10,000 feet; however, we decided that the air at that altitude also makes us giddy. One of us always gets carried away and trips and stumbles in a way we don't lower down.

I teach English every day now. I wish to take advantage of having boring chores done for me by going a bit professional. Will tell you more about my class at the Afghan Women's Institute later. That's all for now.

Love to all,

Janice

Janice at the foot of the Bamiyan Buddha

UPSTATE NEW YORK, 2006

A 175-foot standing Buddha was carved into the cliffs of the Bamiyan Valley in central Afghanistan some thirteen centuries ago — and originally covered with gold and precious gems. Chinese travelers recorded seeing it about 750 CE. With time, bits and pieces of it were blasted off by Muslim warriors because their religion forbids the making of images.

Finally in March 2000, the Taliban totally destroyed it and another nearby smaller standing Buddha shortly before they were ousted from power. They were never, however, able to recruit any resident of the valley to do the job.

During the heyday of the Buddhist culture, monks inhabited the many caves that honeycomb the cliffs around the statues. The power of their prayers and austerities infused the valley with an aura of peace that endured. I found it hard to tear myself away. I had fantasized that we would walk up a narrow stairway to Buddha's head, where we could look down on the whole valley; however, as I describe in my letter, we were forced to make our three-day outing into a two-day one and never got to make that climb.

OUR FIRST *BUZKASHI* GAME:
PRETTY DRAMATIC PREPARATIONS
Tuesday, October 24, 1966
Kabul

Dear Folks at Home,

I should always try to record my impressions when they're fresh, but that's not always possible. Last Friday, we went to our first *buzkashi* game. It is always a guess just how to spell a Farsi word phonetically, and this also goes for place names that vary even on signs painted by Afghans in the Roman alphabet. Mother finally decided that by *Bamian*, I meant *Bamiyan*, as it appears on her map; however, I recently purchased a postcard printed in Germany, and it was spelled without the "y" as I've often spelled it.

We were lucky to go to the *buzkashi* game with Jo Anne, a Peace Corp volunteer, and her older lawyer brother who has come here to meet her Afghan fiancé. We would not have known of the game except through Jo Anne. She speaks such good Persian that she is often suspected of being a spy.

Our ten-year-old Kathryn, ever the observant one, pointed out that Jo Anne even looks Afghan, with long dark hair and very dark eyes. She is stationed in the provinces but has been in Kabul recuperating from a light case of hepatitis. She had kept up her gamma-globulin shots, but during the heat of the summer couldn't wait to boil her water and drank it straight and cold from the well.

First we had Jo Anne and her brother for lunch. We then took a little tour of town, stopping at the Habibia High School — a showplace built by USAID. We wanted to go into the garden and take a picture, so Walter flashed his *taskori*, the little black police identification booklet which we all have with our picture and description of what we are doing in Afghanistan. The soldier at the gate was timid and easily agreed to let us in.

Shortly, another soldier came around shouting and carrying on in a great noisy way. I knew one of them would. The lower the official, the louder the noise they make. I tried flattery in my very imperfect Farsi, saying we would like a picture of the lovely school to take back to America, but he kept screaming that we were breaking fifty laws by being there.

At that point, Jo Anne walked right up to him and in a very low voice let out a stream of Farsi that knocked the wind right out of him. During the intervening silence, we all piled back into the Scout and drove away. Apparently, she told him to shut up because we didn't know his stupid rules, but if he really wanted to murder someone he could pick on the guard who let us in, poor devil. I guess both the fact that she was a woman and that she spoke so fluently stopped him cold.

We have been around long enough now to know, more or less, when to arrive at a public event. This one was scheduled to start at one o'clock with wrestling, so we came around three and still witnessed the final two matches, both in the heavyweight category. They may have been among the best of the afternoon. It was a perfect advertisement for Keds. The only wrestler on the field I saw wearing sneakers — the rest were barefoot — became the heavyweight champion.

The preparations for the buzkashi were pretty dramatic themselves. First, from one end of the stadium, the team from Badakhshan, near the Chinese border, entered. They were dressed in black and looked as if they had stepped out of a set for *Boris Godunov* in the Tartar camp. I held my breath as I watched these narrow-eyed giants with long black twisted moustaches stride seven abreast the length of the field.

"The other team ought to have an extra man to go out against them," I gasped. On closer scrutiny, I saw that one reason for their impressive stature was extra-thick soles and four-inch wooden heels on their boots. The other team, from Kunduz, heart of the buzkashi game, wore pale green tunics and baggy trousers belted with a thin, scarlet cord. Both teams wore caps. The green team's were gray Persian lamb; the black team's, hard skullcaps.

Everyone carried riding crops with very thick leather handles that they used more on one another than on the horses. In fact, when they all crowded together trying to get near enough to grab the beheaded calf with which the game is played, they would beat one another over the head with the crops to keep the other guy so busy, he could not lean over and grab the calf. It sometimes resembled one of the battle scenes from *Henry V* on a very small scale, but with riding crops instead of swords. I found that although this game does not sound ladylike, I got so excited and burned up so much adrenaline that I came home ready for sleep.

The match only lasted forty minutes, but riders and steeds looked utterly exhausted by the end. The game is usually played on an expansive open field with ten riders on each side. There were also three referees milling about trying to keep a semblance of order.

The Ghazni stadium is not overly large for such a wild game. Even with only seven horsemen on each side, I was glad we were high up because I was sure some of those horses would run into or over the low wall in front of the first row of seats. That was exactly what happened. Others also ran into the aisles leading to the gates.

It is a game to view from a safe distance because spectators as well as "dehorsed" riders have been trampled to death. The horses were the most beautiful I have ever seen — all stallions, of course, in this most male of male cultures. Some were white Arabians, some coal black, and others were dappled. I do not know all the breeds. The horses, themselves, are designed to make the blood pound. Must be some symbolism here. I admit to having an attraction to natural violence — thunderstorms, wild horses and such. Seems the perfect outlet for more calculated man-made varieties.

Now . . . to attempt to describe the game. At one end of the field were three circles drawn in the dirt. In the center of one, a black flag, and in the other, a green flag. In the third is placed the beheaded, degutted calf, stuffed with sand. It must have been very heavy because every rider who made a goal and came to bow to the royal box could be seen rubbing his arm as he galloped back to the game. The royal box was occupied by an old gentleman whose identity I never learned, accompanied by someone who might have been his son.

It never seemed possible for the riders to take the shortest route to their goal. Horses cannot turn in a small space, although these could maneuver remarkably well, and often without the rider's control. Many times, the rider would have to use both hands to keep from dropping the calf. At such times, he would hold the riding crop in his teeth and drop the reins.

Often another rider could get near enough to grab the flying reins and turn the horse toward the goal. Once a foursome was galloping toward the goal. A green man had the calf with two hands, and a black rider was trying to cut him off on either side. Another member of the green team was streaking directly ahead, pulling the reins and bridle so hard that it came entirely off.

To our surprise, the game first ended in a tie. Then they continued to play to see who would win the next point. The green team, which actually seemed to be the most polished team, if that word is appropriate, triumphed.

Trying to describe such a game with mere words is really impossible. The whole thing needs to be experienced — sitting in the golden fall afternoon of Kabul with a tremendous view of the mountains all around, sharp and clear now that the dust of summer is settling — amongst the varied Afghan crowd filling the stadium.

One lady in chadri was with her family and four children very near to us in the expensive seats. We paid fifty afs (roughly half a dollar) to sit in the gallery rather than ten to sit in the general section. We never want to be in an Afghan crowd with our children. Their police are not very practiced. If the mob ever gets excited, the police simply start bashing heads in.

Everyone was anxious over what would happen today on the one-year anniversary of the university students' riots when the police rather needlessly caused the death of a large number of them. It seems that this year, the students wanted to have a memorial service for those who had died. Their request was denied, and a number of upperclassmen were sent on field trips and classes cancelled, so the demonstrations were rather weak; however, we live so far from that part of town we do not know for certain. You know, if there are ever riots that reach the dimensions of the *New York Times*, I am as likely to be anywhere near them as any of you are to be near a summertime race riot in the United States.

That's all I have time to write today.

Love to all,

Janice

CHRIS SEES THE NOMAD CHILDREN AS "LUCKY DUCKS" ALONG THE CARAVAN ROUTE

October 26, 1966
Kabul, Afghanistan

Dear Mom and Dad,

I'm so grateful to you, Mother, for typing copies of these letters for my neighbors in New Jersey, as well as for the rest of the family. We've been here five months now and everything is still very new and exciting. It's great to be able to share our adventures with the people we love back home. The feedback we've received is that the letters are widely shared. Yesterday I wrote about our thrilling experience of seeing a buzkashi game. Here follows more on our day-to-day activities.

Basically, I'm learning what needs to be done to get ready for winter. The days are growing shorter and the nights cooler. We're roughly the altitude of Denver, but more southerly. Poor people must really suffer here. Fuel is not that plentiful.

We have three Russian wall ovens each about the size and shape of a refrigerator. On one side of the wall, there is a door at the bottom to access a firebox. One or two small logs warm all that metal, and the heat radiates out into the rooms. We have two in the bedroom wing and one in the main part of the house. We also have a kerosene heater that fits in the fireplace, but best of all is the solar heat that we collect when the sun is out, from the six floor-to-ceiling glass windows and door into the walled garden.

Afghan homes are built to take advantage of the sun. There is a village called Istalif that I've visited that reminds me of some of the ancient Indian sites in our Southwest. Made of sun-baked earthen brick, it backs into the hillside and faces the sun. In Kabul there are new apartment buildings constructed of cement block. They appear gray and drab and are colder in winter and hotter in summer than the traditional homes.

We are currently trying to get the dozens of geraniums from the garden into pots permanently. They will not be replanted in the front garden come spring, as with the previous tenant, because she did not have to keep space for fifty Peace Corps volunteers' bicycles to park of an evening.

When the part-time gardener said he would have to go to Bagi Bala for *paru* (horse manure), I suggested that my friend might give me some that she usually gives her gardener, and he exclaimed that he would be using it now for fuel. So what is he using for the geraniums, if anything?

Human excrement is used to fertilize the fields. I have finally deduced, I think, the reason for Afghan shirts being so long and the pants so baggy. They offer a perfect concealment for an otherwise bare rear end when the occupant squats beside the road. Of course, the chadri is even more of a covering — being such a tent. The only giveaway is the hand reaching out for a smooth rock — left hand of course. The right is for eating. Easterners who are rigidly trained from birth to keep separate hands for separate functions are shocked by our interchange of one for the other.

Walter had an interesting experience on Sunday. We hired a *karachi* to transport a love seat and two chairs to the bazaar to be recovered. A karachi is a wooden cart, supported by the rear axle assembly and tires of a truck, and pulled by one or two men — depending on the load — and obviously invented in Karachi.

While the kids and I were watching the carpenters at the shop, Walter walked away to search for some canned soups in what

100

is known as "thieves bazaar," where all manner of mostly American grocery items can be found. Now that fall weather is here, we crave soup and get tired of Afghan lamb soups as too greasy for our western stomachs. A woman in chadri approached him with a large bag of powdered CARE milk, which she wanted to sell for 60 afs (about 90 cents at the time).

Naturally, we always leap at the chance for some decent American powdered milk — the real McCoy, not the detergent-looking variety. Walter asked her why she didn't feed it to her children. She explained that it hurt their stomachs and that with the money she would buy canned milk instead.

I discussed it further with my cook and I directed him to mix the CARE milk for drinking, and not to waste it cooking. I had thought that because water is so impure, they wisely used the canned milk straight, or in tea. This will probably rile some of you. It's straight out of the book *The Ugly American*, where the powdered milk was decried by the Communists as being an aphrodisiac.

Anwar told me that Afghans think CARE milk is no good because it is so cheap. They prefer KLIM, powdered whole milk from England, which tastes like chalk as far as we are concerned. I nearly shouted to the cook, not that this would make it any clearer, "It's cheap because the government gives it away and our children"— remembering those Halloween offering boxes — "raise money to pay for the shipping!" He shrugged, a typical gesture for the East, and one I now often use when up against a blank wall.

I hope you all won't go on campaigns to stop sending CARE milk because we do need to get rid of it in America. It does serve as a means of barter and exchange, and there are thousands of protein-hungry Peace Corps people and kiddies who are delighted to come by it. I'm glad that I am a realist and not an idealist. I don't think an idealist could take it in the field for very long.

On the other hand, I don't want any of you to feel that I have a tough life. I must have adapted to it because I'm already thinking that two years is an awfully short time to learn as much about this country as I would like.

Actually, we have a more old-fashioned kind of family life than at home. Although Walter works long and hard, the children and I feel a part of his work. He does not have to catch trains, so that commuting pressure is not there. He is home for lunch in the quiet part of the day between one and two o'clock. This is very nice. We sometimes sit in the garden and talk because he is never home again before six-thirty, but then I never remember his *ever* being home before six-thirty.

I will be sorry to have my school close for the winter when the unheated buildings become too cold. I am enjoying the discipline of going out to teach school every morning, even though I blew up at them yesterday for not having told me there would be no class. In the East a servant's time is not considered worth bothering about.

Teachers, although a cut above nurses (who are regarded more or less as whores because they deal with naked bodies), are not respected as they are at home. The girls were very casual about my having made the trip for nothing until they saw that I was angry. Then I think they were frightened that I might not come back.

Today they were very sober when I came in and asked me why I had been angry. I explained that it is important to tell a person in advance that they will not be needed so that they may plan to do something else with their time such as visit a sick friend, go to the bazaar or sew for the children. When a girl asked to translate for the slower students, they all nodded in agreement. I told the *mudir sah* (principal) today that I had received no notice of the cancelled classes. She shrugged and said it had been sent. It was good that I shared with the younger generation. The girls made certain today that I knew Thursday is a special holiday for teachers.

I have told my class way ahead of time that I will be going to Herat on November 7 with my husband and the children. Herat is northwest, near Iran and not far from Russia. There are many beautiful mosques, lots of rug making and many *gawdis* (horse-drawn carriages) for transport. The horseless carriages are mostly operated by the USAID contingent that is living there now in the hotel built by the Russians some time ago. That we are very near to Russia is so apparent by the experience of a military person recently flying a plane and seeing the Oxus River dead ahead even though the instrument panel indicated that he was right on the beam. Maybe all the stories about violating airspace are sometimes actually accidents.

We have finally seen the Chinese ambassador and his wife. She and he both wear pants. His uniform jacket has the high mandarin collar and hers is the standard tailored business suit. Both look as if they had sprung from peasant stock. She in particular must have worked hard with her hands at some time.

We see such a variety of dress: voluptuous Indian women like tropical blossoms in their saris, Afghan women covered in chadri. Many still wear them even though not required by law because they cannot afford coats. Then there are many young Afghan women in modest lightweight dark blue coats. They wear these in every season and always with a filmy, white headscarf. The many German, Russian, and American women dress as they do anywhere and the nomad women appear on the road in migratory season in their brilliant reds.

We took a special ride just to see the caravans making their way along the old dirt road to Jalalabad. In our International Travelall, piled to the ceiling with equipment for the Peace Corps doctors and families now in Jalalabad, we peered out at the women and children who peered back at us equally interested.

Our children all complained that they would rather be in the caravan, even when we pointed out that no one of their ages was riding but rather taking charge of a few sheep, goats, a donkey, or the young camel who was not strong enough to be loaded and frightened of our car even though we tried to creep along and never sounded the horn. Christopher still said, "Lucky ducks."

We were purposely following the Lataband Road, the traditional migratory route. The nomads are not allowed on the *Tangi Gharu*, the modern paved highway that plunges with many hairpin curves down a deep gorge from Kabul to Jalalabad. The Tangi Gharu is also a definite challenge in an overloaded vehicle.

Your granddaughter envied the girls with their silver bracelets, earrings and necklaces, but is unsure if she'd like to have the nose jewel that seems to heighten the beauty of their dark eyes. Many carried their curly-toed, embroidered shoes in their hands. These people look proud and handsome — and not sickly. Their clothes are bright and new. One young man even carried a large transistor radio enclosed in a bejeweled black velvet case.

I have seen that the caravan route parallels, for some distance, a new high-tension electric line like the ones transporting the Niagara power from Buffalo. At several points, one could have captured in a single snapshot the black goatskin tents, the camels and the brightly dressed women next to one of the towers. The governments in the area would like them to settle down. To me, as with the excitement of the game of buzkashi, they appeal to something very ancient and deep within me.

I have been reading with great interest *The Life and Death of Great Cities* by Jane Jacobs, a book I borrowed from the Peace Corps office. She complains of how city planning and planners deliberately set out to destroy the street life of cities — and succeed in doing so.

I had not thought about it before, but I am far less nervous (not at all, except during Jeshen) about the children walking around Kabul than around Westfield, where any auto could knock them down. And then perhaps there would be no one on hand who knows or cares who the child is. I'm not sure all the Americans feel this way, but those whom I know who have lived here the longest allow their children to go all over town.

Jacobs points out that violence usually occurs in the parks and playgrounds where there are no adults milling about. Here life takes place on the streets. A short walk is full of encounters with donkeys, cows, and occasionally small camel caravans. This year, for the first time, they are barred from the heart of Kabul because of causing traffic jams, but our street is part of the circuitous route they take around the city.

A few evenings ago, around five-thirty, just after sundown, Kathryn and I walked to the Blue Mosque Bazaar on the off chance of meeting the boys coming home from a party — and just to enjoy a brisk walk in the crisp fall air. Like all bazaars, there are shops for woodworking, tinsmiths, fruit bazaars, shops where kabobs are roasting for the evening meal — all open to view; part of the heartbeat of the street.

Children are always hurrying along them with the fresh hot loaves of whole-wheat flat bread. Our children also love to go to the naan shop. When we first caught sight of Chris and Greg strolling side by side, each carrying a school book bag, they were taking in the street scene and didn't see us coming. Chris was wearing a mask he must have made in school for Halloween. Its outstanding feature was a very long narrow nose that bobbed ahead of him. He was just another exotic detail in the varied scene around us. No one even stared.

With love,

Janice

When the children played on the street in Sherpur, they communicated more or less in the universal language of play. I loved it when I could get a glimpse of that, as when I rounded the corner in my VW just in time to witness Gregory, one hand on his hip, the other on the handle of our red wagon, telling three little neighborhood girls — mostly by gestures and facial expressions — that they would have to get out so he could get the wagon back on the road.

Somehow in pulling them down the street, the wagon had veered off into a ditch. One could see they all feared losing their place, as no one moved immediately. Later Greg came through our gate much winded declaring, "That's enough rides for today."

Our children had to be bused across town to the International School, but after hours, they biked or walked to friends' homes. At six years old, Greg frequently went to visit another six-year-old whose father was with the US Army. That child was not allowed on the street alone, but sometimes Greg was allowed to escort him to our house.

Our orientation as Peace Corps was to blend into our host-country neighborhood, so our children slipped into its rhythm. They flew kites and shared our little red wagon with the children on the street. When an older boy made off with Kathryn's kite, she began to cry. Immediately, a man rushed out of one of the shops, caught the boy, and returned the kite.

Becoming "streetwise" is not without its challenges. When I was eight years old living in the old section of Portland, Maine, two boys decided that no girls should be allowed to skate on the pond in the park that was blocks away from home. They began to push my friend and me into the snow banks. I fought back fiercely, whereupon the one called out to his buddy, "This one's not a girl." They let us be.

One night, at our evening meal in Sherpur, Gregory was unusually quiet. Finally he spoke up. "I lost my gloves today." When we didn't scold him, he gained confidence and came out with the full story.

As the afternoon warmed up, he had taken off his jacket and put it in his bike basket. A street boy ran by, snatched it and ran off. Greg dismounted and ran after him, grabbing one end of the jacket and fighting until the fellow dropped it but got away with the gloves that fell out of a pocket in the scuffle. "I knew I had another pair of gloves," our son reasoned philosophically.

During our first days in Kabul, we were riding about town with Bob Steiner, who had served four years as director of Peace Corps Afghanistan and grew up in Iran with missionary parents. He asked me about myself. I told of my childhood growing up Down East on the Maine coast. I remembered using an outhouse during my summers on an island, my mother cooking on a kerosene stove, as many volunteers were doing, and reading by kerosene lamps. I could already see many similarities between Afghans and the stoical Mainers. I knew we appeared aloof but warmed up over time and made fast friends. I suspected Afghans would too. "I think you'll like this country," Bob said. I did.

Cricket and "Paul Bunyan"

CHAPTER FIVE

A Landmark Month

GRATITUDE FOR MY LIBERAL EDUCATION

November 19, 1966
Kabul

Dear Folks,

Wednesday was my last day of class. It's now time to evaluate myself as a teacher and to ask myself, "Do I want to do the full year after the school reopens in March?" The schools in Kabul close for winter, as the unheated buildings are too cold for comfort.

The glow has had time to wear off in the six weeks for which we were asked to take the classes. As I was pedaling my bike to class the other day, I thought to myself how grateful I am for my liberal education. After six weeks with a group of Afghan women, I appreciate the fact that someone felt it worthwhile to educate me. I appreciate this now, more than any other advantage I have enjoyed.

On Tuesday, I had an interesting talk with an upper-class Afghan woman who also teaches there. I met her as I was trying to find my class. The two-story building where we usually meet had finally been declared impossibly cold, so the class moved to a low, one-story building facing the sun.

As one volunteer described it to me, the Afghan teachers are part of the grapevine and always know what is going on. The Americans are never told anything, and it is this fact that really burns me up. If it weren't for my really appreciating the opportunity to get acquainted with a representative group of young Afghan women, I would have been so insulted at the low regard for my donated time and talent that I would have stalked out several times. As I have said before, the Peace Corps is no place for the dreamy idealist, or what Peace Corps Washington calls a "bleeding heart."

My newest phrase in Persian is *Ma boisi na mehorin*, which means "You can't fool me." The cook roared when I told him about sending Walter for a *gulden* (a stepped table to hold flower pots) and his getting charged 600 afs for a 200-af item. I told the *rais* (owner) of the shop, "*Ma boisi na mehorin*," and added, "I want two for that price." I got them.

I've amazed myself that I've become the better shopper. Walter throws his money around because he hasn't time to stop and bargain. I'm concerned with the principle of the thing. I will pay my one third more because I have it and because my presence here has driven the price of things, like turkey and beef, up beyond many Afghans' ability to pay for them. I will not pay three times the going price for everything.

To get back to my experience at the school, the Afghan woman I met as I was trying to locate my relocated class arrived at the door in a shiny Cadillac driven by a uniformed chauffeur. She told me that she had lived in New York City when her husband was with the UN General Assembly. She raved about how it saved so much time when one could buy everything for the kitchen and meal preparation in one store. Then she went on to contradict herself by saying she had found little time to write letters home because she had to do her own cooking and child care.

Then she told me that so many of the women at the Institute come just to get away from an old-fashioned mother-in-law, or to combat the loneliness of being a widow or the equivalent, having the husband studying abroad. It reminded me of the experience of so many educated American women of my generation — myself in New Jersey for instance — at home alone miles from any relative, even a mother-in-law, with little or no help with household chores or child care.

With love, Janice

ON THE ROAD TO TEGORI
THERE ARE NO PHONES,
NO COMFORT STATIONS

November 1966
Kabul

Dear Folks,

I had begun to feel a bit trapped here recently before we got to go to Tegori to deliver some desks and benches to a provincial college (actually a school for grades 9–12) that had been constructed with money donated by Ambassador Steeves just before he left. Two volunteers are teaching there now. Sometimes they have a class of fifty boys sitting on a carpet in a 10-by-12 room that boasts a floor, a roof, and one small blackboard.

We could not get underway until we picked Walter up at the airport where he disembarked from the Air Attaché plane. We had been offered a ride to Herat in the north by the attaché. We have several volunteers there. Since it is a few days' trip overland, he jumped at the chance on a few hours' notice. I did not go as there was no time to make arrangements for the children.

We took the Peace Corps Travelall, a larger vehicle than a Scout but just as sturdy. With us were the new associate Peace Corps rep, a real jewel of a fellow named Roscoe, and an Afghan photographer from USIS (US Information Service). We readily overtook the USAID truck loaded with about fifty desks and benches on the Gorge Road known as Tangi Gharu.

There is a new road from Tangi Gharu to Tegori. It's unpaved, but it shortens the trip by one hour each way. However, when we got to the turnoff, we were stopped by two soldiers who informed us that a bridge was out. We would have to go almost to Jalalabad and cross over the dam.

So we traveled on almost to the dam and stopped to eat the emergency rations the men had kidded me for bringing.

It turned out to be the only food we had between breakfast and ten o'clock that evening. It consisted of five tuna sandwich halves (what was left after the children's school lunches had been made), some crackers and peanut butter, a little cheese, two thermoses of soup, one beer, two Cokes, and a chocolate bar.

Such is travel in Afghanistan. There was no possibility of phoning our whereabouts and reason for the delay, so we didn't sweat it. Perhaps the provincial governor with whom we were to have tea after the presentation (six o'clock as it turned out) would receive news of the bridge washout. At the very least, as an Afghan he would be fatalistic about our two-hour-late arrival.

When traveling, I miss comfort stations more than phones, and before I take to the road for Mazar-I-Sharif with Walter in December, I'm going to buy a chadri. It is just not possible for an American woman to take a leak in this country, but many Afghan women do, even the other business, by the side of the busy airport road. One passes this tent of blue, all hunched over, and sees a hand reach out for a smooth stone. One American friend of mine, traveling with her husband and four sons, was so desperate that she leapt into a walled sheep enclosure.

When I was about ready to burst, I whispered to Walter and he suggested a rest stop beside the river; however, thinking to save me steps, I guess, he backed the car down to a spot next to some large boulders. I was sure that Walter and Roscoe would know why we were stopping and would gaze at the beautiful scenery in the distance.

I couldn't be certain about the Afghan, so I spotted a large boulder upstream that was close to the stone retaining wall. I made for it. The grade was steep as I climbed over the wall, but not as steep as the grade appeared to be on the opposite side of the river. I made out, although I had to do quite some contortions to get my panty girdle back in place and not rise above the level of the rock. I rarely wear hose, but I was dressed in honor of meeting the governor.

Well, I was just congratulating myself on a smooth performance when I heard an extremely loud whistle! I had never thought to check across the river, but there, sure enough, was a shepherd with a flock of sheep. He was whistling and waving and followed me all the way back downstream to our vehicle, albeit on the other side of the gorge.

As I told Walter that night, "Can't you hear him when he gets back to the village?" "Yes," said Walter, "all the women will be streaming up to Kabul trying to buy red panties." You have no idea how far a spot of red shows up in the brown Afghan landscape. I had on my brown suit for the dusty road. My only color was underneath.

After we crossed the dam, there was a fork in the road, so Walter stopped to ask two men driving camels which was our road. They did not understand Farsi, being Kuchis, so the Afghan photographer spoke to them in Pushtu and got the directions.

We were now in Lagman province, an area where the nomadic Kuchis go for the winter. It's a fertile valley — beautiful and prosperous. The children looked so handsome in brightly colored, clean clothes. I saw many wonderful-looking turkeys running about and thought how great one would be for Thanksgiving, but we had miles to go and promises to keep, and it was dark when we started back.

Unfortunately, it was pitch dark when we started driving back on that winding dirt road. It was not as washboard as the

Shibar road to Bamiyan, but it crossed riverbeds at two points. The truck had gone on ahead when we stopped to eat lunch. We came upon the driver sitting by the road. He was worried because all the jostling and friction was damaging the desks.

The area all around him sported about thirty camels. I facetiously suggested that we would assure less breakage, but also perhaps complete disappearance of the desks, if we hired the Kuchis to drive them on. I read Michener's *Caravans*, after all. Walter settled for telling him to drive slowly, and we went on ahead again.

As always, the landscape and people of Afghanistan enchant me. There are those miles and miles of scenes from Biblical times — as in low mud-brick villages, with people in colorful flowing garments and many camels and donkeys — but not a billboard in sight or a speck of trash. Three little boys had waited for us to finish lunch and we left the soda cans for them.

They make so many things from that metal. It is valuable just as a container. Phyllis Crowe wanted to know what the Kuchis had of value that required the large dogs to guard, after I reported being frightened by one such dog on our trip north in July. For one thing, they have animals: very many sheep, goats, some donkeys and many camels. Some are also landowners and have winter homes as well as summer homes.

After we finally arrived in Tegori, we sat in the volunteer teachers' living room while waiting for the truck to catch up with us. There are four males that live in a house in the governor's compound, but they will be moved to a house on the campus soon, since the governor has just gotten married. Their house has two stories and has some doorways that are barely four feet high. John Barbee, nicknamed Paul Bunyan for obvious reasons, showed me the way. I am not used to these doorways and cracked my skull fiercely. One just can't believe one's eyes at first, and I never seem to stoop quite low enough. John was very skillful and made it look almost too easy.

I want to go on and tell you about Walter's first speech in Farsi, which seemed to go rather well. He composed it in English while in Herat, and the Army attaché's wife helped him translate it into Farsi on the plane back to Kabul.

Walter and I are both very impressed with the caliber of people that the military sends to Afghanistan. They know that they are coming for eighteen months before arrival. Even the wives have more than a year of language (albeit Iranian Farsi) several hours every day. They have to talk spontaneously in the classes on any subject that the instructor chooses, so they are really fluent when they arrive. Peace Corps courses are only three months in duration for volunteers — sometimes as little as six weeks for staff — but for staff wives, language skills are only what they are determined enough to learn.

The Iranian Farsi is more like the literal written language, so they are really equipped to talk with upper-class people — whereas Peace Corps training is aimed more at getting along in daily life. My teacher wants to begin teaching me the script now, but I have so many demands on my time that I doubt I shall get very far.

I am glad that I can at least navigate with the servants. Part of communication, I can see, is being used to the people. The servants understand me, but their wives, whom I met at a wedding party, kept laughing and saying they didn't understand me. I must be pretty terrible.

I believe that Walter sent a copy of the *Kabul Times* in which the picture was printed of him and the school superintendent sitting at the desks. As I watched Walter maneuver that day with the officials and the provincial governor, fending questions about how much more we were prepared to do for the school with carefully worded counter-questions about how much the governor was willing to put forth with manpower or funds, I felt how much of a politician he really can be.

Perhaps our Gregory, who seems ever willing to make a speech on any occasion, will fulfill this function too. I would not make a good politician's wife, although my husband thinks so. Here in Afghanistan, a wife can just be a part of the background. You will look in vain for me in any of the dozen or so photos that the Afghan took that day. I know my place here and stayed on the fringes chatting with the volunteers. As the candidate's wife, I would not be a subject of general interest, as in the States.

With love,

Janice

UPSTATE NEW YORK, 2006

In our memory album of Afghanistan, there are several photos that tell a poignant story of our own Paul Bunyan's Peace Corps experience. In one photo, "Paul" is standing next to an old Afghan villager known as "Cricket" for his diminutive size. Other photos show two different bridges.

Years ago, Cricket had constructed a swinging bridge over the river with ropes, assorted branches, and found logs. Being the caretaker of the bridge was his life's work. Sometimes, when the river was swollen in spring, a child crossing over on the way to school fell in and drowned. Others would say, "*Khair as*," which I was told reminded the griever not to despair, for it was God's will. Painful as it was, it was accepted.

"Paul" came to the school at Tegori to teach English and then saw an opportunity to do something more practical. He designed a bridge to be built with steel cables, real planking, and sturdy beams. He was able to "comshaw" (as they say in the US Navy) the cable from the German engineers at a nearby dam. He also had to assure the military officers at our embassy that he was not building a bridge that could accommodate a tank.

A day was set for the opening of the new bridge, with visiting government dignitaries. Since "Paul" would be going home, Cricket was to be the caretaker of the new bridge, as he had been of his old one. He would have to guard the planks (so useful for other things) and adjust the cables from time to time. However, Cricket took no part in the ceremony, except perhaps as a disembodied spirit. A few days before the new bridge was to be opened, he went out onto his bridge to tie a loose plank, lost his balance, fell into the swift running water, and was swept away. *Khair as.*

There is a sequel to the story. It wasn't long before "Paul" began to have trouble with his eyesight. Soon he had only tunnel vision. He was evacuated to a hospital in Germany where a tumor was removed from his optic nerve. He recovered and returned to serve on Peace Corps staff in other countries. In fact, he is one of a handful of our early volunteers I'm aware of who have devoted their lives to working in the so-called Third World.

Over and over again I come back to the memory of this story. I wonder how "Paul" views it today. It was so easy for our technology to fix things, often quickly. It made us feel good. What about the Crickets, the ones who could make do with whatever was on hand?

I remember a similar experience Walter and I had driving home from Kandahar in a Peace Corps Travelall, which is a fairly large vehicle. We had taken some supplies to the volunteers there and were returning taking turns driving across the desert on the modern highway constructed by the Americans.

We saw only camels grazing on either side of the road until we came to a bus that had veered off the highway into a ditch and obviously fallen on its side. When we came along, it had been righted to an angle of forty-five degrees. We could see the pile of huge stones that had been slipped underneath one at a time by the busload of Afghan men who presently were squatting on the road taking a tea break.

Time was not a problem for them and patience was on their side. Eventually they would get the bus righted by themselves, but we were driving a powerful vehicle and had a large chain and hook. Walter told me to pull over. He got out and without so much as a howdy-do since, as usual, he was in a rush to get back to the office, he dragged the chain out, attached it to the bus and gave me the signal to go into gear. In seconds the bus was righted. He unhooked the chain and, nodding to the men who stood transfixed, got back into the car. It must have given him much satisfaction, for so many things he was faced with in his work eluded easy solutions.

I always want to know what is the lesson. What did we learn and what did the men learn? Would they learn to wait help-lessly in the future for rescue and forget what they could do on their own? Would we return to our countries with just a little knowledge of how to make do with sticks and stones when noth-ing else was available?

THANKSGIVING: OUR FIRST MEAL
IN AN AFGHAN HOME

November 25, 1966
Kabul

Dear Folks,

On Thanksgiving Eve, we went to the home of some German people. There was one Afghan from the Ministry of Public Works, or maybe it was the Ministry of Planning, without a wife. He had been educated in Germany and spoke very polished German, as well as English. It was my first experience meeting an Afghan from a government ministry.

Our Thanksgiving Day here was a most unusual day and one we will always remember as the first time we ever ate in an Afghan home. The brother of Anwar, our cook, was married on Monday. Knowing that weddings are the most important social events in the culture, I volunteered to give Anwar the time off even before he asked.

This meant that I was here alone, running from the kitchen to the gate of the compound about a dozen times, whenever the bell rang. In the confusion, I left the teakettle on and some of the enamel melted, but I was amply rewarded for any inconvenience.

I had my first lesson in Afghan hospitality. I had not expected it but Anwar invited us all to come for lunch and meet the relatives. However, we got up late the next morning, and Bhaktari, being sleepy from a late night at the festivities, forgot to relay the invitation.

When I arrived home after a morning of shopping, the groom was here in his fancy clothes to guide us. The children were miles away at school, and Walter had a real crisis at the office, so I went alone. It was quite an experience. They couldn't have been nicer to me or taken more care for my health. Bhaktari packed my very own utensils, since Afghans eat from a common bowl with fingers. They made their wives sit beside me and wave away every single fly while I ate. (Anwar has taken a course for servants, organized by the American wives, that features a video about the journey of the fly and how it carries disease.) I was deeply touched.

Then I was taken into the next room to meet the bride — who looked scarcely older than Kathryn, but I'll guess fourteen. Whether because of the presence of the horaji (foreigner) or because of the newness of her role, she looked like a frightened baby chick. She was beautifully dressed and her head draped with a veil of heavenly blue Indian material, embroidered with gold thread. Anwar told me that the groom has to buy at least five such outfits to seal the contract. Kathryn and I can't understand why they don't take better care of women's health, since brides are such an investment.

Next I was placed on a footstool, their only seat, between the bride and her mother, who was nursing a year-old baby boy. If her daughter was fourteen and she married at the same age, she could be quite a bit younger than I am. These people seem to be healthier and larger than Indians. They come from the villages. Growing up there, they had milk products and meat to eat, more than they can obtain here in Kabul. They are earning money now, but much of it must have gone into building this home that was just completed in August. I wondered if all the guests lived in Kabul or if most came down from Bamiyan for the event.

This room — one of two in the house — was completely lined with women relatives all sitting on the thick, padded Japanese-type mattresses. I forget the Persian name for them. *Liaf* is the quilt you put over you. I wish I had had a camera to snap these beautiful young women in their party clothes. Indeed, the bride asked her older sister, already a young matron, to ask me why I didn't have a camera. Now, doesn't that prove that women are the same the world around?

Women are so hidden from view here, particularly from foreigners, and the religion, like Judaism, forbids idols and making images. Of course, she would want her picture taken while she is still young and pretty, in her gold-embroidered clothes, with her little hands stained in bright orange red dye that will gradually wash out.

I did some quick thinking and explained that I was not good at taking pictures and the sun was now too low, at three o'clock. I said that I would return with my husband and children to photograph her, if it was all right with her husband, on another day during the forthcoming *roqsorti*, my children's school vacation.

This is how we came to go out for an Afghan lunch on Thanksgiving Day. These people are so hospitable that you cannot come to their homes without breaking bread. Naturally, we were only able to stay a little over two hours because we had our own guests coming at 3:30. Walter took a lot of slides of the newlyweds so we will have prints made of the best for them, and have the slides for our collection. The relatives had all returned to their homes.

Naturally, the children thought that sitting on the floor on comfortable mattresses, with colorful cushions to lean on, was the way to eat. Christopher and a chair are still not good friends, yet Anwar was so apologetic, saying that it was like a picnic.

The area where he built his house is in back of the fort that sits on a high hill we can see from our front gate. It is just a large barren, dusty plain, albeit with very much water underground. We've been told that the area where we are living looked like that ten years ago.

Many Hazaras are building out there. It seems that a contractor puts up the compound wall. One buys the land and the wall around it and constructs one's house inside. These Hazaras, we were told by our Afghan teacher in Washington, are the Jews of Afghanistan. By that he meant that they are hard working, taking any jobs because they have been persecuted for so long. Now they are accumulating capital, pooling resources, and will one day represent a vital middle class.

I have been very impressed with their honesty. I haven't missed so much as a toothpick. I know now why they are afraid to work in a household with non-Hazaras. They have always been blamed for things and will avoid the police like the plague, even if they have been hurt by someone else. When there are other workmen in the house, they come and ask me to put my pocketbook away. They bawl me out for leaving my keys in the car in a locked garage. When Walter was away, I forgot and left the little VW on the street all night. In the morning, one headlight was missing. Wasn't it considerate of the thief to leave me one? The servants said I was lucky that there were still tires!

I always wondered what they did with the large and sturdy wooden crates I gave them that our sea freight came packed in. One knew, from the look on their faces, that it was as if I had given them gold bullion. I discovered that one of the crates had been converted into a cover for their well, and the other became a sort of outdoor worktable. They cook their bread on a mud-brick outdoor stove. The bread we ate there was more delicious that anything you can buy on the bazaar. I wonder what they do when the snow is deep inside the compound.

As we were leaving the compound after lunch, and the picture taking that had preceded it, we saw the little, new bride squatting over some pots on an outdoor fire. This day, she was in a green satin dress with gold embroidery and pink pantaloons. I commented to Walter how much her facial expression had changed in two days, from one of the frightened, confused new bride to a solemn married lady. Indeed, she looked so much older, I did not recognize her at first.

Anwar is thirty-three and his brother a few years younger. Afghans cannot marry when younger because of the high bride price. The groom is a nice-looking, clean, lean fellow. In fact, I have really discovered that these people like to be clean — not easy in this dusty country.

Even in this cold weather we are having, we see the very poor bathing in the Kabul River. Often at the end of the workday, there are porters washing their tired, dusty feet in the icy juie. Washing feet and other body parts is a must before prayer.

I'm gaining a sense of when I should disappear on an afternoon, letting them know ahead of time. If they have a sense of security that I won't come rushing out to the kitchen, asking for some service or other, they are shampooed, shaved, showered and in clean clothes when I do appear. If I keep people hopping, they will keep at the work and not stop for clean clothes.

So little by little, I learn how to maneuver. It is, after all, their country, and I have a happier experience trying to sense their feelings, rather than insisting on their fitting into my pattern.

For Thanksgiving dinner, we had the new family with their two little boys: Bob Pearson, out from Washington, and Donna Chen, whose husband has to be at the doctor's conference in New Delhi. It is part of our job to make these people, either new to our strange environment or separated from their spouses for the first time on a holiday, feel at home.

We finally found a ten-pound turkey from an experimental farm in Jalalabad. There were three slices left when we finished. I worried it would not feed six adults and five children, but I have great faith in the story of the loaves and fishes. I think it tells something about how people are when they break bread together.

Three weeks ago, I read a recipe to Anwar for pumpkin pie. They have a kind of squash that greatly resembles our pumpkin that is more oval than round. This was his third batch of pies and they were, like all his things, lovingly prepared and delicious. He is proud of his work. We also each had a tiny sliver of mince pie. I had found one can of mincemeat, somewhere, enough to make a small pie; but Chris had been into it the day before.

Dear Chris will be forlorn when he returns to America. He will never be so doted upon again. As the oldest boy, he only has to go into the kitchen and look hungry and he is fed. So Anwar had given him a slice of the small pie, and when he stumbled, going out the kitchen door, and dropped it on the floor, Anwar gave him a second piece. It is an ironclad rule, strictly carried out by the servants, to throw out anything that has touched the floor, because our shoes come in contact with so much excrement in the street. Afghans remove their shoes at the door of their homes, a habit we might well adopt, I might add, even in America.

We also had creamed onions for our feast. We always had creamed onions at home for Thanksgiving when I was a child. I don't suppose I consciously thought about it, but I found myself asking Anwar if there were any onions in Kabul that weren't impossibly strong. He said that he would look for some white ones. When I first bit into them, all the memories of my childhood Thanksgivings around my grandmother's table came flooding back to me. It is strange how a sensory experience will do that.

We also had one of the last melons of the season, sliced in half and cut along the edge with points, filled with the chopped melon meat, oranges, grapes, and a few chopped walnuts. We are now getting oranges from Jalalabad — considered very expensive at 5 afs a pound.

I've described this meal in detail because Mother is always describing to me the delicious foods she prepares and eats. Getting a good meal together here is such a labor, involving so many people and so much preplanning. I hoarded that can of mincemeat for all the time I've been here — six months. If we've had a few days of lean pickings, I have to skip those passages in letters from home, or they will make me feel sorry for myself.

I think it is mainly a protein hunger. We are hungry most every night before falling asleep, because we just can't get the proteins to eat here that we could at home. Even if there is some powdered milk in the fridge, the fires are all out by the time we start to yearn for something, and it is too comfy under our unbelievably warm camel-hair blankets to venture forth, through the long way down the bedroom wing, the living-dining room, across the outdoor pantry and finally into the kitchen. It's not a house for a woman alone, as I discovered earlier in the week on the day of the wedding.

The children helped to entertain our guests with a rendition of a parody we all composed in the car last Sunday to the tune of "The Green Berets." It began with Christopher spontaneously starting to sing from the rear seat, "PCVs in the Peace Corps." Then Walter finished the line with "fighting amoebas by the score." The last verse ends with these words: "What have we accomplished here? Under a chadri, a tight brassiere."

Obviously, these verses had a lot of input from Dad. Chris can carry a tune very well. Since he has the kind of mind that never listens to outside interference, he can carry on even in the face of Gregory's monotone. We think this bit of doggerel, which we signed "The Blasphemy Singers," will be in our Christmas letter.

Finally we have decided about where to vacation. We have reservations and confirmation from Washington that it's okay to take our vacation when the children are off from school — leaving here December 22 for New Delhi en route to Colombo, Ceylon. I will return to Kabul via Peshawar with the kids, and Walter will leave us in Karachi on the way back. He continues on to Tunis for the country directors' conference. Isn't that something though, my flying to my home in Kabul via Pakistan with the children? I can remember when it was an ordeal to fly from Washington, D.C., to Portland, Maine, alone with two babies.

The children are still taking to the experience just beautifully. The day before Thanksgiving, Walter and I attended the program at the school, something we could never do together in New Jersey with him working in New York City. Coming home we commented on how much they had have the advantages of private school without the attendant isolation. They are all in classes of twenty-four children or less. There is only one group for each grade, except for two second grades of about seventeen each.

In Christopher's class, there are Egyptian, Turkish, Iranian, English, and Filipino students, plus an Indian woman for a teacher. She really makes them work. In fact, their play was the best of the programs put on by the fourth-, fifth-, and sixth-grade students, plus a farce written and acted by the high school and faculty. All three now have made some good friends.

Today, the day after Thanksgiving, has been idly spent. We enjoyed the luxury of two days off in a row for a change. When one has Friday off for the Muslim Sabbath, then Sunday for the Christians, it only means experiencing the agony of a Monday morning twice during the week. Fridays here feel very peaceful. The whole country pauses. Sundays are busy market days. We have started having our own family worship on Friday evenings after the servants go home.

The living-room furniture is now permanently rearranged for winter, grouped around the hearth, a kerosene stove set into the fireplace. In fact, we and our guests and children all stayed in a tight little circle for hours and hours after our Thanksgiving meal, clinging to the warmth of the fire, as well as to the warmth of one another.

We may look back in years to come and consider that this year we really experienced the meaning of Thanksgiving. We were far away from home and ate for the first time with Afghans, the native inhabitants of this country. (Peace Corps jargon prefers the terminology host-country nationals.) Come to think of it, I even gave Anwar's boy an American Indian feather headdress. I came equipped with about a dozen for birthdays and other appropriate occasions.

Yes, we may look back to this as one of the really happy times of our family life. Here we are on a Friday evening, with no possibility of television or a movie. Even parties are not held on Fridays. So we sit around the fire together and Walter reads us something from the Bible after we have had a period of silence.

We may not be able to buy a steak, but we have something you can't buy in the States — time to be together as a family. Of course, we are constantly visited by PCVs with problems. We consider them part of our family, although we will be glad for a time to rest our emotions on the beach in Ceylon. Having a family of 205 can be taxing.

Phyllis, you seem to be the keeper of my long-winded journal. Sometimes I wonder if I don't bore folks.

All for now,

Janice

Shrine of Hazrat Ali at Mazar-I-Sharif

CHAPTER SIX

The Old Year Ends, the New Begins

ROAD TRIP TO THE VOLUNTEER NURSES
IN MAZAR-I-SHARIF

December 17, 1966
Kabul

Dear Phyllis,

I am sitting in my sun-warmed living room nursing a new case of
Kabul trots. I was with Walter in the provinces last week. We ate in
Afghan hotels and restaurants every day, so I most likely have a new
infusion of amoebas.

We just received your Santa and letter and read it while listening to the tape we made of a Peace Corps volunteer chorus rehearsing
selections from *Messiah*. We were delighted to be invited to sit in on a
rehearsal, since we will be gone for the final performance.

Phyllis, it really chokes you up when you hear these
young people sing, "Go up into the high mountains." The Hindu
Kush rises up in full view, and life in the countryside still moves
very much in the manner of two thousand years ago. Last week
when I answered our gate, there was someone on the other side
who took my breath away. He could have been an Old Testament
patriarch in his colorful long robes and with the sweetest smile on
his bearded face. Anwar, whom he was calling for, refers to him as
"Old Babeh."

Thanksgiving also seemed closer to the heart of the original
day, being far from home and learning the ways of the new land. I
wonder how long the effect of appreciation will last with us when
we get back to affluent America, which we miss not at all now
— just the people.

It's sad in a way. Sometimes, I wonder how it might be possible to develop a country so that more than 40 percent of its children survive past the age of three, yet not acquire, along with sanitation and medicine, such quantities of the useless junk that crowds our lives so much.

The Camp Fire Girls have not written, but our Christmas cards are just arriving. Yours was one of the first we received. Roberta and her daughter wrote deeply warm letters. A certain few people have really kept our sense of home alive. Not everyone seems able to sit down and write a letter.

If all goes as scheduled, we will celebrate Christmas Day on the beach at Ceylon, not at all reminiscent of the original setting. To compensate, we have had our tree up here for several days. I brought all our decorations, especially the ones made by the children through all their years of school.

Two nights ago, about 120 or more PCVs and staff attended our wassail bowl. Three hundred and twenty of the 350 cookies went, and every drop of the punch we had. We painstakingly acquired six bottles of champagne, six white wines, one cherry herring, one cognac, and one Italian vermouth. We love our big family, even if they send us home broke and aged.

UPSTATE NEW YORK, 2006

On our provincial trip mentioned in this letter, we first visited two Peace Corps nurses in Mazar-I-Sharif. They lived in a drab, gray cement block apartment house. These buildings were colder in winter and hotter in summer than the traditional Afghan mud-brick homes the color of the earth around them. The young women made it cozy with hand-woven *kilims*—a type of inexpensive rug with bright designs not unlike those of the Navajo — hanging in the doorways to keep the heat from the bokari contained in the main room.

The first nurses who came to Afghanistan did not have an easy task. The men would call them whores because, in earlier times, only whores would do nursing. When one of the royal princesses studied nursing, it must have helped bring more respect to the profession. Our nurses took us to the hospital where they worked and then we walked about town.

En route, we passed Mazar-1-Sharif's extraordinarily beautiful mosque. We could not enter, but we stood by the road looking into the tiled courtyard with its flocks of white doves. When they rose up into the azure blue sky, they made a strong contrast with the sky and the blue tiles of the mosque.

The old section of Mazar-1-Sharif was like the Old City in Kabul with many open-sided shops on either side of the dirt roads. The air was filled with sounds of metal being hammered. Workmen were busy making all sorts of items. Mazar-1-Sharif is the heart of buzkashi country, so there were also many shops making saddles, bridles and other gear for horses. Hanging on a post in the front of one such shop was a pair of donkey bells made from a can of 7-UP. The children dearly wanted a donkey. Those bells seemed to say, "Yes, go for it." I bought them and took them home.

The nurses left us on our own to locate another volunteer's home somewhere in those winding streets. Wouldn't you know that it was finally a child who guided us to the home of the American?

Before starting south on our return journey, we rode out to the mile-wide crater that marks where once stood Balkh, Queen of Cities, with great libraries and public buildings, before it was laid waste by Genghis Khan around 1200 CE.

As we stood staring at the desolation, a young shepherd boy came by. He grinned at us, pointed his finger to the moonscape, and said simply, "Genghis! Genghis!" Afghanistan has been laid waste so many times and yet never conquered.

We also stayed overnight in Puli Kumri with a young couple who must have had one of the hardest Peace Corps assignments in Afghanistan. Puli Kumri was a factory town and the Communists were trying to organize the workers, so naturally they resented the Peace Corps.

The couple lived beside the road near the main juie or ditch that ran through town — the source of water for all needs. Every evening after the townsfolk had retired and the garbage from washing vegetables and other items had settled, they filled their buckets with water. For drinking, they strained it first and then boiled it. Such hardiness. Although the wife was frequently ill, she had great courage and a positive attitude that sustained her.

Once the children saw the donkey bells, there was no peace until we acquired our own donkey. That effort in itself was quite an adventure. Anwar told me that on a certain day every week, one could go down by the river and buy any sort of animal.

It was quite a sight. I parked the VW bug, and the boys and I began to walk down to the river. I hadn't thought about how I would bring a donkey home. To begin with, I wanted to see what was available, like going to visit a used-car lot. That was always my chore back home.

There were many camels, oxen, horses, sheep and goats. I could see no donkey, but as soon as I made it known that this was my desire, a salesman materialized. Yes, he said, he had a marvelous donkey, the only one in the field that day, and brought her forward.

She had clearly been worked hard. She stood on three legs, her head hanging down dejectedly. Her blanket was ragged, and her hipbones protruded. Stroking her lovingly, the man eloquently extolled her virtues.

We bargained in Farsi. I agreed that his donkey was great, but I feared that on the morrow, she would be *mord* (dead). Far from being insulted, the man smiled broadly. Afghans always enjoyed a great bargain exchange. "*Ne, Memsahib, ne*," he continued, "*Donkey hub es, besyar hub es*" (donkey good, very good).

I was not to be convinced. I felt that the donkey had too much mileage on her. We returned home and Anwar sent his cousin to the country to walk back with a healthy donkey. The servants were delighted with all those donkey droppings to be dried for their cooking fires. As for "Seven Up" — the name we gave to our new friend — she must have felt she had died and gone to heaven. She lived in our walled garden as a playmate for the three children and learned, in no time, when to appear at the kitchen door for her meals.

UPSTATE NEW YORK, 2006
When Anwar Translates "Spinach Pies" from His Recipe Book, I Know We Hit a Vein of Gold

One of the hardest things for me to adjust to about my new situation was giving over control of the kitchen. Cooking for my family was important to me. I was a so-so housekeeper but enjoyed making healthy home-cooked meals. I was not much of a baker, and as both grandmothers were excellent bakers, I had long ago bowed to them. Every year, Walter's mother made each member of the family a special Viennese birthday cake.

So I was really glad that Anwar, the cook we inherited from the former director, was an excellent baker. In fact, he could learn to make anything; you only had to show him first. He also waited for instructions each day as to menus. In the beginning of our time working together, he never put forth a suggestion.

One day during my first month, I descended on the kitchen to make a favorite family meal. I didn't wait for his day off, and I didn't order him and the other fellow who was doing the housework at the time out. They both stared as if in fascination at my every move, and Anwar stood ready to assist. Anxious to finish and leave, I took a pinch of the red powder from a dish on the back of the stove and sprinkled it over my production. A little paprika, I thought, would do well. Then I brushed the hair out of my eyes and discovered the red powder was hot red pepper.

The men roared with laughter as I ran for the cold-water faucet. I never again cooked when Anwar was around. We kept eating the few things I knew he could make. Whenever I asked him if he could make something from the many different varieties of pulses I saw in the bazaar, which I would learn how to cook with later in my time in India, he would say, "You teach, I cook." A Peace Corps volunteer's cook made a delicious soup using several different kinds of beans. He called it crazy soup, but I could not get the recipe.

After Anwar and I had our fight over the subject of his clothes and we moved to our new house, we began to develop a working relationship. When we needed someone to handle the front gate and to be there all night since I would be alone so much, we hired Anwar's nephew.

As for the question of Anwar's clothes, I gave up. He would shower and shave and put on fresh clothes Thursday afternoon in preparation for his day off on the Muslim Sabbath. When he returned on Saturday, it was clear he had slept in them. Bhaktari lived in, and could shower and change more regularly. He was the one who would be serving should we have company on Saturday night or Sunday, and Anwar would usually remain in the kitchen preparing the food.

I went with the flow and so did Anwar. I asked him for his advice and opinion on different situations as when I despaired of the dhobi, the washerman, a really slow-witted man. He was a better gardener than he was a washerman. When a friend told him some Americans had machines to do the wash, he came to me and said he wanted one. It was news to me. In every household I knew, the dhobi did the wash by hand. Besides, I knew Abdul Ahmed with a washing machine would be a disaster. "I get a washing machine," I told him, "I do the wash, and you go." Sensing my frustration with the man, Anwar pointed to the side of his head and with a shy smile said, "Abdul Ahmed for head not so good."

When I got the impression that the servants lived all day on green tea and whole-wheat naan, I set aside a certain amount of money for their lunch. So a couple days a week, when there was nothing going on, I believe their friends came to eat with them, but I got a lot more mileage from the deal as they seemed to have more energy in the afternoons. I got the impression that every penny Anwar made was going into his new house.

One day, after a few months, I decided to find out what else Anwar could cook. I asked him to sit at the dining-room table with me and make out some menus. "Bring your book with you," I said. Anwar had a stenographer's notebook. In it, all the recipes he had learned were written in beautiful Arabic script. It looked like notebooks I'd filled with shorthand as a young secretary.

"Now read to me what you have in there," I said, after we were settled. Anwar turned the pages, selecting what he considered his American dishes. The trouble was, we were not typical. We didn't even like casseroles. Our tastes were fairly eclectic.

Finally I asked, "What did you make for Mr. Ahwad?" His face brightened. He frequently spoke fondly of a Mr. Ahwad; I had always thought he was trying to say "Mr. Howard." Then, when a guest recognized Anwar as the former cook of a Lebanese merchant, I made the connection.

Anwar turned his book over and flipped through several pages. When he read "Spinach Pies," I knew we'd struck a vein of gold. "We love spinach pies!" I exclaimed.

He promised to get pine nuts the next day. They grew wild in the mountains of Afghanistan and there were baskets of them on sale in the bazaars. I promised that the children and I would shell the nuts, although, truly speaking, we were used to buying pine nuts already shelled and in a plastic bag.

After school the next day, the children and I sat at the table. Anwar demonstrated how to remove the shell from the tiny nuts, and we went to work. It wasn't easy. We broke or crushed most of the nuts and ended up eating the pieces. Twenty minutes later, Anwar came back to see how we were doing. He picked up the glass container with our results — barely a quarter cup. Squinting for a close look, his eyes brimmed with tears as he tried to hold back his laughter.

"So little," he said. Then quickly followed it with "*Parwa nayss*," meaning that it doesn't matter. "My family will do them."

Parwa nayss was the second most important Farsi phrase to learn. After *enshallah*, "God willing," it handled many situations. I found that it made for a friendlier relationship with our host-country nationals if we didn't try to act as if we had all the answers. I eventually used only Farsi in speaking with the servants, and they corrected me. It relieved Anwar of the stress of trying to understand and translate my English correctly, and it meant that any one of them could approach me directly.

Sometimes I made bloopers, and they got a great laugh, as in my instructions to light the fire at *chor baja* — four o'clock. "Oh, Memsahib wants us to light the sun," they would roar. I invariably mixed up the words for "fire" and "sun." *Parwa nayss.* A shared laugh cements friendship.

Jack Vaughn visits volunteer nurses

WORLD PEACE CORPS DIRECTOR
ARRIVES IN KABUL

January 27, 1967
Kabul

Dear Mom and Dad,

We returned from vacation on Thursday, eight hours after the worldwide director of Peace Corps, Jack Vaughn, and Bob Steiner (former Afghanistan country rep) arrived.

Again, we were immediately in a whirl of events. I haven't had time to unpack my suitcase yet, but spent the morning with our new doctor's wife, planning a farewell supper and staff wives' skit for our departing doctor, who returns to the U.S. on Sunday, and our field officer, who leaves in February.

All the girls fell in love with Jack Vaughn. He says what he feels and delights in giving the Foreign Service types a hard time over protocol. He had a rather bad cold while here and was craving our wonderful oranges, so early on the day of his departure, I drove to the ambassador's residence where he was lodged with a large bag of oranges I had cleaned in the regulation way. He was on his way to Katmandu, and Nepal has no oranges. He referred to them as his aphrodisiac.

As Walter was loading the Peace Corps vehicle with the luggage, Jack took charge. "I'll drive with Janice," he said, and hopped immediately into my VW bug. It startled me, as I was not in the required female attire for an official airport departure. No hat, gloves or high heels. It was a cold morning, and I was bundled up in a wool cap, muffler, mittens and thick wool stockings with walking shoes. I fully expected that I'd be driving directly home, as there was only room for two people in the Scout. At the end of the driveway, I stopped, as the chargé d'affaires and the embassy protocol officer were pulling up in the official chauffeured limousine ready to escort Jack to the airport.

"Keep going," Jack said. I commented that after being around Quakers, I found Peace Corps similar in its lack of protocol — that respect for the person was shown instead, but I guessed that it threw Foreign Service types into a dither. "It's good for them," he said, and then told me he was a Quaker.

Love,

Janice

Letter from Chris

Dear Nanny:

Four days ago, we got back from Ceylon. Ceylon was great. We saw elephants, peacocks, wild boar, deer, water buffalo, turtles, monkeys and even crocodiles. Gregory and I helped pull in fishnets. The fisherman paid us with fish. We helped ground catamarans. Most brought in small fish, but one brought in a big stingray, a codfish and a shark. For Christmas, I got a crossword puzzle book, a zero-M snapshot, a chocolate king, a spoon and 2 walkie-talkies. We saw a magician do some tricks. I had a cobra around my neck. When we got back, every one had stomachaches. I, myself, have just gotten over one.

Sincerely,

Christopher Blass

I LOVE THE BRITISH

Late January 1967
Kabul

Dear Phyllis:

Walter will be in the States in March. I am enclosing a check for $80. If it is not too much trouble, could you call up Randall's Shoe Store and see if they have one pair of white and one pair of black dress shoes, size 8AA, in the style that I got when I left last May, with very low heels and rounded toes? It is the only type I can wear on Kabul's rough roads. The shoes here in the bazaars come mostly from Italy and Germany. They still feature pointed toes and needle heels that I have not been able to manage, ever since I injured my foot in the modern-dance recital two years ago. Maybe it's just that the old styles are sent out to the far corners of the world.

Could you also stop at the music store opposite Woolworth's and get one alto recorder (wooden flute) and one soprano. They are about $20 each. We also need the Trapp Family book of instructions for same, if they have it.

We had a vacation during Christmas and New Year's in Ceylon for three weeks, counting travel time. You'd never know it now to look at Walter. He looks ten years older. We got back about eight hours after Jack Vaughn and had barely recovered from his visit when the new ambassador arrived. Now Kabul is settling down again.

Also the rainy season seems to have started. We had no snow, but we will soon be awash in mud. Gregory is beside me, writing to his grandmother about how his bicycle slipped in the mud today and ended up on top of him. The cook just left early because his bike light depends on the wheels' turning fast. It doesn't operate in mud. The road to his house is just a track with two deep ruts, and there are no streetlights.

One of the reasons for Walter's fatigue is that he has joined the "I have a Kabul cold" club. It seems that if you don't catch one, you have a good winter. Once you do, it's hard to shake, particularly when you attend a function put on by the British in a building without heat.

I love the British. The Americans abroad wallow in luxury, but the British can take it from the long years of being abroad under the Empire.

The American lady who sat in front of me at the film we were invited to view in the unheated hall was wearing a low-neck gown. I could see goose bumps on her flesh, but she kept her composure. I speculated that she had been a cheerleader in high school and used to performing in cold weather while being scantily clad. I wore a very warm wool suit with a karakul collar, which I had made for me on the bazaar. I'm told there is a saying in the Foreign Service, "You can tell she's lived overseas. The clothes are homemade but the jewels are real." In that regard, we bought a nice pair of earrings in Ceylon, opal — which is my birthstone — surrounded with pigeon-blood rubies.

I had a wonderful time shopping on vacation and have some mementos of Ceylon for you and the girls.

Love you. Miss you.

Janice

FEELING AT HOME

FEBRUARY 1967

Camel caravan in snow

A Camel rest stop

CHAPTER SEVEN

A Month of New Experiences

KABUL WOULD RATHER HAVE SNOW
THAN GOLD

February 6, 1967
Kabul

Dear Folks,

Today two letters came from Walter's parents dated the 26th and 28th of January. Otherwise, we have recently received very little mail. This also goes for the Peace Corps office. There seems to be doldrums everywhere.

My response to this cultural experience seems to follow that of the volunteers, so it seems I'm having a case of the eighth-month blues. The children are also restless since vacation and bored with their surroundings. There has been practically no snow — which is despairing, since the country depends on it for its water supply as it melts and runs down from the mountains throughout the summer through handmade ditches and terraces. Here in Kabul, folks say they would "rather have snow than gold."

Basic food prices are high and many Afghans have told me it is because the U.S. is not sending any more wheat. "We will just have to starve," they say. The staple whole-wheat naan is smaller, and some shops have little wheat with which to bake it. The white flour, which is consumed mostly by foreigners, is also scarce. The cook cannot buy any on our side of town. Potatoes, another staple, have risen from last winter's price of 30 afs a *seer* to 40 afs for the same amount.

On top of it all, I am depressed by what I feel is the second-rate quality of so many of the people who serve abroad. Since life requires more of one abroad, it would behoove us to recruit our best. But there is so much to keep that best at home that many people seem to come abroad for years and years, and live in a style that their talents could not bring them at home.

We have just finished reading *The Zin Zin Road*, by the same author who wrote *The Ugly American*. The potboiler plot is purely the imagination of the novelist, not to be taken seriously, but the types of people one finds in the Peace Corps, USAID, the embassy and CIA are all spelled out. Of course, the director of the PC in the book is not the self-starter that our director is, but all the PC types, their foibles and attitudes, are described in a way that we recognize.

By the way, the new ambassador reminds us so much of Walter's father. He is only about ten years younger: urbane, witty, and speaks with the same Viennese accent. He claims he is argumentative because he has been married a long time.

Naturally, everyone now is out to earn brownie points. The amount of anxiety before the new ambassador's arrival was something to behold. I sat through some unbelievable meetings for the ladies at post recently. At home, I used to avoid this kind of thing and choose activities where I could run my own show. Here I am stuck, and yet I can't resist sometimes saying what to me is the obvious thing. But then, my husband has a job to return to and is not in mortal fear that someone won't like him.

I actually get the feeling that many people worry more about the impression they make on others at the endless parties and receptions, where so much business seems to get done, than on how they perform their jobs during the workday, and even less on how they relate to the country nationals. As *The Zin Zin Road* put it, they know the palace gossip but try to hound the PCVs to learn what is going on in the backcountry — yet they can rarely tear themselves away from the cocktail circuit to even visit such places. The Army attaché here does pretty well at that. I would say that here the Peace Corps and Army Corps know the country better than anyone else.

So you can see that my mental outlook has not been conducive to letter writing, and I've recently received little mail. So the cycle goes on. Actually, the States seem a little remote to me now. I have not been back as Walter has. Until we have been here a little over a year, I won't be thinking in terms of "Next year at this time we will be . . ."

Gregory recently said that he was missing the States too, so it seems to be running in the family. When pressed as to what he missed most, he replied, "Drinking out of the tap." Then he went on to say that he supposed that when he was in the States, he would miss things about Afghanistan. I think that was an astute thing for a six-year-old to say. He continued this theme. "Of course, it will be awful at first." "Why?" I asked. "Ohhh, everyone will be so excited and hugging and kissing us and all that."

With much love,

Janice

UPSTATE NEW YORK, 2006

Gregory was particularly sensitive to hugging and kissing after he asked to go to my school with me one morning during his vacation. As a four-year-old at home, while the other two were in school, he went with me several afternoons a week to my modern-dance rehearsals. There he was completely at ease with the ladies; however, when we walked through the door to my classroom at the Moise Naswan (Women's Institute), several of the students jumped up at once and clustered around him.

Each one wanted to gather him up in a warm embrace. One lady waiting for her turn looked at me and said, "He's not yours. He's ours." (I wondered how they meant that, but Phyllis used to say that when he had his summer tan, he looked like he belonged to another ethnic group entirely. Well, perhaps Richard wasn't kidding when he said his Bessarabian grandmother was a gypsy.) I had not expected such a show of affection, although I had come to realize that most Afghans seemed to favor boys. On the way home, a subdued Greg opined that never again would he ask to come to class.

The fact that I was a mother was a plus with the students, as several of them were also. The Women's Institute was a form of adult education as well as a place where girls were transferred after they became engaged. The most scholarly student was a young married woman who sat in the front seat closest to the door. She carried a bulging briefcase and obviously didn't need any English lessons. I've wondered what became of her. I feel that she had the bearing and the intelligence to become a prime minister. Across the aisle from her was a young mother who approached me one day before class and opened the front of her coat to show me how slack her stomach muscles were. "I've only had one child, and you have had three," she said. "What can I do?" I had no answers.

From visiting some of the volunteers who taught school, I learned that it was difficult to start a sports program for the girls. They feared being in the sun as it would make them less fair and, therefore, supposedly less marriageable. On the other hand, I had seen our newest student, recently engaged, at the International Club in a bathing suit.

Then there was Miss Noor, the only one who wore a chadri. I could see it folded over the back of her chair. She appeared to be in her forties. I admired her spunk for pursuing an education, but when a video crew from Poland wanted to film the class, she became very upset and asked permission to leave. When I granted it, she picked up her chadri and her books and hastened away down the hallway.

WHAT CONNECTS ANISA AND ME
February 7, 1967
Kabul

Dear Phyllis,

Your letter just came today, lifting my spirits immensely. Walter also read it over lunch. You just don't know how much your letters mean to us.

I'm sitting under a hair dryer around the corner from our home. My Afghan friend, Anisa, runs a beauty salon in her home. She learned her skill while she was in England with her husband, who is with one of the large banks. Two businesses that Afghan women can have are beauty salons and dressmaking shops. So, there are several of each in town.

Walter asked me what connects Anisa and me. I didn't have to think long. It stems from the fact that we both came from small towns and went away to the big city. I left Maine and went to work in New York City as a young woman. She tells me that she went to Pakistan to catch the boat for England in a chadri that she no longer wears. The best thing is that she lives nearby and has a great sense of humor.

I will try to answer some of the things you asked in sequence: Yes, vacations with just husbands would be nice. Upon return from our last vacation, we almost needed another one. As to servants, we have three, and I find that all human beings have problems. When you are the mistress of the manor, so to speak, you are very often looked to for assistance — often monetary. When a machine breaks down, you call a repairman. When a servant is moody or morose, you have to figure out what the problem is, all the while operating in an unfamiliar language and culture.

With regard to my learning Persian script, I got bogged down after the first five letters. There are so many demands on my time and always the unexpected breakdowns of electrical functions, frozen pipes, and all the rest, to consume my time and energy.

I've noticed that Kathryn is now beginning to have unexplained (to herself) blue spells. I suppose this presages becoming a woman next year. She is now ten and a half. She has changed quite a bit, and although our three still sometimes play together, she prefers the companionship of another ten-year-old girl. Her friend was a constant companion and confidante for Kathryn until she left for Honduras this week. I don't know what will replace this relationship. It's a whole new world to me, but it makes me realize that even if we were still on Whittier Avenue, our children would be changing from that two-through-nine-year-old pack (everyone with a role in the act) to the preadolescent need for a close confidante to talk privately with about, most likely, mothers who don't understand them. It's taken a lot of wild guesses on my part to start a conversation that would open her up to discussing her feelings.

I'm glad you are trying to get Becky to stand up for herself. It's sad that the world can't be trusted to be nice to a sweet little girl, but it can't, so we have to train our girls to handle the snake in the grass when he appears. I had to answer some of Kathryn's questions about rape this summer when she overheard what happened to a British volunteer who walked out alone late at night. Knowledge is armament, I feel, but I always try to speak to her level. Well, the hair dryer stopped. I'll finish this later.

Next day:

I can't match your stories about the flooding on Whittier Avenue because the rainy season hasn't started, but we did have our first earthquake of any size, enough to send us out of our beds for coats. Then this evening, we were supposed to be at the PTA "Back to School" program, but while Walter was resting, the lights in the bedroom wing went out and he smelled smoke.

We had wet snow last night, so the telephone line is down, and Bhaktari was at the bazaar eating supper. In five more minutes, we would have left for the program. The kids were going to practice being alone until nine o'clock. The dog would have been with them, but she is only a good alarm sounder, no electrician. Walter has gone to the Marine guard at the embassy to phone the electrician. There is a large black spot on the wall near one of the many circular openings that mark a way into the wiring.

Well, I should have fun while Walter is in the States. This is the season for earthquakes, fires, and, next month, rain and mud.

About my quoting Jack Vaughn's use of the word "aphrodisiac" . . . I believe that it means a love potion, or something that makes you attractive to the opposite sex; but with his moustache, he doesn't need anything else. Serving in Latin America for so many years seems to have given him that old machismo. That's what Latinos call the male's conquering genius.

I am presently on a rug binge, not necessarily buying but lots of looking. After six months, I finally fell in love with some Afghan carpets and have enjoyed bargaining for them. I must be getting the feel of this place. I've been invited to share tea and naan twice in one week — once at a tiny jewelry store where I purchased Kuchi earrings, once by a donkey vendor from whom I purchased oranges.

To locate rugs I'm interested in, I go in and sit down on the floor and chat for an hour. It's best not to show too much interest in one thing too soon, or you'll never get the price down. In the winter, there are no tourists, so there is an eagerness for cash and plenty of time to chew the fat.

Kathryn's knee bandage that you noticed in the photo was from falling on the cinder track while running across Ghazni stadium after her class had danced on the green at the children's Jeshen celebrations.

Walter was using his binoculars and saw her being taken by an Afghan Boy Scout to the first-aid station. They would have poured strong iodine onto a pretty nasty cut, but the Peace Corps nurse on duty recognized Kathryn and held off for her dad to arrive, suggesting the American dispensary instead.

My greatest fear is of accidents, particularly on the road. We could never live through an Afghan hospital experience. We are too soft for that, I fear. There just aren't the supplies and equipment to use, even though the knowledge is often there. Our Peace Corps nurses get very upset, but they realize it's often a stone wall for the Afghan doctors too.

Our children have also been down with colds and sore throats this month. There is no TV and little to do outside because of the weather. There is a decent movie at USIS (United States Information Service) on Saturday. I hope they are all okay to go. USIS is also the source of our news about the astronauts' deaths while in their training simulator. Sometimes, I think these kinds of events tell us something about life: Don't hold yourself back from the bold, adventurous step. When your time comes, it may be in the most unlikely, or even supposedly safe, place.

I dare not tell the kids about the weekly skating at home. There have been no winter sports this year. There was some skating while we were swimming in Ceylon. Of course, they seem to have already forgotten that! How come their memories are so short and appreciation nil after the fact?

Lots of love,

Jan

THE AMBASSADOR'S WIFE MEETS
STAFF WIVES AT OUR HOME

February 8, 1967
Kabul

Dear Folks,

I have to write a sequel to my gloomy February 6th letter to say how proud I am of the Peace Corps — while I'm still brimming over with it! This morning it was my turn to have our new ambassador's wife to coffee, to meet the staff wives and our local hire, the executive assistant and cashier.

Mrs. Neumann changed protocol, which states that every American wife should call on her within the first forty-eight hours. That means more than one hundred women. Instead she had the senior wives, whose husbands were the head of an agency, to coffee — to meet us for the first time in a small group of less than twenty. At that time she asked each of us to give a tea or a coffee for our department or agency.

I don't think I have ever done anything in my life along these lines that did not turn into an adventure. Last night, we had an electrical burnout of one whole line — luckily the line involving only the bedrooms and adjacent hallway, not the kitchen stove or hot-water heater. The embassy electrician must have been waiting for Mrs. Neumann's car to leave because he came in five minutes later to investigate what the night-duty workman had not been able to unravel by 11:15 PM.

Anwar cooked some nice goodies for the affair yesterday afternoon. Then his friend died in the night, and he had to go to the funeral this morning at some distance from town. His nephew

Bhaktari, who lives with us to do odd jobs and answer the gate at night, was to warm everything up. He did quite well, except for putting the butterscotch rolls on the plate upside down, hiding all of Anwar's lovely work with the nut-butterscotch topping.

I was to make the coffee. I discovered that we had just barely enough pure water in the house to make the first pot. Walter had taken one of the cans out this morning to be filled and returned late morning. (The Peace Corps driver takes all empty staff house and office water cans and fills them from the embassy's deep well.)

For some reason, our second can was almost empty. People in the undeveloped lands are so used to living a life close to the margin of want that they never think to say that something is low. It's always after it is finished that they begin to worry a bit. So I sent the dhobi with a note to the closest Peace Corps family's house for a small water can that they keep in the bathroom and that he could bring back on his bike. It's a good thing I did send a note, because on her invitation to the coffee, I had written the wrong date. At the time Walter was arguing with me about the correct form I should use. On invitations that one must attend, one writes, "Regrets Only," but it gives me the creeps not to have the confirmation required by RSVP.

It turned out that we had the most marvelous gathering that has yet been given! Ours was the last except for a gathering of all the Americans not associated with government agencies. So the orphaned child turned out to be the most interesting. Word is out that the Peace Corps staff wives are an unusual bunch.

Some of our wives are professional in their own right. One is an economist, another a psychiatric social worker, another a nurse. We seldom get time to talk to one another because of the press of Peace Corps responsibilities. Mrs. Neumann asked everyone to talk about themselves. As a woman who has taught and done a variety of interesting things herself, she was so excited and interested that she stayed overtime and forgot to go look at a car she wants to buy. If she drives her own car that will be another break with protocol. We have two wives with the Peace Corps staff who are Viennese; the ambassador is also. The protocol officer's wife, who escorted Mrs. N., made a slip, saying something about someone being "all-American."

Mrs. Neumann deftly put that remark in perspective when she shared with us about her husband's background, including being in a concentration camp because of some student political associations — a history familiar to more than one person in the room. Then she said something like, "You know, this is what is so fine about America, that a man who was a refugee in 1939 can later become an ambassador, representing America to another country in 1967."

I am so proud to be associated with a group of people who are doing a job and not just sitting around worrying about protocol or whether the wife of their husband's boss approves of them. I've said this before. The people of the United States get one hell of a bargain out of the Peace Corps.

It was so obvious, listening to each story, that here were families that could make it in America. They are often on leave of absence from other jobs, choosing to be here because of their convictions and busy doing a job that does not require attending many official functions.

As ever,

Janice

WITH A VACCINATOR TEAM I COMPREHEND
THE WORD *PESTILENCE*
February 15, 1967
Kabul

Dear Dr. Gloria,

It was just about a year ago that you were vainly trying to produce a real hot "take" from our smallpox vaccinations. Today I saw my first case of live smallpox when I accompanied a combined Peace Corps-Afghan vaccination team into the old section of Jalalabad. I was greatly comforted that just last week I got a really good "take" on the first try.

I had always supposed that smallpox was a slightly stepped up version of chickenpox. After being taken to the hospital by our volunteer doctors to observe a young mother and her baby with full-blown cases, I feel that I now comprehend the full meaning of the word *pestilence* — a word which has largely dropped out of our present-day experience in the West.

In fact, the whole morning's experience was rather like stepping back into the fifteenth century. I am dimly reminded of some of the old diaries that we used to read in English Literature classes — descriptions of conditions in London before the days of sewage disposal systems and running water. One of the Peace Corps doctors' wives commented the previous evening that her husband, in his short walk from house to hospital every morning, diagnosed various diseases from the stool specimens he observed along the way.

I never realized how many different colors feces could come in until I spent these two and a half hours going on foot *khana* by *khana* (house by house) in a sometimes unsuccessful attempt to get the occupants to accept vaccination. Walter was unable to tag along because of being asked to meet the newly appointed dean of the medical school to discuss next year's recruitment of Peace Corps doctors. Are you interested?

Asia Foundation recently donated a Land Rover for the use of these teams. In our team there was an Afghan driver, an Afghan nurse, one male Peace Corps nurse, one Peace Corps volunteer doctor, two Afghan medical students, and myself.

The PCVs spent some weeks this summer in rural Afghanistan vaccinating with a team and reports that it was infinitely easier. If the local *mullah* or village headman was sold on the idea, he or his agent would accompany the team and the whole village would line up and be done within an hour.

Jalalabad was definitely a different kettle of fish. Situated near the Pakistan border and at a considerably lower altitude than Kabul, it is a favorite winter resort for Kabul families, many of whom have second homes there. When we rode into town the evening before, we could see that the streets were crowded and had little of that lazy small-town atmosphere we sensed on an earlier trip in the fall — great setup for an epidemic, eh?

Finally, the Land Rover was loaded with the right people and the UNICEF vaccinating kits that included the alcohol lamp to sterilize the needle. The same needle was used on about fifty people. One Sikh woman refused on the basis that we didn't wash. Where would one wash! These people often have such faith in the efficacy of washing even in the dirtiest of water. Many of the children that day I supposed might never have been washed in their young lives. We saw one little four-year-old boy whose feet closely resembled the blackened, wrinkled, toughened hide of an elephant.

We were supposed to join up with another team that went out earlier. Communication under these conditions is often word-of-mouth only. We spent some time driving around asking children in the streets playing jump rope and young girls in doorways how long ago the had team passed. Starting with the first reply of *aires* (yesterday), it finally narrowed down to *yak sort pas* (one hour ago).

We were finally on target and got out of the car. Scrambling down an embankment, walking around a resting camel train and then up a narrow winding alley, we came to the very heart of the mud-walled old city. We did not stay for long. The captain of the other team assigned us an old babeh (it's an affectionate term for "old man," some of whom have such character etched in their faces they could pose for illustrations of an old Isaac or David) to escort us to a street on the fringes of the old section.

Here some of the Kabul families have built two-story houses with marble-slab facing — common enough building material in this marble-rich country. Otherwise, the noticeable difference in these homes from those of the less affluent was the number of fine carpets on the floors and a Mercedes Benz (definitely not fifteenth century) in the yard.

The women usually insist on being vaccinated by a woman, so I helped to support babies for the Afghan nurse. I met one beautiful fourteen-ish mother, who was no taller than Kathryn — now almost eleven. She was holding a really bouncing baby boy.

At another well-off home, the nurse and I went into the women's quarters where there were three mothers, one whose face was badly scarred from the pox, and about a half dozen or so children. They were thinking of going along with the idea when first one and then another of the children took up a tremendous wailing at the sight of the needles. Everyone under ten was also being injected with BCG (for TB). Suddenly, the grandmother burst into the room and said, "*Ne mehonin*," "You will not do."

She was somewhat startled and fascinated at the sight of a female horaji, a foreigner. Since I discovered that my English students are intrigued by the combination of my youngish face and silver hair, I have taken to going bareheaded again instead of bowing to the Afghan tradition of the covered head. My Farsi has caught up by now with many of the volunteers', so I explained to her that I had three children and they took shots every year and did not get the sickness. I even showed her my own fresh vaccination.

She looked and listened, and I suggested that since she was the grandmother she was the boss. She thought a few more seconds and repeated her first instruction. I really think it would have been too much loss of face for her to reverse her decision. Since these people are used to following an older person, or a mullah, it would be good if somehow the natural leader of each block of a city could do some spadework beforehand so that such a great number of people would not have to spend almost three hours to vaccinate only fifty persons.

In contrast to the attitude of those people who had a little more of this world's goods — and perhaps felt themselves more under God's protection — the poorest people would grab their children, screaming or not, run after those who attempted to scoot, roll up their sleeves and get that free vaccination. Porters, always from the poorest class, would run up in the street and request it.

I have been in Afghanistan now for about nine months and I know what I am going to see. I know that dirty water is channeled in small ditches to a larger ditch where all sorts of refuse and garbage are added. Many fowl and animals scavenge in the ditches for their food.

In Kabul there are infrequent trucks that collect garbage. We have a barrel for ours outside the wall that is constantly raided by cats, dogs, cows and donkeys. As we were walking in the narrow streets of old Jalalabad, Dr. Hamilton gallantly put me next to the wall and trod along the ditch himself. I seem to remember reading that in Old London, there was a saying about a gentleman "taking the wall" — that is, giving the lady the space where slops hurled from the rooftops would not strike her.

At this time of year, the odors are at minimum. As we were making our rounds, the housewives were baking loaves of flat bread by pressing the dough against the sides of their clay-pit ovens. Perhaps because of the current shortage of wheat, these loaves were made from ground corn, and the odor of the freshly baked loaves wafted above the odor of decaying offal.

Not all is depressing. There is always some heartwarming incident. The women wanted to share their delicious freshly baked bread with us, and we accepted the first offering. The tradition of hospitality is strong here. In the provinces, each village puts up the vaccination team and gives them their best. As we moved down the street, if a woman was baking when we entered her compound, Dr. Hamilton would say, "We have not come to take your tea and naan but only to give the shots and vaccinations."

At the end of the morning, I had very much the feeling, "This is long enough." I could well understand why the vaccinators told Walter that every few days they should be removed and locked up somewhere away from all local people to get ready for the next exposure. Making oneself see the state of affairs can be an exhausting process, and probably the reason why many of the native inhabitants and foreign-assistance types put on blinders after a while. I once knew a Quaker man who had spent much time in Europe for CARE right after WW II. He spoke of lying in his hotel bed and crying like a baby after returning from a protracted mission in a badly destroyed area.

Back at the hospital, Dr. Rogers spoke of how they could not manage without the relatives who stay constantly with the patient. There are so few nurses. We saw an older husband bent over his young wife who was almost unrecognizable under the pox. The baby, lying on the foot of the bed, had his hands bandaged to prevent scratching. The man was spoon-feeding tea from an ever-present teapot to them. "They will go home," the doctor assured us.

As we stepped back into the courtyard, through the gate swayed a pair of those remarkable beasts on their big spongy feet, tossing their heads with that particular haughty expression that only a camel can assume. They were carrying the hospital's firewood supply. It's always like that here: the depressing and the romantic in one big capsule.

As ever,

Jan

From that day with the team in Jalalabad, there is one image that remains with me still. As we were leaving the area where we worked, we turned a corner and found ourselves mounting an ancient garbage heap. From its summit, we could see down into the local mullah's compound. He did not see us because his back was turned as he frantically barricaded his gate lest we try to enter.

Another image that comes to my mind is one from my childhood. I am sitting alone in my fourth-grade classroom. All the other children are lined up with rolled sleeves fearfully marching single file to receive free vaccinations. My parents were the only ones who had not signed the release form. It was during a period in our lives when we attended a Christian Science church. I received my first vaccination as a requirement for entrance into the University of Maine. The government made up for my lack of shots when we went overseas. They vaccinated all of us every six months. Surely that was a bit much.

AN EVENTFUL MONTH WITH
THE NATURAL ELEMENTS

February 17, 1967
Kabul

Dear Isabelle:

We have just finished our Meeting for Worship with the kids. We finally settled on Friday evening when the servants are observing their Sabbath, while the whole country basks in that vibration, so we can make it a habit to always be together at this time. Now we are reaping the rewards of this established discipline.

This one has sorely missed your friendship and presence, and the nearer it comes for Walter to leave again for the States, the more desolate I feel in my soul. Not that I would really want to take that trip, but my heart cries out for the comfort of old friends and faces.

To date, yours is just about the only Christmas present that has made it through to us. I know that the Havilands mentioned a package on their card but there are also several from Maine that are as yet not received. Someone saw the customs shed recently and reported that it was stuffed, but right about the time most Christmas mail should have been coming in, no packages were received at all by the entire Peace Corps. Whether it was held up elsewhere or whether it avalanched on the Afghans and produced their fatalistic response, who knows?

Anyway, the books *Zlateh the Goat* and *The Wolves of Willoughby Chase* have been very satisfying. I have enjoyed introducing them to the kids by reading aloud, but good old Christopher

170

has decided to plough ahead on his own. We are having a great time trying to prevent him from telling us the plot of *The Wolves*. "The First Schlemiel" is a repeat favorite and we all do thank you from the bottom of our souls.

Belle, when I decided to take what almost seemed to be a "walk in space" because I felt it was in the true spirit for us, I did not realize I would meet so many who seem "lost in space." The Foreign Service and foreign aid seem almost to be constellations of their own. They become worlds apart as they exist too far from the gravitational pull of their own culture.

Perhaps it is this realization that has produced the desolation in my heart. I have still too long to be here to continue to live in the past. Our role here is a strange one, straddling the immediate cultural confrontation of many volunteers — the need they have for us to visit and see their world — and being also the contact with the official world, as well as smoothing our family rhythm into the whole.

Recently I was invited to spend the day with some vaccinators in the old part of Jalalabad. It was a real step into the fifteenth century, including a view of the true meaning of pestilence: two live smallpox cases — a mother and her baby.

It seems to be fashionable to approve of the Peace Corps today. Perhaps this is not so good — a sign we have become too respectable. On the other hand, I sometimes resent the attitudes of some volunteers, knowing the world will not coddle them, as they often expect us to. Our new staff wife is a psychiatric social worker. She was a welcome addition, but I become increasingly less envious of her "professionalism."

I feel she suffers from always having worked with the disturbed mind and would turn the Peace Corps into a kind of clinic. Our doctor's wife recently said to me, "I feel we are so lucky to have an older woman for the boss's wife. Someone steady. We have so many young wives."

I'm rather amused at this view of me and still, although I don't feel that old, am aware that even our volunteers who are older than us need this image. They all need someone to admire what they are doing and to listen to their problems. I should think Walter would be drowned from listening. And of course, the leader or parent figure has to also be there to blame for troubles, test one's strength against and sometimes curse.

Also, the children often long for their familiar paths. Although they are aware that when it is time to leave, they will miss much that they have had here — being a foreigner is to be constantly reminded of one's outsider status.

A sort of abrasion results from that constant rubbing up against all of the cultural differences. Perhaps this will make the rest of us understand Walter and his parents better. Much is gained by the experience — sophistication, as well as a triumphant feeling at having merely survived and mastered unfamiliar details of language, customs, and money.

Checking with Walter about how the books managed to arrive, he says: "Keep it up. Not only doesn't Pearson in our Washington, D.C., office object, he reads them too." *Handful of Rice* arrived with his bookmark in it.

We have had our first big snow this week, but because the sun is already on its way to the spring sign, the ground is muddy underneath and the snow wet. We've spent much time getting ourselves out of juies (ditches). Even the school bus rounded our corner too wide and ended up tilted way down into one.

All in all, we've had an eventful month with the natural elements: one impressive earth tremor, three days of snow in a row, knee-deep mud on an excursion last Sunday, an electrical fire in a junction box, and a telephone that works incoming but not outgoing. It sounds tapped.

When I pick up the receiver, I hear Indian popular music from a radio. The former tenant was the CIA!

Tell me, what's going on at home? Has the U.S. become as overrun by the radical right as it sometimes seems from a distance? Has the Quaker Meeting resolved the issue of building a new meetinghouse? When do you leave for Europe — next fall, or this summer? I'm having some hearing difficulties which, if unsolvable here, could take me as far as Frankfurt.

Love and kisses,

Jan

Spring thaw

Mountains and poplars

CHAPTER EIGHT

Our First Kabul Spring

UPSTATE NEW YORK, 2006

Near Arrest by the Kabul Police

In January 2003, the *Christian Science Monitor* printed an article about an international project to train Afghan police entitled "Law Lessons for Afghan Police." In this piece, the reporter, Gretchen Peters, quoted a foreign official who " . . . would be scared to be arrested by a (police) conscript."

This brought to my mind the one frightening experience that I had in Afghanistan. I had been in the country about fourteen months and felt quite at home as I drove around town in my VW bug doing my round of errands.

My last stop was usually the fruit bazaar a few blocks from home and luckily, as it turned out, within sight of the Peace Corps office. I was anxious to get home and so I brushed off two young boys who were swinging incense pots containing a foul-smelling concoction. They wanted to wave them inside the car and looked at me in disbelief as I insisted, "*Ne, ne.*" Later I learned that the boys' job, which they would do for a pittance, was to chase out any *djinn* or evil spirits that might be lurking inside. If I had understood their intent, I might have gone for it.

Twenty minutes later when I came out of a shop, there was a policeman lounging against the driver's side of my car. Holding up my key, I gave him a rather weak but hopeful smile and waited for him to move. There was a patrolman like him on almost every block. If they fell asleep at their post in winter, they fell prey to the packs of hungry wild dogs that roamed at night. Unpaid or poorly paid, some of them resembled distrustful stray dogs themselves. This one's wide leather belt was pulled in tightly around his gray uniform, highlighting a waist as slender as a young girl's.

When he realized that I was the owner of the car, he began

to shout loudly and wave a document in my face. I caught just one word, *horaji*, foreigner. He obviously wasn't going to let me get into my car, so before he might gather a crowd around us, I began to scurry down the block toward the Peace Corps office.

I may not have taken care of any djinn in my car, but my guardian angels were still watching over me. Seemingly out of nowhere, the suave Afghan translator for the Peace Corps program, immaculately dressed in a western suit, materialized over my shoulder and directed the policeman to follow us upstairs to his office, where he took charge of the situation.

During our first days in the country, we were instructed, if we were ever in a motor-vehicle accident, to drive immediately to the embassy. We would, most likely, be immediately evacuated by air. Motor traffic was new for most Afghans. Arriving in Kabul from distant villages, their nervous systems attuned to the pace of animal traffic, they often stepped off a curb directly in front of your oncoming vehicle. If you, the stranger, hit one of them, an angry crowd could gather instantly. To minimize the risk of such an occurrence, only Peace Corps staff were allowed to drive motor vehicles. The Peace Corps volunteers rode bicycles.

Our translator read the police document. It claimed that there had been a hit-and-run accident recently in Jalalabad. The numbers on the license plate of the vehicle involved matched mine; however, it was a Jalalabad plate. My car was registered in Kabul province — a fact my rescuer pointed out to the patrolman. The translator next turned to me and asked, "Do you drive a Mercedes Benz?" "No, my car is a VW," I replied.

Again the translator sought to explain the confusion to the patrolman; namely, that he was to look for a Mercedes Benz with those numbers on a Jalalabad plate, but the words seemed not to mean anything to him. He refused to budge. The light in his eyes reflected hatred and resentment. Once again he shouted an angry complaint about the horaji.

Walter heard the commotion from the other end of the corridor and came to investigate. After listening to the story, he went back to his office and soon returned with a brief letter he had typed on official Peace Corps stationery. At the bottom, next to his signature and title as the Peace Corps country director, he had melted a blob of sealing wax and pressed it with a Kennedy half dollar. Finally, he'd rolled and tied the document. Presenting it to the policeman, who now looked very confused and deflated, he said, "Take this to your boss. The lady is not coming with you."

After I parked the car safely in our garage, I left it there for weeks and opted to ride my bicycle just in case there were more patrolmen in other sections of Kabul on the hunt for a car with my license-plate numbers and not recognizing the difference between a Mercedes Benz and a Volkswagen.

A DAY SPENT AT THE AIRPORT
April 4, 1967
Kabul

Dear Phyllis,

The shoes are gorgeous — a perfect fit and so comfortable. I hope to initiate the black ones tonight, but it looks like rain, and I don't want to wear them under boots. Parts of Kabul are a sea of mud now. It is an experience to learn what cities must have been like before paving and street lighting. There is a story about the bad winter three years ago, when policemen were eaten by dogs on their night watches.

That is probably an exaggeration, but it points out why they hate dogs. We have also been told that not so long ago, as in the biblical times, bodies were thrown outside the village walls for the dogs when the ground was frozen. Remember Jezebel in the Bible? This winter was mild. The snow never covered the garbage heaps that are outside every compound wall for more than a few hours, so the street dogs are still fat and sleek.

Our doggie slipped out of the garage unnoticed on Easter Sunday and was lost for forty-eight hours. We were all much relieved when she got back to the compound safe, but very dirty and with a scar on her head. Bhaktari heard her barking early one morning and let her in. She raced to all our beds to express her joy to each one of us.

By jiminy, it is snowing! Spring breaks through for a few days, and then rain or snow again. We have had the ground ploughed up for a vegetable garden. I look forward to salads again. Meat I've learned to forget about, because the fruits, vegetables, and nuts are so good, and we can buy Danish butter for $1.50 and cheeses. Walter brought home a beef roast from London. Just imagine! Although it was not the best, it was an experience to eat rare beef. Yes, we are well supplied with dips, sauces, and sour-cream mix. I have about one dozen sour-cream packages now, so I will try a dip Thursday night with one of the training groups. We've been told we can eat the delicious carrots raw if we soak them for thirty minutes in iodine solution.

Was it fun seeing Walter? I kept him talking for hours about all our wonderful friends, and I almost felt I had been there. While he was away, I attempted to take the children to Peshawar during their school vacation, but we ended up recuperating from contaminated airport food in our sunny garden. Travel in the East always presents stomach problems.

The dental trailer is now installed permanently here. We used to have to go to Pakistan for dental work — one trip to make the appointment, another for the work to be done. The dentist will keep very busy in Kabul. He's the only one. You know, we may have a whopping food bill for the people we feed, but we do not pay for housing, or medical/dental. Isn't that awful. No wonder some people never go home.

Greg was bitten by a dog this morning, luckily in someone's compound, so we can observe the animal. His bite is in the same place Chris was bitten by the Trends' dog — in his arse.

I have a doozy of a cold today. No Afghan public building or school is heated after February. The schools close until spring. I was chilled to the bone three times in a row: at the Women's Institute where I teach; at an Afghan sit-down dinner in an unheated building; and again during my one-and-a-half-hour morning class.

The rainy season is late and we still have frost at night. So I'm afflicted with what the volunteers call "the second pestilence of Kabul." "The runs" is number 1 and a cold number 2. Needless to say, I've arranged a substitute for tomorrow. Even wearing woolen knee socks, skirt, sweater, and a lined raincoat, I perish. The girls all have colds, and they have to sit. I can at least move around.

Please don't worry about the children. They enjoy all the little tidbits that come their way. Gregory loved the "dot-to-dot" books. You know, I feel it's good for them to be removed from so much surplus. They have had so much in their lives and I brought most of their things with us.

For the Afghan New Year, which was the first day of spring, I gave jump ropes and matchbox cars (forty cents here) to the children on our street. One little boy, whom I missed, stood on tiptoe next to my car window, pleading "*motora hord — motora hord*" (meaning "little car") as he looked up at me with those limpid, brown eyes. I had to tell him I would remember him next Nauroz (New Year). I believe I bought the whole supply of "little cars," such as it is.

Bhaktari saved his "cowboy pants" (jeans) for a party. Jeans are a status symbol here. Thanks a million for doing those errands.

Love,

Janice

UPSTATE NEW YORK, 2006

MORE ON OUR ABORTED TRIP TO PESHAWAR

When the children and I arrived at the airport for an early morning departure, we learned that the Ariana Afghan Airline plane was grounded in Pakistan due to their heavy spring rains. When it finally reached Kabul in late afternoon, it was beginning to fog over, so they decided to stay overnight. Those of us waiting for the flight to Peshawar were told to report back at six in the morning.

The airport officials were most hospitable and had given us a delicious lunch. When accompanied by my boys, I was given the greatest respect. They related to Chris as if he was the man in our group. When they invited us to come into the airport dining room for the free lunch, the official spoke to him directly. Who knows? Perhaps that's why he was the only one of us who didn't get sick in the night! On his own, he went out the next morning to the bazaar and shopped for canned sodas to settle our stomachs. He returned and stood next to my bed showing me three cans of 7-UP. "They've not been pierced," he said. It seems he'd learned to check if some of the contents had been replaced with water and then the can resealed.

When we heard about the great trips their school friends took on vacation, I feared he would feel cheated. "I'm sorry we didn't make it to Peshawar," I said. He looked at me in amazement: "We spent the day at the airport," he exclaimed. He obviously counted that as an adventure worth having.

HITCHHIKING ALONG THE FORTIFIED
KHYBER PASS

April 20, 1967
Kabul

Dear Folks at Home:

We're still marveling over our most recent Afghan adventure so it's time to type one of those long letters that Grampi says are more noticeable by their rarity these days. Partly, it's because I feel so at home now in Kabul that what used to seem exotic now seems normal. Then too, I've often been labeled as being somewhat eastern in my outlook and concept of time. On the other hand, as you are all aware, my husband is very western. He is up on the very latest world events, the absolute correct-to-the-minute time straight by shortwave from Radio Moscow every morning, and has on his fingertips all names, addresses and telephone numbers. Thank him that he reminds me how long it's been since I sent you an update on what's happening with your children and grandchildren in this mysterious remote corner of the globe.

Last Friday, we took off for Peshawar across the border in Pakistan. Walter was scheduled to meet with the Peace Corps doctors on Saturday afternoon in Jalalabad, which is halfway between Kabul and Peshawar, so I suggested that we let the kids skip school on Saturday and come with us. We celebrate two Sabbaths out here — Muslim Sabbath on Friday and Christian on Sunday — so the children attend school on Saturday but not Friday or Sunday.

It turns out that although mile-wise it is not very far from Jalalabad to Peshawar, time-wise it is far. Parts of the road are washboard. Passengers sitting in the back of the stretched-out Peace Corps Travelall take all the bumps. Your granddaughter says she needed a cushion on her head as much as one to sit on. She had a pretty uncomfortable trip. In checking our vaccination cards to make certain they were up-to-date so as not to face dirty needles at the border when we reentered, we discovered she needed a typhoid shot, so she was pretty miserable for a few hours. Walter volunteered to sit in back on the return trip. Then, in spite of the fact that I drive slower than he does, he bounced so hard that his watchstrap broke.

We had to stop four times — twice in Afghanistan and twice in Pakistan — for passport and other checks. Since we have official passports, we don't get our luggage checked, but it takes just so long to go through all the palaver involved concerning what we are or are not carrying or have purchased.

At the border station in Afghanistan, we discovered that although we had our health cards and our passports, we did not have a document that allowed us to take our vehicle into Pakistan. What to do! Undaunted and in true Peace Corps spirit, we decided to leave the car at the border station overnight. After all, it was guarded. Besides, the border would close in an hour, and we were much too far from Kabul to return for the missing documents. We decided that we would walk across the border into the little village of Torkem in Pakistan and hire a cab to take us through the Khyber Pass into Peshawar.

The border was marked by what I can only describe as a hawser, one of those thick ropes used Down East to tie a steamboat to the dock. It sagged in the middle so I could easily step over it and follow after the family who streaked on ahead. A porter, who was carrying some of our luggage, walked beside me and at one point inquired, "*Germani astin?*" Are you German? "*Ne, America astom*," I replied and asked him why he thought we were German. Wouldn't you know? His answer was that "all Americans have big motorcars." He had obviously not seen us drive up in the Travelall and was curious about our walking into Pakistan.

Naturally it was also the Muslim Sabbath in Pakistan, so we were dismayed to discover there were no taxis plying their trade. Walter scoured the bazaar for a vehicle, found a couple of fellows with a rickety stake truck, and bargained with them to take us to Peshawar. He sat with the driver. A second man sat on the hood of the car feeding water into the radiator from a jerry can. The children and I climbed into the back and sat on a bench. As we drove through the historic pass, I glanced up at the mountains backlit now by the late-afternoon sun. "I hope Walter's paying them more than they think they might get for our luggage!" I thought. All was fine, however, and we got there safely.

The Khyber Pass is certainly fortified. Everywhere in the now-dry streambed are great concrete blocks to prevent trucks or jeeps from avoiding the road. On top of many hills are forts from various ages that once (or perhaps even now) guarded this historic invasion route. On the Pak side, we passed tribesman after tribesman with bandoleers of ammunition across their chests and shouldering one and sometimes two very efficient looking rifles. The only guns one sees in Afghanistan are the handsome but ineffectual relics of bygone times, all intricately inlaid.

There is such a hunger for modern rifles or revolvers for protection against thieves that our cook asked me to get Walter to bring him one from the States. I had to tell him that as Peace Corps we couldn't get involved in this but that if a friend of mine wished to sell a weapon when leaving, I'd let Anwar know. He lives out beyond streetlights and police protection, both of which I have a new respect for — and also paving for mud season. I have literally skied in mud to reach the Turkish naan shop this spring.

We were only in Pakistan for twenty hours and were more than happy to return to Afghanistan. It was hot there, and even the few people who spoke some English could not understand us, or we them. One can't know all languages of course, but it is frustrating not to know any words. We did go to the American airbase for our three meals. It was fun to have a rare steak, fresh creamy milk and ice cream. The salad was wilted so ours will be better when our garden comes in. Our hamburgers are about as good too, I thought. Actually, the homemade ice cream our cook can make in the hand-crank freezer we brought is good too. What do we have to complain about?

There was also closed-circuit TV for the base, and the kids got to look at that. The reception was poor, but it was a novelty. The children were the first to comment as we walked around the grassy walks past officers' bungalows and brick apartments, "Why, it's just like America." After observing all the overfed, under-culturally exposed folks in the officers' club, we were certainly glad we had waited for the Peace Corps to come into being. The bulletin board was full of notices of dances and free-drink nights at the bar, one-cent steak dinners if you bought the first one at regular price, and cookouts with your own steak, but everything else supplied. A real tough life! I see nothing to distinguish it from the colonial life of the old empires, and I think we are kidding ourselves that we are democratic abroad. We look and act like the well-off ruling classes. Becoming a sahib or memsahib can really puff up one's ego.

At one point during our short visit, I got involved in conversation with a British woman who told me that the American wives at the base were unnerved by the anti-American feeling being expressed in Pakistan, and shared her advice with me. "Cheer up. Once they've kicked you out, they'll invite you back." What wisdom!

We had little time to shop in the bazaar because we kept getting lost. The roads were very narrow and crowded with animal-drawn vehicles, more crowded than in Kabul where we have many very wide roads on the outer rings of town — probably because Kabul expanded only recently. We did purchase some canned fruits, some Wheaties, woven baskets for our bikes, and a large punch bowl we can use for the groups of Peace Corps volunteers we entertain. After lunch we started back to Jalalabad, where Walter had a four o'clock appointment with the volunteer doctors. I want you to know, Walter has adjusted to Afghan time so much he actually did not fret, at least outwardly, when we were delayed.

We picked up our vehicle at the border station in Afghanistan and drove out into the desert. We had gone about halfway to Jalalabad when we coasted to a stop. We were out of gas.

We all piled out of our vehicle while Walter stood beside the road holding up our empty gas can ready to flag down the next passerby. In no time at all, a sedan came roaring up apparently headed for some remote unguarded mountain pass, for, as he approached us, he took his foot off the gas, leaned out the window and, with a perturbed expression on his face, waved toward his back seat shouting "*Smuglaar, smuglaar.*" He was loaded to the ceiling with brand-new tires still in their wrappers. His expression seemed to say that he regretted not being able to fulfill the sacred duty of aiding a traveler, but he was in a bind. He gunned his motor and took off once more at top speed. We were still laughing when a truck going in our direction stopped, and the driver gave us enough gas to get us into Jalalabad at five o'clock for Walter's four o'clock appointment.

I have more to tell you about this trip later. This is all for now.

Janice

SIKH WEDDING FESTIVAL:
A MORE REASONABLE EVENT THAN
THE ENTIRE AFGHAN SYSTEM

April 20, 1967
Kabul

Dear Folks at Home:

When we got back to Jalalabad, Kathryn went to the home of one of the volunteer doctors whose little daughter is very much starved for the company of American girlfriends. The boys and I went to the home of a young Peace Corps couple and washed off many layers of road dust while Walter had his meeting with the doctors. That evening the thirty-odd volunteer doctors, nurses, and English teachers stationed in Jalalabad had been invited to a garden outside town. There the Sikhs, who are numerous in this area, had set up a tent village for a full week of marriage ceremonies. About a dozen couples were to be married every night.

Spring is the season for love and marriage, is it not? This group event is much more reasonable than the Afghan system, which is so extravagant that grandchildren are often still paying for their grandparents' wedding. The Sikh bridegroom contributes about 500 afs, a fraction of the cost of an Afghan wedding. It includes some for the priests and some for the sweetmeats and refreshments.

Walter decided to retire early, but I piled into the rented Afghan bus with the others and went to a ceremony that would last all night. We made our adieus or rather *Bomona khodas* to our Sikh doctor host at about 2:00 AM.

This was my first experience on an Afghan bus. They are high and wide, and every inch is intricately painted in bright pastels, depicting every imaginable subject matter — temples, jet planes, flowers, animals — but no humans of course! This is all in that fine, detailed technique like the old Persian miniatures. I found it took the bumps better than the Travelall except it was very stuffy inside. I realized this was the reason most of the volunteers rode on top Afghan-style, so I tried that coming back at 2:00 AM. Then we were mostly silent as the stars, undimmed by any sky glow, enveloped us and bats swooped gently by. The top of an Afghan bus has a guardrail about ten inches high to keep animals, bags of wheat, and people all together on the roof. In this case, the cargo was about fifteen volunteers and myself.

There was a very joyous atmosphere in the wedding garden, much like a carnival with all the family tents and the temple pavilion strung with paper leis. The wedding festivities themselves went along at an eastern pace. We were first taken to the doctor's tent where we sat around on cushions for about an hour and ate all the gooey things I often see in the bazaars, but never buy because of the flies. There were no flies on them when we ate them, and they were delicious — particularly a kind of honey pretzel I've often wanted to try.

The electricity was not functioning, which was not a surprise. Still, every family seemed to possess one of those very effective German lanterns; they are so large and powerful, they can heat a whole tent. Then we were led by lantern light to a bathing pool fed by natural underground springs. One could see the water bubbling. There were four stone walls to contain it, and in the center of each side was a flight of steps that allowed the bridegroom to descend to bathe for his wedding. All this was done in view of the whole congregation.

On the other side of a high wall at the end of the garden was an identical pool. It was crystal clear and uncluttered by any debris;

this was where female relatives privately bathed the brides. There was also a group of male dancers who circled up to the bridegroom's tent, beating an intricate rhythm on sticks. They surrounded him and led him to the pool where two bearded grandfathers waited to assist him. The first bridegroom scooted under the dancers' arms and ran back to his tent. Hopefully this was only embarrassment at having to go first, because the marriage was inevitable at this point.

The grooms seemed to range in age from about fifteen to twenty. At least one boy had no facial hair. Some of the Afghan fellows from the medical school at Jalalabad had tried to scramble aboard the bus, but been told by their teachers to return to the dorm 'and study for the next day's finals. They turned up around the pool and kept a close watch on Mrs. Rogers, our oldest volunteer of over sixty-five years and one of their teachers, to see how she was taking watching these young men being bathed.

Afghans are so puritanical about seeing the body. True, they go to the bathroom anywhere, but their clothes are so designed that one never sees a bit of flesh. I can go around the house all day in my bathrobe, and the servants never bat an eye, but let me wear a sleeveless dress, and they are embarrassed to talk to me.

As it happened, the bridegrooms bathed in their short drawstring underpants, but the rest of them was showing before all the ladies. The Afghan fellows were not sure they would like this. First, the old gentlemen rubbed the boys with some cream and then washed their long hair. Sikh men never cut their hair and it is hard to distinguish who is a little boy before the age he dons a turban.

Finally, the bridegroom is plunged in the water. Then he is wrapped in a towel and given a new pair of underpants from the bride's home. Clad in these, he is hoisted onto a table and handed his new long pants, shirt, jacket, turban, many leis of roses and other leis made of fifty-af notes. All wore western-type suit jackets over their long shirts and either baggy Afghan-type pantaloons or western suit pants. Their turbans were of soft material in shades of pastel blue, pink, or lavender.

The brides were so enveloped in their gold-embroidered red or green shawls that one never got a glimpse of them. They were escorted from the pool to the temple by female relatives. At an Afghan wedding, I was told, no woman is present. There's only the agent for the bride, and the agent is a man.

Dr. Singh told us something about the Sikhs. They are recognized by certain articles of clothing: a turban easily distinguished from the Afghan turban, special underwear, a comb for their long hair, a small knife, and a silver arm bracelet. There are four things they do not do: go to other women, get circumcised, eat beef, or take tobacco.

But the most interesting thing was how like a Quaker service their worship is. That is, there is no priesthood — only gurus, or teachers who are deeply respected. Anyone else, even a child, can give a prayer, and some children did so at the weddings we saw. The prayers are supposed to follow a certain format that also includes a section for improvisation. After everyone prayed for the various couples, each couple was tied together. That is, their bright shawls were tied together. Then they walked four times around the guru, who sat under a canopy and read from a book after each time around. The bride was still all covered up and very bowed over, as if in grief to leave her mother, on whose arm she leaned, as she followed her husband around the altar until she met her new mother-in-law at the last corner.

Much love to all,

Janice

Pakistan tribesman

Over the Khyber Pass on a stake truck

Greg on a backcountry outing

CHAPTER NINE

War Looms in the Middle East

WAITING TO SEE WHAT BECOMES OF
ANTI-AMERICAN SENTIMENT

May 12, 1967
Kabul

Dear Isabelle,

My Royal Afghan International License arrived today, but Greece is not one of the signing countries to the agreement. According to my little book, encased in pale lavender plastic, it was signed in 1949. This being Afghanistan, there could be newer forms that have added Greece to the list, but we shall see. Anyway, it could be that your mother is right, and that conditions being still unsettled there, we should hire a driver with the car.

We are having some trouble here. The ambassador has requested wives not to drive across town alone. A couple of days ago, a German woman was badly stoned after a child ran out into her car. The redeeming part of the story is that it took place in front of the Ministry of Finance, where she was calling for her husband — and the Russian translator rushed to her rescue. Once you pass Rome, you are in the East. It seems that the old Bible tradition of stoning is very much observed. I am a little unnerved at this point.

We are still waiting to see what will become of the anti-American sentiment that the published *Ramparts* article about the CIA in Afghanistan stirred up. Some papers have carried articles denouncing Asia Foundation, as well as the Peace Corps. The present prime minister, Maiwandwal, was cited as accepting CIA funds. The whole thing could easily flare up.

The present shortage of naan and the long lines at the bread shops, in spite of the PL40 wheat shipped by the United States, doesn't help to make one feel easier. Bhaktari, our cook's nephew, claims that Maiwandwal has given it out as baksheesh. Yesterday the prime minister was to appear before Parliament, but so far we have heard nothing. Riots were expected, and we women and children were asked to stay off the streets. Asia Foundation had several policemen stationed in front of it. They are down the street from us, and the Scout meeting at the home across the street was cancelled. But as usual, when you carry your umbrella, it doesn't rain.

It was an awfully long afternoon, longer because, contrary to homes in the States, where we can flick the switch and get six newscasts, we have no channels of communication to speak of. Our servants are Hazaras who stay out of politics and, as a persecuted minority, benefit from the foreign presence. Only the young nephew seems to have any opinions. I doubt if Bhaktari's uncles, who also work for us, would have any comments, since they are family men and stick strictly to business. They have their wheat sent from their clan that still lives on the land, so they are able to ride out the wheat crisis.

It's at times like this that one feels so very much the foreigner, although I have warm, and I think reciprocal, relationships with some of the young women I teach and the men who work for us. Still the total picture is so complex. And for the life of me, I will never be able to decide how much our presence is for the benefit of the Afghan people.

For one thing, I would say that we have driven the price of choice meats out of range of the common man — the old law of supply and demand. But we are bringing in vaccinators to a country where, much as the government hates to admit it, smallpox is endemic. With the students, I feel I open a small window on the world, but that may only increase their frustrations. When everyone has little, one accepts what is as God's will. When things start to change, many people cannot make the necessary leaps and adjustments and so the gaps widen.

Walter is envious that I will be able to travel with you. He almost considered inviting you here, if time allowed. We now know from our experience that it is a journey that would tire even Isabelle. It's an awfully long way East. I'm sure that you will be a point of focus for me because, unlike Walter, I have not been out. The States have rather a dreamlike or sometimes nightmarish quality for me at this point.

We women empathize so with our surroundings and, like mother birds, take on the color of our environment. In that regard Kathryn is charming and amazing. She is soon to be eleven and after spending a social evening with a group of the new volunteers, she picked out the one who "looked sad all evening." This was almost before Walter realized the person was someone who needed a little private and personal attention.

As I plan to join you in Greece, I can't help but remember that it was just after the Cuba crisis that we went to Pendle Hill, the Quaker retreat center, together. I certainly hope that events will be equally resolved both here and in Greece when we are there. Is not this, then, the world that we must live in! The other world, what some call the "good old days," was a world where I would still be sitting on a rock off the coast of Maine. And you would be speaking German as your native language — had not the world changed and gone through an upheaval.

I have finally consumed all the pills I was given to get myself on my feet again, but the doctor says it takes eight months to really get rid of amoebas. If needed, I can just pick up another bottle and keep right on taking them through Greece. I have now had bacilli and amoebas, as well as roundworms and pinworms. Our Chris is the only other one to match my record. It seems, in Kabul, Walter only gets flea-bitten.

See you soon,

Jan

ISRAEL MIGHT FORBEAR HAVING A WAR
JUST AS YOU GET THERE

May 22, 1967
Kabul

Dear Phyllis,

Janice left last Thursday for Greece and Israel, and so far she seems to be making out all right. We have had no cables from her, which is a good sign, and Israel might even forbear having a war, just as she gets there. I hope so. She's due for a vacation from the razzamatazz around here. Every day it's something new and surprisingly that "something" often involves Janice, even if only as a sympathetic listener to my troubles. The rest of the time, she has to get involved with additional duties or parties or the myriad of other things she takes care of.

Reading papers from the U.S. is a terribly depressing experience. From what we can observe, the U.S. is steadily drifting into a bigger and bigger war. Five doctors who had accepted the Peace Corps invitation to train for Afghanistan have been drafted to go to Vietnam, and we understand that all doctors under forty-one are being picked off by the draft. I don't dare tell my six here who have accepted residencies, for fear of ruining a beautiful vacation they have planned at the end of their tour. The letters I get from colleagues in the U.S. are similarly gloomy. What do you think and feel about it all?

We all miss your company so much. Chris is starting to talk again of "when we go home" as a considerable number of his friends at school go home at the end of their time here. Janice has come around to agreeing that we will not extend. Actually at the rate this program is seeing troubles in specific ministries, I seem to be presiding over — as Winston Churchill declaimed — "the dissolution of the Empire."

It still looks like I'll be back in September, so let's get together again.

Lots of love to all of you,

Walter

WALTER HOLDS SOMETHING BACK;
PLUNGING BACK INTO KABUL

June 1, 1967
Kabul

Dear Mother and Dad, Richard and Malvi,

This air letter is to all four of you because I want to say the same things to everyone, but can't face the typewriter. Everyone says I look tanned and handsome. I certainly found that the sea life agrees with me. I'd like to earn enough myself to go to the sea during hay-fever season instead of buying shots. Too bad it is also the stormy season at sea!

The Greek Islands all seem a million miles and years away right now. I arrived in Teheran late in the evening and spent most of the next day sleeping so I could be up at 3:00 AM to catch the 5:00 AM seven-hour, non-air-conditioned flight on the old Ariana DC-4 to Kabul. The twice-weekly flights on the Iran Airlines jet are booked solid with new Peace Corps arrivals.

Walter met me at the plane steps and I plunged right into Kabul. These times outside are so necessary — to be among people one understands and away from the tremendous pressure of all the many people who depend on us here.

I could feel that Walter was holding something back that was not directly related to the family. We unpacked, chatted and lunched, and then he gently led me into the story of a horrible accident in which my very best Kabul American friend's two boys were badly injured — one requiring an emergency flight, via the embassy's attaché plane, to Beirut.

It seems they are going to be all right, but the accident was a pure nightmare of a situation. When I went to Susan as soon as I possibly could, she threw herself into my arms and sobbed, "Just when I needed you, you weren't here. Oh Jan, I missed you so." Can you imagine how I felt?

However, she is a young woman with great hidden strengths, much like Jackie Kennedy, and without any knowledge of Farsi (this is not required of the USAID families) was able to get an Afghan at the scene to help extricate her son, who was pinned inside a friend's car. Then she proceeded to sit on the floor of her own vehicle, with her two very critically injured boys, for the forty-minute ride back to the embassy dispensary. Finally she stood by while a great gash in her oldest son's skull was sewn. Bruce is a year older than Kathryn.

The problems of getting help in a foreign land, with few phones and emergency measures, are tremendous. On the other hand, her children were cared for by no less than nine American doctors — including great men in their fields, who were passing through on short CARE Medico assignments. The whole community cancelled all social engagements and pitched in to help. Many even donated their blood. This is another side of the Peace Corps experience!

The sad part of the story is that Bruce, who was so badly injured (spleen removed, liver damaged, and convulsions), has been having a horrible year and had just flunked sixth grade. They came from Southern schools and all of the children have had trouble keeping up at AISK (American International School of Kabul). This boy is such an appealing boy — good at sports and good with his hands. His dad was handling the situation with constant deprivation of privileges, so the boy was in a real box. The good part of the story is that his father went with him to Beirut. From what Susan says, the whole tragedy may be the beginning of a new source of strength for the entire family.

After I kissed my children, had supper and opened my mail, I received a newspaper clipping from Phyllis Crowe of a tragedy involving our good friends at home that has no happy ending. Their thirteen-year-old son had been sent to his room for fighting with one of his sisters on Mother's Day. Later he was discovered to have accidentally hanged himself from the closet pole with a length of clothesline. How often have I found that Christopher, having been sent to his room, has either tied himself up round and round with clothesline or tied the door closed so I could not get in!

Children today are so painfully aware, from mass media, of the many possibilities for ultimate destruction, either from a dictator, or our own armed strength, or a madman firing into a crowd. How must these young minds feel overpowered by having to cope with a world that adults cannot? Not that children can't cope with realities, including tragic realities. Our children seem so much calmer away from the constant overstimulation of TV. That's true even with this winter when they have experienced people dying of famine, servants' children perishing from lack of medicine, and a bad automobile accident in a land where people didn't know what to do, except kneel and pray. Perhaps the prayers did help.

The parents here have blamed themselves too, for this was the first time they have ever let their kids ride with another person. Their boys begged to ride in the car with their school friends. Susan and her family were following four other cars, all driving north for a weekend. They had just passed through a rain shower and had to stop for a band of nomads and their animals crossing the road. The Afghan driver of her son's vehicle was speeding to catch up and crashed into a bus.

The father in that car died within two hours, the driver is·badly off, and the other family's son has just been discharged from the infirmary. Susan's older boy will be back from Beirut next week and the younger one will be in traction for five more. The wife of the man who died had not come on the trip and blames Susan's husband for not bringing her husband in the first car that returned to Kabul. But he was the only one who was conscious and could sit up.   ·

The doctors all said later they could not have saved the man who was killed, even had they been on the spot. His injuries were all internal. We learned this noon that the two boys will definitely be okay.

Sorry, but the description of Greece will have to wait. It is a beautiful, friendly country. I could scarcely believe there were political troubles. Isabelle and I had it all to ourselves because the military coup had scared tourists away. When I left a week later, Athens was flooded with American dependents from Egypt and Israel — and tourists who had no other choice because most of the rest of the Middle East was closed due to the outbreak of war in Israel.

The children are home now. We are all fine.

All my best,

Janice

POSSIBILITY OF WAR:
ACUTELY AWARE WE'RE IN THE ARAB WORLD
June 6, 1967
Kabul

Dear Folks,

This is Walter — and Janice, who will add her comments later. So much has been happening in recent weeks here that I think you might be owed a letter that explains why we have been doing relatively little writing and why it may get worse. This letter will be mailed from somewhere where Dr. de Maine feels it has a good chance of getting to you. I wouldn't be surprised if mail inbound as well as outbound gets slowed up.

The daily press is full of righteous indignation at the Gulf of Aqaba, and the students as well as populace are very pro-Arab. By contrast the professional military has a deep respect for the Israeli military — in particular the capacity to fight when other countries' troops cave in. Whether Afghanistan joins in the melee appears to be a moot question since their troop-movement capability is extremely limited.

It's a very touchy situation as you, who have far more access to news than we do, realize. We mostly listen to the BBC for the straight scoop. Voice of America is nearly unobtainable, though occasionally you will chance upon the Swiss Radio or *Die Deutsche Welle*. India Radio and Radio Karachi are both quite biased. I haven't yet heard a single Israeli station. The *London Economist* arrived last week with some further descriptions of what's doing, but the *Christian Science Monitor* is weeks late. We are so short-staffed that the mail isn't even getting out. The new *International Herald Tribune/Times/Post* isn't getting sorted either.

Walter just left for the office. This is Jan now. Yes, I brought a paper from Athens, the new *International Tribune*, and although I stayed two nights in Teheran, the paper was still new to Kabul when its twin caught up two days later. And I thought I was enjoying the relative remoteness and lack of constant bombardment via mass media! Tomorrow, at the end of his tour, Dr. de Maine says he will have to leave the country to learn what is really going on here. Jack Vaughn, the head of the Peace Corps, wired yesterday to remind staff and volunteers of the apolitical nature of our work here. Indeed many of the volunteers were out in the streets and at many points walked through the crowds.

Some of them are probably teachers in the very schools, if not classes, from which these students were playing hooky to demonstrate. In the developing countries, it's always the very young who seem to be the most ready to apply political pressure with their sheer numbers and enthusiasm for change from the centuries of stagnation.

So far, there has been no gathering in front of the Peace Corps office although we are a stone's throw (some image!) from USIS, the United States Information Service. This should answer many people's questions as to why, when we are so cramped, we do not move into the empty offices at USIS!

Last night there was a Peace Corps party for the de Maines. About thirty-four volunteers also depart next week. Unless the airport in Beirut reopens by then, there will be a lot of rearranged travel plans.

It seems that when Malvi wrote to me last spring about the similarities between my experience and hers at the same age, she was truer than I thought. I had to remind her that I was not going to a war zone, but we are acutely aware now that we are living in the Arab world. Although the Afghans do not consider themselves Arab, their Muslim ties are strong.

As you might expect, the children are aware that we are concerned, from the way we are so attuned to news via the short-wave. I imagine that Walter will instruct you to sit tight. You will get the news faster than we will and may get itchy and want to wire. I do not think this would avail you much at this point. We will continue to send mail out next week as the volunteers leave for Europe. Remember one important cardinal rule. We are living in a situation where instant reaction is not possible with any form of communication.

As it is time for me to teach my class, I must get dressed now. The Peace Corps carries on. I must say the Afghans that I know personally are still very warm and friendly in their greetings, including the father next door. Perhaps they don't get all the news either and, like most human beings, separate the individuals they know personally from the stock newspaper images.

Here is Walter back from work on Wednesday evening, June 7.

I want to add my strong endorsement to what Janice has said. No matter what happens — even if the Peace Corps gets thrown out of Afghanistan or the Americans are evacuated, don't call Washington or telegraph. Just sit tight.

Love from us both,

Walter and Janice

CHRISTOPHER SCREAMS BLOODY MURDER FROM HIS BEDROOM

June 16, 1967
Kabul

Dear Richard and Malvi,

It is a cloudy Friday afternoon and getting ready to thunderstorm — very strange weather for Kabul. This spring we had hail several times, once the size of golf balls. I've been very homesick since coming back to Kabul in a way that I never was before. Then I remind myself that I have been away from home for so long and so much has happened that is impossible to convey.

We are all reasonably well. Kathryn is being treated for amoebas that I knew she had picked up. We just never seem to hit this situation when there's a lab technician available. The covering doctor for the summer is new and won't give the treatment without a positive specimen. Finally the PC doctor, the only one left for the next month, did the test as a special favor. The battle with the amoebas continues!

While the doctor was phoning me to give me instructions, Christopher screamed bloody murder from his bedroom and ran to me, holding up a finger bleeding from teeth marks. The servants had given him a fairly large rodent, which had been raiding the kitchen for some time and was secured in a two-pound coffee can. I think it was the sort of mole that tunnels under our garden. But Chris took it to his bedroom and removed the lid, although they had wired it on, and stuck his finger in. The animal was quite wild and was furious at being captured.

Said rodent is now in our unused birdcage, being kept alive and observed. The servants all say they have been bitten many times by these rodents, even in their sleep, and unless you're a baby, no harm ensues.

But I just felt as though I had had enough of being a foreigner and trying to understand. So I did the natural thing for me and burst into tears. When I explained to them that I was homesick because so many things here are strange, they were immediately sympathetic and that surprised me. I had not thought they considered me a human being with feelings, but a sort of all-powerful mother figure who dispensed the dough, clothes, and favors, and listened to problems. This has shown me that they are an empathetic bundle of human contradictions like every other human being.

Of course, I arrived back right at the beginning of another anti-American scare due to Nasser's calling on his Muslim brothers to go after American and British installations. Walter is a very acute political animal and had figured out what later came to be true — the government here encouraged and indeed organized, with police escort, the student demonstrations as a way of allowing them to let off steam, but not against their own government. It had much the quality of a football rally. Still, because our two cultures are so many miles apart, one can never be sure.

I am sorry to disappoint Richard with my pro-Israeli sentiments. Of course we only get the bare bones of the news from day to day, until a bunch of papers arrive, so we are not so instantly assailed by who said what, when and where. I think Richard will have to admit that the Israelis have style. I cannot help but cheer for the boys who are willing to commit themselves to creating their own destiny, rather than leaving it up to Allah with a shoulder shrug saying, "It makes no difference."

Walter and I were talking about Richard the other day and how he had planned to come to Nepal at one time. We both agreed that he would have stayed little longer than a month. Of course my morale has also been quite low because some of the staff have quit before their contract is up. And now it's rumored that another wife will do the same thing. It may be just a rumor. This term of service isn't easy for any of us, but we did commit ourselves to this job and to doing it in a certain style, without the conveniences that many Americans depend upon abroad.

If there is one thing my dad instilled in me, it was not to be a quitter. I may grumble and complain and get very discouraged and blue, but I don't believe that I have it in me to be a quitter. Richard, I don't mean to imply that I think you are, but I do think you would rather spin theories than live with the consequences of trying to see any theory through.

I'm sorry this is not a cheerful letter, but I know you worry if you don't hear from us. As I said, we are all as well as can be expected. Walter and Greg are the two who have never had amoebas, but Greg was told to take some medicine for worms. When told, he nearly fainted, clutched his stomach and felt he could hear things crawling inside, until we explained that the doctor had seen only their eggs not yet hatched.

Jim Pines, a visiting fireman from Washington, after spending five days in the country, remarked that if he ever sends us another piece of paper from Washington, he hopes that we send it back as a reminder that we have enough trouble just surviving out here, without having to reply to everyone's bright ideas from a desk in Washington. He served once in Ecuador, which he said had a "couple of holes," but he added, "You have a whole country of them!"

212

Still, they may all survive long after we are dead from the fumes of our factories producing our soaps, disinfectants, and medicines. If I sound bitter, it isn't that. I just wish more armchair theorists could get away from their desks and radios and TVs and try to put just one of their pet ideas into practice, in the midst of dirt, sickness, apathy, and language and cultural barriers.

As ever,

Janice

PHYLLIS'S PROPHETIC DREAM

June 18, 1967
Kabul

Dear Phyllis,

I feel I should write some words of comfort for you folks in the States who are so constantly bombarded with the details of worldwide conflict. We had one day of nerves when we stayed off the streets, except for the PCVs who walked everywhere. This was when Nasser called upon his Muslim brothers to destroy British and American installations.

The students demonstrated at the American Embassy and United States Information Service, but not outside the Peace Corps office. The government organized and escorted them, as it was a good outlet for anger they had stored up earlier over the CIA exposures implicating their prime minister.

I don't know if your dream about our having to be evacuated is prophetic. I have mentally rehearsed what I would pack, if I was given short notice and allowed one suitcase per person.

Afghans have strong Arab loyalties, but do not consider themselves Arabs. My Afghan friends still invite us to their home, although the husband would have been drafted had the conflict enlarged. They were worried about me when they thought I was in Tel Aviv. Actually I had to cancel my visit to Israel, but my Greek vacation was fabulous, Phyllis. I never worried about anything for a minute, but when it was over, it was definitely over — no doubt about it.

With your letter today came one from Roberta and a five-page description of how their son died. Ken and Karen were nearest the truth. After the police left, Frank found a comic book, *Spooky Spooktown*, in the closet behind the carton the boy had been standing on. The cover showed a monster-man hanging little ghosts on coat hangers by their sheets. He was a creative boy, and like my Chris, loved to stage jokes and imitate things he read. He had just been studying Boy Scout knots with his dad, and knew a hangman's knot, which he did not use, but rather the kind of non-slip loop with which you'd lower a person down from a burning building.

Frank tried artificial respiration when he found him tangled, and the boy vomited. Roberta summoned the rescue squad immediately. They used a suction tube and respirator, but failed.

I will be happy to forward her letter to you when I know where you are, but you might want these few facts to help you with your own and other people's questions.

I hope your vacation turns out well. You are obviously overstrained by the heat, the war news, and the general razzamatazz of suburban power failures, train schedules, and the constant moving away of friends. Perhaps it's easier to keep a quiet center here, even though I feel terribly isolated at times. We can sometimes hear a short BBC newscast, and we get week-old newspapers.

I also very much experience the pressure of living in a culture that I cannot penetrate very deeply. I'm sure it takes years. We hope to go to Israel next spring upon our return. I should like to see if they have really made the desert bloom. As far as I can see, the Muslim philosophy is based on *enshallah* (if God wills) and *parwa nadera* (it makes no difference). You can't run a modern country on that philosophy. I have no objection to people not wanting to be modern, but apparently we ALL want modern medicine and motorcars.

The boy who had his spleen removed was here yesterday with his mother and will be able to swim next week. Ask Karen which other organs take over some of the spleen functions. All in all, nine CARE Medico and Peace Corps doctors worked on that boy.

The whole American community acted as one. It's my only answer to the riddle of life. In your dark hours, individuals are always so wonderful. Maybe it's human to forget during the sunny hours and let injustices slide along, unnoticed, until they fester and explode.

Love to you, Dave, and the kids,

Jan

FINDING A HOUSE
FOR OUR SUCCESSORS

June 24, 1967
Kabul

Dear Laura,

This is to be a little progress report on our efforts to locate a house and a car for you. Walter will be adding a note to the effect that it will not be possible to find a car out here with less than 10,000 miles on it.

In regard to finding a house, it is obvious now, with only ten days left, that we will not be able to have a house ready for you in which you would want to live permanently. We are cleaning up the doctor's small house so that you will have a roof over your head and not have to be in a hotel in the hot weather. The water in the hotels is not safe to drink and lugging water for the number you are would, in itself, be quite a chore.

Laura, the Peace Corps is low on the totem pole of agencies overseas. We do not get the first and choicest of anything. Although as staff we live on a much more comfortable level than volunteers, there are still many adjustments for a wife and mother to make from what she is used to in the States. In some ways, we have more luxuries, if you can call servants out here luxuries. The way we do things at home is still easier. We hobnob with the other department heads, including the ambassador and the chief of missions, all of whom are wonderful and fine people, and we take vacations in exotic places. But when you are first in Kabul, just because it will take so long for your things to arrive, and just because it takes so long to get things done out here, you will have to sort of "camp out." If you are aware of this beforehand, you will be better able to face it once you are here.

We talked yesterday with the head of Asia Foundation about a house they will possibly be relinquishing. There is a good chance we can get it for you. It would be very fine if we could. It is a roomy house and even has room in the yard for horses. Since the streets are only dust, it is nice to have some space in which to toss a baseball or football or do a little badminton. The house you will be in temporarily, just vacated by Dr. de Maine and his wife, is small with only two bedrooms, but Helen O'Bannon is loaning two *charpoys* (Afghan rope beds) for the garden. Many Afghans, and indeed American teenagers (including our younger children), enjoy sleeping out in the garden during the summer. It never rains. The garden at the de Maines' is spacious, and I am sending my gardener three days a week to keep it watered and looking inviting.

Our biggest stroke of luck is that we have been able to hire a good cook, and I will give him money to go out and buy staples so that he can bake bread and have a meal ready for you on your first night. Naturally, we will all be having you to meals, but it has been our experience that a family should have a place to be private, to relax from the rigors of the journey, and to absorb the strangeness of Afghanistan. Please understand that if you do not like the man, you can fire him later, but it is not easy to come by someone who can really cook and one just cannot do it by oneself under these conditions. He is highly recommended by Jan Morris's cook, who is one of the best in town. Both know how to cook from what is available on the local bazaar, which is a must for us, since we cannot use the commissary.

Walter will be in Turkey when you arrive, but there will be lots of us at the airport to greet you. Plane days are always festive occasions in Kabul, and scores of Afghans and Americans go to greet every arrival and departure. Landing at Kabul Airport is like no other landing anywhere. You will have flown for hours over the most desolate country and may even wonder, when you glide down in the Kabul valley, with the majestic Hindu Kush all around, if you are indeed arriving at the capital of Afghanistan. The airport itself was built by the Russians, is very attractive, and there are usually lots of flags flapping in the bright clear air. I have never forgotten my first day. There is an exhilaration one experiences at this altitude unlike any other.

By the way, if you are interested in dogs — everyone out here has loads of animals — a friend of mine has seven thoroughbred Alsatian five-week-old black puppies. Sometimes before one's personal belongings arrive, folks acquire pets to fill in that empty place. The yards are all walled, so pets can often live outdoors and not be underfoot inside.

That's all for now. Godspeed and happy landings,

Janice

UPSTATE NEW YORK, 2006

Laura and her family were the replacement for the Binghams. Mr. Bingham had asked early on to be rotated back to Washington, but he needed a transfer since the regulations were that if you decided to leave before your tour was up, the expense was on you for airfare, shipping of belongings, and so forth. When Laura's husband John applied for a position in the Peace Corps, he had in mind being appointed director. Washington convinced him to take the deputy position in Afghanistan and be prepared to take over after a year, when we would be leaving. It seemed like a win-win solution; however, at their farewell party, Mrs. Bingham appeared to be quite angry.

When I shared my confusion with Laura, who was also there, she wisely posited that Mr. Bingham had most likely not told his wife he had asked for the transfer. She might have been feeling rejected. When I thought about it, it made sense. I had read that Southern men put their wives on pedestals. What if Walter could have or would have taken me seriously my first week in country when I was so sick! I would not be writing this book.

Christopher at the garden window

The boys with our donkey

Kathryn and her friends on the street

CHAPTER TEN

Lull after the Six-Day War

THERE IS NO POLITICS
WHERE OUR SONS ARE CONCERNED
July 2, 1967
Kabul

Dear Folks,

Walter is away in Turkey. A little under the weather myself. Bad sleep these nights from my allergy, but if I do the same as last year, it will be over in a month. Maybe the sandstorms or something else in the air.

Chris and Katie have earaches, and I suspect the pool at the International Club. It is too small and imperfectly cleaned and maintained. Chris was to have gone with his friend Ibrahim to a picnic in the king's garden and a swim in the pool but has to stay out of the water. Ibrahim is a name we've heard much recently. When Chris was first invited to sleep over at Ibrahim's, Walter took me aside and told me that Ibrahim's father is the Egyptian ambassador. This was news to me. Walter said he didn't feel right about his son sleeping at the embassy during the Middle East crisis.

A couple of days later, I received a phone call from a very pleasant lady who asked me to come to her apartment nearby. There, her husband, Dr. Aboud, explained that his ancestors had had some unlucky accidents sleeping in the Kabul embassy, so he keeps a private apartment.

The boys are warm friends. As the ambassador puts it, "Where the boys are concerned, there is no politics." Sitting on his sofa under an oversized picture of Abdul Gamal Nasser, I said that I agreed completely.

The Abouds served recently in the States. Ibrahim went to American schools for two years, has a large supply of Beatles records which he brings over to our house, wears blue jeans, and looks for all the world like a Jewish boy. Mrs. Aboud reminds me of Malvi — warm, ebullient, sitting on the edge of her seat, talking and joking excitedly.

Dad always worried about how Chris would make out. It seems to me he makes out like a robber. He's hardly at home these days, and I find out only later from Mrs. Aboud that she's taken the boys with her on a visit to the Polish ambassador's house. So he travels about Kabul in either a dusty Peace Corps jeep or a shining chauffeured limousine with diplomatic flags. "I just love your boy!" Mrs. Aboud said. Perhaps it's his nonaggressive style that endears him to these foreign ladies. His Indian teacher also liked him. Perhaps he'll have reverse culture shock when he returns to the U.S.

Before I go any further, may I thank Richard for the excellent delivery on the bike tire. We were all amazed and Greg was simply delighted. Bike tires take a beating out here. Greg's bike is the original secondhand one Malvi paid for that was Katie's first bike. You paid more in postage than for the tire, didn't you? I have another item we sorely need: worm medicine for the dog — preferably capsules. She is losing weight and must need to be wormed again. Hope that's all, because there is no veterinarian here now. She only weighs about twenty-five pounds. This could go through the diplomatic pouch if marked "medicine."

Kathryn is learning to sew by making a pair of sailor pants. The children are always surprised at the time things take. As for myself, I'm dead tired again. I suppose it means the amoebas have sprung back to life after the last round of medicine. Anwar is making yogurt for me every day now — today with apricots. It's every bit as good as Dannon's, and I hope I'm learning how to make yogurt myself.

You all keep asking me about Greece. It was wonderful, particularly the boat trip to the Greek Islands, but it seems like a dream now. There is nothing here to remind one. This is another world. I find everything in my past life is rather remote. I am so absorbed with our present life and just trying to keep well. After Christmas the idea of a home in New Jersey will seem more real.

Malvi dear, could you please forward this letter to Maine for sharing? Kathryn's dying to see what's in her birthday box from there. We still get airmail, but I believe no ships are docking at Beirut. I wonder how folks' household goods will get here. The Karachi port is tied up with many weeks' backlog of wheat shipments. There's no doubt about it. Everything takes more time here.

Love to all, and I hope the heat waves are dispersed,

Janice

LISTENING TO DESCRIPTIONS OF LIFE AT HOME
WITH ATTENTIVE INTEREST

July 26, 1967
Kabul

Dear Doctor Gloria,

We were certainly glad to get your recent letter. Sometimes the States feel about as real as the moon to us.

Our new deputy and his family of four large boys arrived two weeks ago from San Francisco. A successful businessman with his own business, he wanted something different to do in middle age, and they will be staying on after we leave, to head up the program. We find ourselves listening to descriptions of life at home with the same attentive interest we used to reserve for travelers from foreign lands. We do hear the BBC newscast almost every day, but magazines and newspapers are almost ripe by the time we get them. In fact, during the Near East crisis, the government withheld that type of mail.

At a recent dinner given by the *Kabul Times* for our Fran Hopkins — can you imagine a capital-city newspaper owing so much to a twenty-four-year-old woman who gave three years of her time to them that they honor her when she leaves with obvious regrets and warmth on both sides?

I found out why. Although Afghans are not Arabs, Afghan men traditionally have sold their carpets and even their homes to raise the money to make the *hajj* or pilgrimage to Mecca. They have a deep spiritual bond with the Muslim world and indeed are probably the most deeply conservative and faithful to their religion of any of the Islamic countries.

Since I haven't traveled in Arabia or Iraq, I can't say, but surely they are among the most faithful. This government was afraid they would rise up at Nasser's request and attack the foreigner and his installations. In fact, the students did march en masse to the USIS (United States Information Service) offices around the corner from Peace Corps, but it was a demonstration, not a riot. The volunteers walked freely all over town that day and mingled with the crowds — many of them their students — but the ambassador asked other Americans and their children to stay at home.

What a long day with no radio or TV to know what is going on! How I would rather have been like the volunteers, but still I have a car and am identifiable as one of the Establishment. There were some funny little anecdotes, including the Italian ambassador's remark that if the crowd of demonstrators headed down the intersection past the Italian embassy for the new American embassy, he would run out all his cars and trucks and block the road. In fact, some few did demonstrate at the embassy; some of the PCVs who were there cashing checks and getting papers to terminate had to remain and eat lunch in the new snack bar until they dispersed — on the embassy's instruction to remain, of course. If left to their own devices, they would have plowed through on their bicycles most likely.

Walter has a good political nose, and he felt at the time that the government was letting the students blow off steam. Sure enough, all the police of Kabul escorted them. The month before, the students had threatened to topple the prime minister after the *Ramparts* article was published, in the government paper no less, implicating him with the CIA.

At that time, some papers wanted to know what the hell all these foreigners like the Peace Corps were proliferating for. We were pretty nervous that day, I can tell you. Walter had told

Washington last fall that there would be anti-American feeling soon — that the country just had to go through a xenophobic stage.

But as usual, Washington is several lightyears behind any other human institution. I'm afraid that I will never again put any faith in their intelligence. As far as I can see, the CIA only hobnob with the power elite and are aware of the palace gossip, but if they want to know what the people in the hinterland think, they try to flatter some poor little Peace Corps volunteer. The Russian agents also make a play for them. Can you imagine yourself at age twenty-two or twenty-three having to be that savvy?

The Russians don't talk to us, but Walter, who has just come back from the Kabul Hotel, where he was asked to talk to a group of traveling schoolteachers, says he felt very inhibited because there was an obvious eastern European in the audience.

I'm afraid that the volunteers and even our children have much more entrée to some of these other worlds than we do. During the height of the crisis in the Near East, Christopher was sleeping at the Egyptian ambassador's house with his friend Ibrahim. Walter was going to put his foot down until Ibrahim's mother invited me over to tea.

But by and large, everything is all working out better than I could have hoped. The children are calmer, more centered and lacking of that former jazzed-up quality that used to make my mother comment, when they arrived in Maine, "They act like they've just been let out of prison!"

Your comments on your experiences with children's emotional disturbances are interesting and frightening. I remember Pearl Buck in her autobiography saying how as a child she saw death very often in China — even trying to bury the little bodies of children who had starved in the field during the famine. But somehow a child could cope with this direct experience.

My mother has been concerned that the children will get some dread disease. We all have had and have presently conquered, at least temporarily, amoebas — with the exception of Gregory. He must have a cast-iron stomach or something, but then he is my only yogurt eater so perhaps his good bacteria overwhelm the others.

The children were aware that there was famine in the country this winter, that there was smallpox, and daily they saw the large crowds of men fighting for naan at the shops. They were also taken out of school and routed around the mountain on the days when there were demonstrations, but somehow this is an experience you live through and cope with. The experience only strengthens your equipment. The contagion of the violence that is seen and felt in the mass media must make them feel helpless, as it does us.

Certainly, Dr. Gloria, we have noticed that there is an air of deep anxiety and a·sort of nervous weariness in many of the letters we have received in the past six months, yet those who have written are more worried about us being more on the spot.

I was actually on my way to Tel Aviv the day all the Americans in Israel were asked to leave. Walter sent me out on a vacation to Greece to meet a friend as a possible way of snapping the amoebas that had dragged me down for about a month. The morning I left, he listened to the news while I was packing in another room. He only told me when I stepped on the plane, "Don't go to Israel until you check if there is a war going on."

He has relatives in Tel Aviv and we do hope to visit next spring when we leave for home. I'm afraid I was mentally and silently cheering and hoping the Israelis might go straight to Cairo and really show them how to run a modern country.

I'm afraid that I'm still too much of an American to ever adjust to *enshallah* and *parwa nadera* ("if God wills" and "it makes no difference") as philosophies to base life on. Still, these people have survived a long time and perhaps we are wrong to change them. I only know that change seems inevitable in our time — and that only those who can adjust seem to survive. Of course, in the process of trying to bring about change, we ourselves are changed.

With best wishes,

Janice

Kathryn in Kashmir

The Gulmarg valley (Vale of Kashmir), above the English church

CHAPTER ELEVEN

Fleeing Dust Storms in Kabul
for the Green Vale of Kashmir

ASCENDING INTO MARLBORO COUNTRY,
WE RECOVER WITH SADDLE SORES

August 26, 1967
Kabul

Dear Phyllis,

Walter will be leaving in less than a week now, so he can mail this in New York, or even deliver it to you in person en route to the dentist's office. He's planning to spend Labor Day weekend in Deal with his parents — to make amends for not having spent much time there on his last trip. Also, September 4th is his mother's birthday.

Your letter arrived today. I'm glad you were in Canada during the worst of the riots. Honestly now, the tables are turned. A volunteer in West Africa wired Washington to inquire if his parents in Detroit were alive and safe.

We are still reeling from the shock of the resale of our house for $27,500, which we sold for $23,000 less than a year ago. We couldn't afford to buy it back! Guess we'll set up a tent, line it with our rugs and cushions, and live like Kuchis. We know we are kooky in the way we live, but perhaps if we could reform, we would make more money. They certainly didn't lose any on that transaction.

I'm afraid we will never reform. The world is too big and interesting and in another few years, we may be off again. Walter has already had an offer to work for the UN in Indonesia. Once it is known that a family can make it overseas, there are so many agencies that want us.

On the other hand, three weeks ago, I felt my days were numbered. Kabul is exceptionally dusty this summer, due to the lack of snow this past winter. Also the temperature drops suddenly when the sun goes down. Invariably that's when we are at a required official function in some garden. The dampness begins to rise from the ground. Suddenly, I cannot speak — only gasp and wheeze. I have not only hay fever, but also asthma attacks. I was taking so many pills that my mouth cracked with sores.

So Walter, having ten days leave coming to him, packed us up — he and Katie with really bad colds — and we flew to Kashmir. You know how he loves to study those government maps that show every little village on them. Well, he could see that at 9,000 feet up from Srinagar, where you land in Kashmir, there is a place called Gulmarg. "That's where I want to go," he said.

First we had to deal with the tourist office in Srinagar. The clerk there was promoting the luxury houseboats on the lake. He assured us that a day trip to Gulmarg was included in a week's rental, but Walter was adamant. No day trip for him. We would find a way to get up there and stay for at least a week. There were not many tourists around, so we were being pressured to stay on the lake in luxury and spend our money on Kashmir's wonderful handicrafts: carpets, papier-mâché, and woodcarving.

I began to get the feeling that westerners never rented the second-class boats, which could be had by the day, but we always go second class on trains. There is a great difference in the outlay when you are a family of five. I finally asked the clerk, "What's the difference between the first- and the second-class boats?" He rolled his eyes skyward and sighed, "All the difference between heaven and earth."

We chose to stay on earth, and for sure there was a great difference. The second-class boats were moored pretty close together, close to shore. We visited a Peace Corps couple in one of the luxury boats. They were anchored out in the middle of the lake far from any other boat. There was a dugout for our use with our houseboat, so we paddled over rather than hire one of the fancy, canopied *shikaras*. Their boat sat high up off the water.

We tied up at their front steps and walked up. Inside, their living room was covered with silk carpets and many cushions, as well as a divan and low tables with lamps. It was most elegant.

Our boat was the size of a single-wide trailer, but the woodwork, like all the woodwork we saw in Kashmir, was hand carved. Unfortunately our living room was on the same level as the lake, so whenever I sat on our couch relaxing, I was exposed to the view of many peddlers paddling by, calling out their wares. In the morning, I watched a *mahout* (keeper) bring an elephant to the lake for a bath, not far away.

Meanwhile Walter had taken Chris and Katie to town to investigate how we could get to Gulmarg. The family who owned our boat lived in the rear and cooked our meals, so I had no kitchen duties. I could focus on resting up for the next leg of the journey.

Greg had asked me to read to him. We were enjoying a quiet time together, ignoring the calls of the peddlers, as they paddled at a respectable distance calling out their bargains, when suddenly there was a merchant stepping right into our room.

I hollered at him to get out! He bowed low and said, "Furs Madam." I could see that his shikara was piled high with them. Again I ordered, "Get out!" Again he repeated, "Furs Madam." After I ordered him to leave the third time, he backed out looking very bewildered. On the other hand, Greg looked up at me and said with great tenderness, "You're allergic to fur, Mommy."

On the third day, we made ready to take a taxi to the end of the road to rent ponies and porters to carry us and our luggage up to Gulmarg. I had been dragging my feet about going until I finally realized that the dampness on the lake wasn't helping my allergies. I went to the kitchen to say goodbye to the wife. I felt sorry for them because we would not be staying longer, so I gave her a Kennedy half dollar. Silver is very valued in Asia, and Kennedy was also well respected. She glowed.

At the end of the road, Walter got out of the taxi to investigate. Suddenly he was mobbed by pony boys. We were the only customers in sight. At six foot two, he towered over them. Out of nowhere a short stocky man pushed his way through to him from the edge of the crowd and flashed a homemade badge that read "Number One Guide." He convinced Walter to hire him to take charge of our expedition. In no time, he engaged ponies for us to ride and porters to carry the bags. Soon we were all saddled and ready to ascend. The porters took off straight uphill. Our trail wound around at a gentler angle.

Halfway up to Gulmarg, we came out of the woods into a clearing that overlooked a beautiful valley with many ponds. The mountains rose on all sides. The air was fresh, and drier than the hot, muggy air on the lake. "I can breathe," Katie exclaimed with great joy.

As we ascended into "Marlboro Country," we all recovered our health — except now we had saddle sores. The guide proved to be a wonderful masseur. We submitted to his care. Then we sat in tubs of hot water in the rustic facilities of a run-down hotel from the days of bygone British glory. It boasted, however, a marvelous chef, who has remained from their time, even though business is scant and will probably continue to be, until they construct a road for buses.

We had fresh-picked raspberries and real cream. Excuse me, but it nearly makes me wild to think of fresh, safe dairy products. We assumed it was safe because an elderly British gentleman and dowager who had never gone home when the British Raj left India were also indulging themselves in the salad grown in the hotel garden.

During our stay, I would hear her scolding the servant for not turning down her bed for the night and closing the curtains. She seemed to demand and eventually receive the level of attention she had always enjoyed. Hard to imagine, isn't it, feeling outraged that someone has not turned down your bedcovers? No wonder she never went home!

The place reminded the children of a Wild West town, with all the abandoned wood-built summer homes (called huts, even though quite elegant looking) left by former colonials. Chris learned to ride beautifully, but I was content to sit out many of the rides and admire the view, rejoicing in being able to breathe again.

Sometimes only Walter would go off on horseback with our guide, Mohamed. Then I would sit on the grass reading and looking across the lush green valley as the children ran in and out of the woods on the other side — playing whatever it was they played. I could see them and hear them as clear as a bell. When we were off by ourselves like this, they explored together and probably learned more than we ever did.

I only went to the shops down in Srinagar for one day. It is such a tourist trap, but a tailor friend of the guide brought some dress pieces to the hotel when I told him what I wanted. I bought myself a gray piece with pale flowers. Kathryn chose a red piece, also with flowers. She picked the piece we bought for Becky. I shall try to get ours made up this winter, but if I don't succeed we will come knocking on your door for help in 1968. Walter will bring your pieces. I'm getting jealous of his trips, particularly because he is stealing all the thunder with his slide shows. Whatever will be left for me to talk about?

Phyllis, do you still talk of returning to Canada to live? I wouldn't blame you. Sometimes, I think it will be such a shock when I return. Mostly it will be shocking that nothing has changed, as far as people's thinking goes. The BBC news we receive headlines the new racial outbreaks in America. How different our country appears from this distance.

We will probably look in Summit for an older home. We need a school system for Chris where he can read with his interest and ability level, which according to this principal is ninth grade. I've suspected that he's been reading some of my books! He's almost ten now. He has made some good friends, as have they all.

It will be the usual wrench to leave. My Afghan friend told me yesterday that when she even thinks about it, she knows she will cry for three days. I think more than any of the official folderol I've participated in, I'm proudest and happiest to have made one friend in this country. I so much need my women friends. Only another woman understands the female heart. If our husbands love us, they never understand us, and I don't suppose we'd love them if they did, because then our female mystery would be gone.

We are really paring down now rather than accumulating. The kids, however, love getting Classic Comics to read, and they are wonderful to leave with Afghans when one goes. They now have *Oliver Twist*, *Robinson Crusoe*, *Mutiny on the Bounty*, *Gulliver's Travels*, *Robin Hood*, *Black Beauty*, and *Rip Van Winkle* — but there are over a hundred titles.

Please, Phyllis, the illnesses you folks have had terrify me. It's worse than Kabul, I swear. Such bellyaches we get, but few fevers; however, the night before we left Kashmir, I did get a lulu — probably drinking the water on our day's shopping in Srinagar.

Walter had already flown back for a wedding. The kids and I were still up in the hills with our competent and attentive Muslim guide. He treated me like a baby, Phyllis. First I had chills, so he got hot-water bottles. Then when the fever came, he took away the hot-water bottles and brought water and aspirin and slept on the floor in the living room to be sure we could get up at six in the morning to mount those ponies for the ride down to town where one catches a taxi to the airport.

When he was kneeling on the floor, rubbing my ice-cold feet under the covers before the hot-water bottles arrived from the kitchen, Greg came in to go to the bathroom and asked, "What are you doing, getting into bed with her?" Luckily, my fashionable streak of white hair has earned me the title of Mother or even Grandmother in Asia — and the respect that goes with it!

During the time I was alone in Kashmir with Mohamed and the children, we had lots of time to talk and I learned much about him. He remembered when all the huts were occupied with the British, coming to the higher altitude during the season when it is unbearably hot down below in India.

The dining hall was filled every night. A dance band played. Now, only an occasional Indian family rode up on the ponies. There was a plan for a road to accommodate buses. When it's completed, he will no longer have work as a guide.

One day he organized a picnic for the children and me. We rode up to a higher altitude and he cooked out. The picnic spot had a tent in case of rain. At one point it began to drizzle. He herded the children inside, but I continued to sit on the ground outside and watch a line of Hindu pilgrims, not far away, walking uphill to a sacred lake.

Suddenly Mohamed rushed out of the tent and began to scream at a man that I had not noticed, sitting on the ground just in front of me. Further down, his family was photographing us. I was wearing dark red flannel baggy pants and a long tunic. When Mohamed had learned that neither Kathryn nor I had anything comfortable for riding horseback, he'd taken us to the bazaar and the tailor had made up these local-style outfits in no time. Here as in India I believe they are called *Punjabi*. We are wearing them now around the house as pajamas.

It turned out that Mohamed was furious at them for photographing me without my permission. I have to say that I appreciated that. It was quite brazen, I thought. Who or what do you imagine they thought I was that they wanted my photo! It made me reconsider times that I have tried to sneak a photo myself.

Riding down the mountain our last morning, I had to dismount near the end of the trail because it was so steep that I couldn't face staying upright on the horse. The kids all rode ahead. Mohamed and I walked together. I put my arm around his shoulder, as he is shorter than I am, and I was wobbly from the fever that had broken just before dawn.

He openly began to cry. I realized how much we had bonded in all the time we had to talk and share stories of our lives. Our fees came at a good time for him, as his son was getting married. He is only fourteen. "He wants to get married?" I asked. "Of course," he replied. I thought of Kathryn, going on twelve. At one point, he observed how young Walter looks. Then he looked at me and became speechless.

As for the fever I got in Kashmir, now I know why the Peace Corps application form asks, "Have you ever treated yourself for anything other than a common cold?" When I couldn't stand the pain in my stomach any longer, I opened the Peace Corps medicine kit and started with the appropriate antibiotic to go with "persistent stomach pain, diarrhea and fever." Seems I live on that stuff, but no more than the residents of Whittier Avenue, it seems. Indeed, I feel blessed because the children, unlike the Crowes, have had less startling symptoms. In short, what is happening at home? Please do keep writing. Your letters are food for me.

Love and kisses, Jan

P.S. Seven Up, our donkey, had a son born while we were away. While she is gray, he is dark brown with white rings around the eyes. The children named him Dr. Pepper. We're told he will nurse for some time.

THE GUIDE WOULD HAVE KEPT GREGORY
FOR HIS OWN BUT I SAY HE'S NOT FOR SALE

August 26, 1967
Kabul

Dear Malvi,

Here we are back in Kabul. The children and I returned early Tuesday morning from Kashmir, after a two-night stay in Amritsar in the sweltering plains of India waiting for the delayed flight on Ariana Afghan Airlines. It was good to be out of Kabul's dust for nearly three weeks. It was the only thing that snapped me out of intense allergic symptoms and asthma attacks.

So we learned that you had a good trip to Maine and that the fog cleared for you. It is always good to see my folks at the Island. They are at their best then, being among the oldest and most respected members of that small community, and my mother is a warm and efficient hostess — better than I am.

I'm always somewhat oppressed by having people around for very long, being at rock bottom a solitary person. I like to think about things and events in between the active, outgoing sessions.

I have appreciated your many letters, Malvi. Both Kathryn and I found the one you and Emily wrote most enjoyable. We came home from Kashmir, by the way, loaded with little gifts for people. Kashmir has many lovely crafts. One only needs someone who knows the ropes and can be trusted to lead you around the worst of the tourist traps.

Since we are so near the end of our tour, I have just a short list of items we need. For Gregory, school pants. Also, we need two pairs of dungarees for Bhaktari, the houseboy. Anything else, he ruins quickly. I have included his waist measurement. We would like two or three containers of dental floss, also a tube of Rhulicream for bites and rashes, and three jars of good paprika.

For Christopher's birthday, would you subscribe to *Boy's Life* and have it mailed to you for forwarding through May? He was given some copies by a friend who left and has truly devoured them. It is a good family magazine. Katie and I read the articles too.

Otherwise, I suggest money at Christmas. There is also little for them to do to earn money, but I'm getting very tough as the kids get older. We give them 2 afs for the first "A" on their report cards and double it (4, 8, 16, 32, 64) for each subsequent one, so that the most difficult effort pays the most. This has been their only source of income, since servants don't leave much for chores.

I am enlisting all grandparents not to stand at the boat dock with showers of presents. The children are — you will be surprised — greatly grown and not exactly in the toy stage any-more. They will probably be needing bikes, but we feel they should do chores and save for them. The world is just changing too fast for them to get used to a "feather-bed" life.

I must say that they have done us proud in our travels. They may not be polished ladies and gentlemen, but they have a kind of friendliness and ease with people of all colors and back-grounds. It is so completely unforced and natural that the guide in Kashmir was in tears when we left.

We had to mount the ponies before seven in the morn-ing for the two-hour ride down from the hills where we stayed in Gulmarg. Even the head chef from the dining room was out in bathrobe and nightshirt to see us off. He said, "We are all missing our own children up here, and it was good to have these children around." As the youngest, Greg is the chief one who melts all the men's hearts. The guide would have gladly kept him for his own but I said he was not for sale.

So, it's Jeshen (Afghan Independence celebration) time in Kabul. We will go early tomorrow morning to see the exhibits. Yesterday, the children and I went with Anisa, my Afghan friend, and her family to a picnic in Paghman. Two siblings of the queen were there, plus the minister of tribal affairs, a handsome gentleman with iron gray hair. Anisa joked, "Everyone in this town is related to the royal family, except me."

AUGUST 28, 1967

Malvi, I just received your first letter after your vacation. I know what you mean about not leaping in right after vacation. The other two times I returned to Kabul, I couldn't help leaping in. I had to. This time, I returned the day before Jeshen, and there were no official functions, so I have had a few days of almost normal, "housewifely" life. I'm not going to sweat it, if I can help it, but most likely, I can't help it. With Walter leaving for a month, I can take a back seat, as the deputy family can do the official appearances. I'll just teach that month. That keeps me plenty busy.

As for my birthday, Malvi, we are coming home soon, but we do want to buy a couple more rugs — a large one, of a long-wearing variety, for under the dining-room table for a medium price. Walter was in love with a beautiful Mowri at Jeshen. So, I think money contributions would be most useful.

I hope you like what we picked out in Kashmir for you. It's small but personal and very much a work of art. We also look forward to finding out if the riots really changed anything or anyone. Maybe we are just like the German people when Hitler was coming — too attached to our own small life and small things to bother.

With much love, Janice

UPSTATE NEW YORK, 2006

Paghman was a summer resort out in the foothills north of Kabul. Anisa's family owned a garden there. I vaguely remember there was also a small structure, not one of the palatial homes of the wealthy, but the flowering garden was fresh and green with a stream running through the center, making a rocky pool that the children played in one afternoon. It was a refreshing retreat from the heat and dust of summer in Kabul. Today Paghman is in shambles, having been destroyed by the fighting.

Sherpur school-bus stop

CHAPTER TWELVE

Hosting a California Teacher after Her Close Call in Iran

CHRIS GLAD TO HAVE SOMETHING TO DO
AND READY TO LEARN SOMETHING

September 5, 1967
Kabul

Dear Malvi,

Today was the first day of school. The children were up early, and of course the first day the bus is always late, so they were frazzled by the time they got off. Katie and her new friend Kieren were carrying on like Sarah Bernhardts. It's quite an age — very dramatic. Chris was only glad to have something to do and ready to "learn something." His sister calls him Professor Blass.

Malvi, does Richard know Marshall McLuhan, the man who wrote a book called *Understanding Media*? Is it in paperback? I'd like to read it.

It's a nuisance having to trouble you for things like jars of Sanka coffee and chicken-broth stock. It's just difficult to know when one can get them. You might ask Walter to bring another cheese. For months nothing has been coming from the West. There's been no tomato sauce or paste for months on the bazaar. Anwar cooked a big batch from fresh tomatoes and peppers yesterday and then froze it all. If I only knew how to can, but we spoiled the bottles we made last year. Walter would like to have green tomato pickles, but I don't have the know how or jars and lids to do it. My mother and grandmother used to can when I was very young.

CARE is no longer sending UNICEF milk to Afghanistan, and do we feel the pinch. It's hardest on the small Peace Corps children in Jalalabad.

In spite of the problems, I will be very sad to leave the friends I've made, Afghan and otherwise. The children have also made some wonderful friends. So many unusual families go abroad. This world is so interesting and varied. I doubt I can get bogged down in one place again. Just think! Our children have learned horseback riding in Kashmir and snorkeling in the coral reefs of Ceylon! Will Scout camp ever be exciting again?

I'll be interested to watch them. They are exceedingly resourceful and adaptable. Last night they were enumerating all the servants in their prayers. They will go on to the next thing I'm sure, but it will be interesting to see who and what they will miss. One of our embassy wives told me she wonders if her children aren't homesick for a dozen different places.

Malvi, I hope your weekend with Walter went smoothly. What changes do you notice in him, if any? We do miss Walter this time. Also you might tell him the phones were fixed this morning after only four days out, and the embassy came on their own and cleaned the stoves. We are going to put the donkeys in the woodshed for the winter and extend the roof overhang to protect the wood.

I hope you are all well, and we miss you folks. It will be nice to see you all — what, eleven months from now? At the end of July?

Love,

Janice

RUNNING OUT OF SOY SAUCE
WITH WALTER OUT OF THE COUNTRY

September 7, 1967
Kabul

Dear Malvi,

The Afghans never plan ahead for anything, and when something is gone, they rely on Allah or the Americans to provide. With Anwar gone to his home province to get his work permit straightened out, I spend more time in the kitchen, so I notice things we are almost out of. I don't mind going without many items, but when I don't have spices to make the food we do have tasty to our fashion, I get frustrated.

We're almost out of soy sauce, and I wonder if you could send a plastic bottle out with Walter — a large one. We use a lot since fried rice is a good favorite of the children and a tasty light lunch for visitors, just off the plane, who don't want much.

I have had no word from Walter yet, so I assume he had to race across the field in Teheran for his connection. I've been a bit edgy this time with him gone, and look forward to the end of these long absences. It gets harder as the children get older and need guidance with homework and a firm hand. It helps to have Peace Corps volunteers around whom they respect, but they ain't "Father."

I talked with Katie's girlfriend's mother (who is much younger than I) about these emotional upsets that Katie's been having. According to her, it seems to be par for prepuberty.

As for the "I may not even be your child" bit, the tactic this mother used was, "We haven't told you before, but you're the child of your father's first wife." The girls have a good sense of humor. It's worth a try.

Much love, Janice

CHERYL ARRIVES *SANS* ENTRY VISA

September 27, 1967
Kabul

Dear Malvi and Richard:

Walter is due in the morning, and we are all very excited. It has been too much that he's been away, but we wouldn't really exchange any of this experience — even the difficult moments. It is perhaps hard to explain that we have become closer as a family, one to another, and more truly alive than ever in my life.

It is with some trepidation and much real regret that I think of leaving. I am a much different person and live in a different dimension in my relationships with other people — that is, the amount I can give emotionally — because here I am free to be all that I can be as a person.

Cheryl, whom I met in Greece, has been with us for two weeks. It has been a great joy to have her. She is a magnificent young woman who took her sabbatical leave to study and travel in Europe — also to get away from her boyfriend who could not seem to grow up to her level of maturity, even though they are both thirty-one. It seems he remains a boy who is somewhat dependent on Mother.

She is really terrific with the children and has even won Christopher's heart by helping him with some school problems. She is traveling to Kashmir with some of our Kabul women tomorrow, and returning in a week. Several people have expressed interest in her possibly helping out at the school, and I hope something will work out. She asked her school for a second year's leave without pay. After almost a year of traveling, she could benefit from a stay in one place, particularly in this part of the world where travel for a woman alone presents special challenges.

It is impressive to have become the kind of family unit in which outsiders can find solace. Or as Cheryl said to us, "You, your home and children are like a tonic." Not that she is not giving as much to us, keeping me from loneliness and the resulting brittleness and shrillness of operating as a single adult with three young children. We have truly made good use of our days, seeing what we wish and quietly relaxing when we need to. She is calm but responsive and vital.

We went to the ambassador's residence last night to a private concert for the diplomatic families of all nationalities, performed by a famous harpist who is on a concert tour. The ambassador was most attentive to Cheryl and showed her all of his paintings. She recognized many of the scenes from Vienna, such as the opera house and other scenes. These Viennese men! I had to smile as it reminded me so much of how Richard would behave.

Thank you for your letters, books, and tapes. I'll wait for Walter to make your tapes. He's the one with the mechanical mindset. So glad you found him centered and not fractured. He was reluctant to leave and I was much worried for him this month.

Love,

Janice

Soon after Walter left for the States in early September, I was at home alone one afternoon when our phone rang — itself a minor miracle.

An airport official was on the line. "We have a young lady here who says she is a friend of yours," he explained. Cheryl had not known that it was necessary to have an entry visa to come into Afghanistan. They were about to put her back on the plane to return to Teheran when she'd pulled out Walter's business card.

I always carried Walter's card in case I needed the office number to call when I was out of the country. When we'd parted at the end of the Greek Islands tour, I wrote our Kabul home phone number on the back and told her that we would love to have her visit with us if she ever got to Kabul.

Walter was well known to the airport officials, since he met almost every arrival and departure when in the country. I said I would be right over to pick her up, not knowing at the time what an exception they were making to regulations.

It turned out that Cheryl stayed with us during the several weeks it took for her to get an entry visa that allowed her to be in the country legally before she could then apply for an exit visa.

After she related to me her experience in Iran, I understood how badly she needed a place of safety. On a day bus trip to visit some ancient ruins, there were two men traveling together who paid her a lot of attention. On the return trip to Teheran, one of them sat beside her and the other in the seat behind.

It was then that she overheard a conversation one of them was having with the person sitting next to him. They were speaking in French, which, luckily, she understood. When asked what his business was, he replied that he and his friend "dealt in women."

She prepared herself with her one piece of light luggage to make a dash for the door as soon as the bus stopped, intending to grab the first available cab. It was two in the morning and there were no taxis.

The two men implored her to let them take her to a hotel. It was then that a young Iranian man traveling with his sister came forward and invited her to go home with them. He later shared with her that until she'd bolted for the door, he felt she was going along with the men's plans — for he also understood French.

Learning of Cheryl's experience gave me the background to better understand why Anisa could not travel alone to Mazar-I-Sharif to visit her brother who was very ill. When I offered to travel with her, she replied that a male family member must accompany her, but both boys were having exams and her husband could not leave his work.

It was then that I realized how blessed I was in having sons and understood why I was treated with such respect, since one or both of them was usually with me. This was a great boon when Walter was out of the country. In fact, he and Cheryl kept missing one another as they both came and went for some time. After missing him for the second time, she laughed heartily and said, "I believe your Walter must be a ghost!" Eventually, he returned and was available for her final rescue.

During her many trips to the passport office to straighten things out with her visas, she was often asked to sit for long periods of time in the corridor — fully aware she was being looked over. When her exit visa was finally ready, the minor official in the office said that the director himself was waiting for her "at home" with her visa.

Naturally she was not going to go there alone, so she called me, and I phoned Walter. He rang the director, whom he had met before, and said, "I understand that you have an exit visa for my houseguest. Would you mind sending it around to my office?"

I'm happy to say that she had one reassuring experience with the male species while she was with us. A government official invited her out to dinner one evening. Naturally, I was feeling very protective and plied the poor man with all sorts of questions when he came to pick her up. I wanted to be certain I knew his name, rank, and serial number, so to speak — just in case.

What Cheryl learned about him was that he had been educated in the United States. Now back in Kabul, his wife was refusing to give up the chadri, so he could not take her out in public. He was missing talking with an educated woman, so the evening passed very pleasantly.

I feel that this story is a good counterpoint to all the stories we hear about how awful it is for the women to have to wear those chadris. It's hard to give up something you have always known, something that has made you feel secure on the street, and some could not do it.

A chadri also did have its uses even for some western women. I was told about one American husband trying to catch his wife as she went to her lover's home, but since she was wearing a chadri, he was unsuccessful.

Kathryn and neighbors in Afghan national dress

Side street near our house

CHAPTER THIRTEEN

My VW Becomes an After-hours Taxi

I FEEL I HAVE
A NINETEEN-YEAR-OLD SON

October 14, 1967
Kabul

Dear Mother and Dad (please share this
with Walter's folks and with Phyllis),

Well, Walter is off on another trip — supposedly the last alone for
a while. We hope to travel together in country when he returns. I
tried again to go with the children on my own with very little more
success than last year's abortive attempt to go to Peshawar. My friend
Cheryl, the teacher on sabbatical leave whom I met in Greece, is
here with me. I felt that together we could manage. We boarded the
Ariana Convair two-engine plane for Herat at 8:30 AM yesterday.

The first stop was Kandahar, where we were told there
would be a twenty-minute delay. We took bets on it. I bet one-and-
a-half hours, but we all lost. A gear that controls the nose wheel was
mashed to pieces. There is one other Convair in the country — our
ambassador's! If they could get a new gear from the American air attaché, they said the plane might fly on Saturday. This was Thursday.
Otherwise the flight was cancelled until the next scheduled flight
on Monday. If the part has to come from America, then "the other
Monday" — read week after next — is more like it. Ariana cannot
afford to keep spares of all things — maybe most things.

So we slept at the Kandahar Hotel and went to the USAID
compound for some American food. We kept ordering turkey sandwiches, cheeseburgers, and BLTs until they came out of our ears.
Everyone had two of something and topped it off with sundaes. We

had to buy a five-dollar chit book, so the kids spent the remaining seventy cents on the one-armed bandit, winning initially — but losing all eventually.

We rode back to the hotel with a taxi driver who drove without lights so his radio would play better. I insisted he turn them on, so he then bore across the desert and into town at 100 kilometers an hour. We decided that Ariana was safer, even though our flight back to Kabul would be on Friday the thirteenth.

The DC-6 that was to take Walter to Teheran took us up to Kabul, where one of its four engines conked out. So it happened that Walter and I spent the day together sitting on the grass near the field in view of the plane as the crew tried to find the trouble. It was a gorgeous autumn afternoon with hawks circling in the clear blue sky and tiny blue butterflies flitting through the grass. We only had to reassure the worried policeman that we were not about to bomb the airfield but were only taking the sun.

Last Sunday, Walter was taken for a second time in his life for a spy. (The first, I believe, was when he and his mother were trying to get out of Belgium after the Nazi invasion. Ten-year-old Walter, his name being very German, asked too many questions of the soldiers as they were waiting to cross the border into France and aroused their suspicions.) This time, we were driving a different Peace Corps vehicle than usual on our way to the restaurant at Karga Dam for the termination banquet of the Group VIII volunteers.

When the car sputtered and came to a halt, Walter thought we had a clogged gas line. Since we were already late, we abandoned the car and walked the final couple of miles in the starlit night.

After the banquet, I returned to town with other staff. Walter, John Barbee and his new bride went back to get the Scout. They found it surrounded by twelve soldiers from the nearby base, six mounted, six on foot, all with drawn bayonets. Aside from a military base back in the hills from the road, the area is not settled or lighted.

After they extricated themselves from the suspicion of spying (so they thought), John pushed Walter to the outskirts of Kabul where the police lieutenant, to whom the soldiers had reported, tried to take the car and Walter to the police to see if the car was really out of commission.

Walter refused to push the car over the mountain when repair facilities were nearby. He suggested that the lieutenant try the car, and handed him the keys. The officer replied, "I am not an engineer." Finally, Walter suggested they put a guard around the car for the night.

At the police station, the chief bawled the lieutenant out for giving the foreigner so much trouble. Walter is well known now to most officials, at least by name, but Nancy Barbee, young bride of three months, was pretty unnerved. It must have been quite a night for her. When her husband had cautioned her not to eat the gorgeous strawberries at the restaurant, she asked, "They wouldn't serve them if they weren't all right, would they?" Unlike fruit with a smooth skin, strawberries cannot be safely eaten raw. We must stew them.

Walter arrived home just about the time I had begun to wonder where on earth he was. The climax to our story is that when he sent the Peace Corps driver for the car the next day, the trouble turned out to be that Walter hadn't known about opening a valve on the floor to switch into the reserve tank, so . . .

We weren't even out of gas. The sputtering had been the last gasps of the first tank. The switch on the dashboard was not enough, as in some cars, to change over to reserve.

Luckily or not, as you look at it, there were no longer any soldiers guarding the vehicle and the tires and lights were still on board.

So ends another chapter in our exotic life. Never a dull moment, but I look forward to a few in 1968. By the way, Walter has made reservations on the *SS United States* for us to sail from Southampton on July 18. We should dock around July 22 — or hopefully before next year's riots.

Next morning:

This writing is crazy because I took half of one of Walter's Seconal (sleeping pills). Usually I sleep with one ear cocked and one eye open when he is gone because I have so much more responsibility, but last night I decided to sign off for one night. The least bit of Seconal makes me sort of drunk, since I rarely take them. In fact, I still feel a bit giddy eleven hours later, but I must get up and teach school this morning.

I had expected to be gone for five days from Kabul. The truth is that no one else likes to take my class, so the minute I'm seen back the note comes around, "I hope you are teaching — it's very hard work." I happen to agree that it is hard. So is operating in another language most of the time around here, but I always wanted to try that too.

I want to thank the grandmothers for the things sent even though Walter couldn't remember what was from whom. The pants and dungarees were a godsend to Greg and fit perfectly — also the new shirt for Chris. He was low because the ones I brought with us for this year are way too large. The light blue work shirts for Bhaktari are fine but the dungarees would fit, in Anwar's words, "some restaurant owner who eats much *pilau*" or two of the average Afghan people around the waist.

Bhaktari swapped them for some cloth trousers made in the bazaar from imported cloth. Together with the navy denim shirts, he looks mighty handsome. I feel like I have a nineteen-year-old son. He has great energies and does much for me, but the rascal had my VW keys copied at the bazaar and was caught by his uncle, Anwar, driving to the movies in style. Just like a nineteen-year-old. I'll tell you how I handled that one later.

The school dress and pink pants and shirt for Katie, I believe, came from Walter's mother. She loves them. I've had several dresses made for her here: one from embroidered Kashmir cotton, another with Kandahar embroidery, which I love.

Now I must get a cup of coffee to wake up entirely but it's been some time since you had a letter, and I want this to make the jet tomorrow if possible. With Walter home for such a short time, life was very hectic. In other ways, our life is more like my childhood, with home entertainment and so on.

On the other hand, our life does not follow the pace of the country but the demands of Washington and the needs of two hundred PCVs who at their ages sometimes seem unforgiving and ungrateful. I feel that I will miss Afghanistan but not the Peace Corps.

Love to all,

Janice

Bhaktari's VW Caper

This is the missing link that I had no time to supply back in Kabul:

Soon after his nephew Bhaktari was hired to live in and handle the gate and some housework, Anwar asked me to keep his nephew very busy. He didn't want the youth who came from a village in the remote Hazarajat to have a lot of time to run around Kabul on his own.

So I had to come up with lots of chores. One of them, which Bhaktari obviously loved, was to wash the car. Since there was so much dust, it could be done weekly. I don't know where or when or how he had learned to drive, but he obviously knew. I only had to show him once how to do something, or operate some gadget he'd never seen before.

I imagine the world is full of young men in undeveloped countries who fall in love with the motorcar and somehow learn all about them. Certainly Bhaktari had great ability to focus his attention. For instance, we bought a couple of little birds and a hand-made cage from the bazaar. The bazaar also had strings of dead birds that young boys caught and were used in a special kind of pie. Bhaktari must have been a bird catcher. When ours got out of the cage, I would open the kitchen door and motion for him to come. He would freeze like a statue, staring at the bird, then suddenly swoop it up in his hand. He grasped most things quickly.

In order to wash the car, he had to park it on the street. Possibly this is when he took the key to the metal shop on the block and got a copy — crude to be sure, but workable. What amazed me most about the event was Anwar's obvious anxiety. Certainly, he was concerned for his job security, but perhaps he was also fearful of Bhaktari, who was now taller and stronger.

One evening after Bhaktari left to get his evening meal in the bazaar, I was surprised that Anwar had not gone home. It was unusual for Anwar to stay unless we had guests to feed. His eyes looked moist as if he'd been weeping.

"Memsahib, Bhaktari not good boy," he said.

"What do you mean, Anwar?"

"When he come to Kabul, he boy. Now man, but not good," Anwar said. Then he handed me the key and made me promise not to let Bhaktari see it. He had caught Bhaktari driving the car in the late evening, possibly to see a movie.

By agreement with Walter from the beginning, I handled all the servant problems. How I would deal with this I had no idea at the moment. I had assumed that as the uncle and the elder, Anwar had absolute authority over his nephew — life and death even — based on a story told me by one of our PCVs. She lived in an apartment over the chai khana, the teahouse down the street from the PC office. Like all shops, it was fully open to the street. One day, a young man rode by on a bicycle and shot his uncle, who was sitting inside at one of the tables.

The volunteer spoke excellent Farsi, and she phoned the police. When they arrived, she followed them around as they questioned several people. "Aren't you going to do something?" she asked. "Why?" was the reply. "It will all be taken care of by sundown."

We had been informed that the ancient "eye for an eye" justice had prevailed for centuries in Afghanistan but that street executions by families settling scores were now forbidden. Her story made it sound as if private justice was still being carried out.

Anwar was a Hazara, and therefore a Shiite. I didn't know how closely his group followed the patterns of the ruling class, but I knew he was frightened, and I was pledged to secrecy. I could not fire Bhaktari over his transgression. Besides, I really liked him. He did a lot of work and was most agreeable. I needed to find a solution that put me in control of the situation.

The next day, I went around the corner to see my friend, Anisa. I found her in great spirits. Afghans, I found, laughed easily. Although life was hard, they did not stay down for long. Anisa was still chortling over a story her brother, who was in the police department, had told her that morning. A gang of thieves from the north had begun to operate in the neighborhood. Disguising himself as a thief, he infiltrated their group and told them, "I also thief." Anisa imitated a man's voice as she related the story.

Since he knew how to drive, he volunteered to drive a getaway car. Beforehand, the sign identifying the police compound was removed. The undercover policeman drove pell-mell about town and then directly into the police headquarters with the loot and the thieves.

I now had a plan. I returned home, gathered the servants and told them of the need for heightened security, sharing what I had just learned about thieves from the north operating in our midst. Then we replaced the slide bolt inside the garage doors with a lock to which I kept the only key.

Bhaktari walked away with his hands thrust deep into his pockets and his head down. Now, even if he had a copy of the VW key, he would not be able to get it out of the garage.

Overlooking our neighborhood in Sherpur

Aboard the SS United States

CHAPTER FOURTEEN

We Buy Our Tickets
for the *SS United States*

WE JUST SETTLED IN
AND WE'RE ALREADY LEAVING

November 15, 1967
Kabul

Dear Malvi,

In response to your question about the fate of your generous birthday check, for which I thank you again, it is safe in Walter's briefcase, and Walter will deposit it in his next mailing to the bank.

As I recall, I used my birthday as an excuse not to go to a boring reception. We sent the deputy in our place. So I did stay home with family, friends and pets. There is not much to blow fifty dollars on, but I am planning on having a karakul muff made, which will take about half of it. By the way, the furrier man was very pleased with the stylebook, which you sent. The Afghans are terribly clever, much like the Japanese. They can copy anything that can be made with their hands, just as long as they have a picture. And they are utterly fearless!

Our Bhaktari tried to get a job as a chauffeur with a friend of ours. He has never had a license but can operate the car. I'd never trust him with our lives, but I wouldn't trust that to any Afghan driver. Still a teenager, he's decided he doesn't want to be a servant any longer. The true innovator, he came to Kabul at age fourteen or fifteen from a village where there is absolutely nothing by way of modern conveniences.

Cheryl left yesterday morning on the new bus for Pakistan. We all miss her. She was jolly and had infinite patience with the children. Walter and I suddenly feel like we are surrounded by a parcel of screaming brats. Such a big house should hold a resident auntie.

Well, we have our tickets for the *SS United States*. It makes us feel like we're already on our way — and I've just settled in! Moving every two years is just not worth it to me. Kathryn and I would like to go on "home leave" and then return, but the men are restless, as usual, to move on.

Walter is the perennial discontent. He forgets how low he was the year this job offer arrived. Of course, he's not doing economic planning out here, but he does have to use many of his other talents, particularly his political acuity.

What a change in gears I will personally have to make, starting immediately, to do all the grubby chores again and see my children exposed to all the corruption and violence of the present American scene. They are so calm and unhurried over here. Not tense or wrought up. Katie wants to stay in this small school with her same classmates. There is only one classroom for each grade, and they move ahead together. She does want to see her old friends at home too, but she is worried about going to a large American junior-high school.

It is going to be a cold winter out here — looks like snow any day. Of course, it is already there on the mountains. How I will miss the quiet — no traffic by our house. To think I couldn't sleep at first from the animal noises. I must not hear them anymore.

Bye for now,

Janice

THE PROSPECT OF TWO HUNDRED
BOXES IN STORAGE

November 17, 1967
Kabul

Dear Malvi and Richard,

Richard's crack about the rarity of my letters deserves some candor, and this time I will seal it from "Snoopy" so it will be mailed without being read by him. We have been over this ground many times, and as with your own marriage, it is always a stalemate. Walter is a talented man with great energy and drive. His powers of self-deception are also great, and the more he suffers from success, the more insufferable he can become in his closer, personal relationships.

Walter and I call it his tendency to "walk off the top of the mountain." He said, during our last battle over this, that I should let him. Perhaps it will have to come to that, because the energy involved for me to try to get through to him, as I get older, is becoming not worth the effort it costs me.

We have talked about it often, and the fact that when the children no longer need me and are grown, my alternative may be to leave. It's just that I have never felt I had anywhere else to go and that standing and fighting to preserve my family has seemed the more noble way. I have often prayed to God that He will remove me before that point. I will have had a full and rich life and no desire to start over on any new one. I've often wondered what a younger, different kind of woman could do for Walter.

My not writing to you is part of a whole lot of things I do not want to face about going back to the States. It is also easier to live with Walter with three servants, however inefficient, to cushion his disruptions of household organization. So, aside from the fact that I feel it will be harder to raise my children in the atmosphere of violence which exists in the States, I do not relish the isolation in a house all alone pushing those dials, loading those machines for washing dishes, clothes, and so on. Here, our home is a hub of significant activity, and as its mistress, I don't even have to leave the house to be involved with human needs.

Right now, I wish that the warehouse in the U.S. with all our things would burn down, so we could start over with just what we bring back. It seems to me that Walter, on his side, has never made a compromise keeping down the accumulation of junk for me to look after. I am also referring to grandparents who give children a lot of plastic stuff they don't need but cringe at the thought of a good set of encyclopedias that they could use. My goal would be to have a few nice things, some beauty to look at and the basic essentials of living so that I, too, could be a person, and not a cataloger and picker-upper of the accumulation of five persons.

Cheryl and I joked that she will come and help me unpack those two hundred boxes now in storage. Perhaps it's no joke. I really feel sometimes that the only way I can face them is with a match. I threw away all I dared. I always face these packings and movings pretty much single-handed because I am efficient at it and Walter isn't, so I should think he would let me do it my way, but he won't. It's his way of being a man, to be assertive and dominating. This is all right in love, but I cannot convince him that the woman should be queen in the house.

Well, the staff is coming to supper. Unfortunately, I'm just getting over a bladder infection and don't feel like girdle and stockings. Do you remember, Richard, the picture of the ladies in the long silk caftans you sent me last year? Well, I had one made, and since I have desperately wanted to wear it, I've decided to christen it tonight. It is made of a beautiful black and gold Indian material. It is loose and flowing, and I can wear it over my flannel pajamas and be all ready to fall back into bed.

Thanksgiving is a week from today, and we have invited our Afghan friends. I will see if I can get a recording of a lullaby as you requested. All Persian songs I have heard so far are love songs, but if there are lullabies, and there must be, Anisa will know. Her five-year-old daughter's favorite song right now is "*Chesem Abi*" (blue eyes, pink cheeks). "Pink" is *golabi* and rhymes with *abi* (blue).

Where will you spend Thanksgiving — with the Hoopes?

Love,

Janice

UPSTATE NEW YORK, 2006

Hosting Anisa and Her Family for Thanksgiving

Thanksgiving is the nearest thing to a sacred feast we have in our culture, so I looked forward to sharing it with my Afghan friends. I had eaten with them more than once. I particularly remember the meal during Ramadan. Shoeless, we all sat on the floor on the traditional carpets. I sat next to Rashid, Anisa's husband. She hovered close to the radio listening for the signal from the mullah in Mecca that the fast could be broken.

Somehow participating in the ancient ritual made me remember Walter's report about the Jewish tradition of sitting *shiva* with the family of the deceased. He told me that at the moment he had to take off his shoes and sit down, he felt connected to something very ancient. Until that night during Ramadan, I had never had the experience of participating in any ritual, and hungered for it. I asked Rashid if what we were doing was at all similar to Jewish practices.

His reply was interesting. "Afghans believe we are the lost tribe of Israel." We didn't know that evening that his family would flee their homeland in the eighties as part of an Afghan diaspora.

Anisa and Rashid had the same number of children we had, two boys and one girl, only their girl was the youngest, ours the oldest. I felt awkward at first as we gathered around our table, but Anisa broke the ice: "I want to hear the song." In our family when we had grace, it was a silent Quaker grace, as my Jewish husband had been raised in a Quaker Meeting.

Unfortunately, Quakers are not hymn singers, but I knew the Thanksgiving hymn and hoped Walter had learned it at Choate. I knew that Christopher could always be counted upon to carry a tune, so we offered up "We gather together to ask the Lord's blessing." I trust that our joy at having dear friends with whom to share the meal made up for what we lacked in musical talent.

For a dinner party earlier at her home, Anisa had hired a drummer. I can never resist a good drumbeat. When she stood and raised her arms overhead to dance, I leapt to my feet and followed her movements. The drummer responded enthusiastically. Now, once again in our living room, she and I began to dance while her son played Afghan songs on a harmonium.

As we circled, I saw the shadows of our servants standing behind the screens taking it all in. I never felt more at home in Kabul than I did that evening, but I forgot to ask for a lullaby for Richard, even though Walter tended to his recording machine the entire time.

A GROWTH EXPERIENCE FOR US ALL

December 23, 1967
Kabul

Dear Malvi and Richard:

The clouds of rain that have hung around a good part of the week seem to be lifting, so the outlook for the jet's arrival on time tomorrow looks good. Tonight we went to the compound of the Community Christian Church to see the outdoor pageant of the Christmas story — complete with Afghan costumes, live sheep, donkeys and camels.

It was sensitively done and quite moving out under the Afghan night sky, with so many more stars visible than at home. As Gregory explained it to me, "I say 'boo' *and* 'yay' for going home. Last year I was homesick every night for America, but next year I'll probably be homesick for Afghanistan." Kathryn regrets leaving all her friends before the school year is up, but says that they are so far ahead of schools in the States that even if we travel for six or eight weeks, as I hope we will, she will not be behind.

Chris, our archconservative, wants to return to the products of affluent America. He longs for a "Sting Ray" bicycle. He will probably be our most financially successful child, because material security means much to him. I somehow have failed to help him achieve the kind of inner security that the other two have, though they are far from having his intellectual brilliance.

I will not be sad to leave the Peace Corps. In a nutshell, I have often felt that the Peace Corps was initially successful yet seems unable to grasp the problems of its needed evolvement. Two things that would have helped here would have been more staff and a staff that were adaptable to Afghanistan (if there could be such a thing!)

I will be sorry to leave Afghanistan, and I do hope that we can return one day to work for the Afghan government or university.

When we started out in Peace Corps, we felt we might be coming in too late, as we have more in common with the original volunteers from earlier in the sixties.

I did feel it was very likely that Walter would experience his personal shortcomings in exactly the way he did. Our friends the O'Bannons have said, "He is really very flexible, but the way he states his views, he gives younger people the impression that it is useless to talk to him, that his mind is made up. Naturally, those who get to know him realize that he will go all the way to help a person."

Part of the difficulty is that half of him is very European and has that kind of masculine assertiveness and intellectuality that make ordinary people feel he puts himself too far above them. If one is going to lead, one has to lead the common folk as well as the loners.

As the ambassador put it, I have a softer exterior, but I too am too much of a loner to relate well to those who are not. It has been a growing experience for all of us. The children and I have really become stronger all around and learned to stand alone together during his absence, leading fruitful lives without self-pity.

The young of today have not known the war experience that Walter did, so, in a sense, the experiences that motivate him to service, to pay the debt he feels for having survived, are out of their range of experience. All they know is that they feel adult culture excludes them from the decision making, and they do not feel like having the decisions made for them.

Of course many young people have not yet gone through the rite of passage that gives them the perspective to judge what is happening to them. They simply have not had much life experience yet. Since they are such a major part of the population, parents and adults do have to learn to relate to them.

Countries now want more than a batch of very young people who are going to do so much of their growing up at their expense. As I see it, we have a thin slice of very competent people representing us abroad and a greater number who tend to be as colonial in their way of being with host-country nationals as any of the empire builders were. It is true, in large measure, that we are neocolonialists.

Our Christmas tree is large and beautiful, the nicest we have ever had. The children decorated it for a large party we gave for volunteers just before Walter left for Washington. We have truly learned to make ourselves at home, and I do pray that some of the stability we have acquired as individuals and as a family will last the reentry into American life.

From this distance and with the news reports we get, our culture sounds like a true Sodom and Gomorrah. I have to keep remembering all the wonderful people I know who are holding down the center through their prayers and right actions.

I hope that your trip was a happy one and that Malvi's cold evaporated in the sunshine. I can never understand how you can take penicillin for a cold. Isn't this dangerous?

As ever,

Janice

The family on the Ladaband trail

CHAPTER FIFTEEN

A Look in the Rearview Mirror

UPSTATE NEW YORK, 2006

The final weeks in Kabul sped by. During the month of January, I wrote no letters. As the time for departure drew nearer, the daily drama didn't slow down, but I became less caught up in it; however, as I read back through the letters, there are a few incidents I recall that are worth recording.

To begin with there was the final examination to be administered for my ESL students. Their schools would be closed for the winter, and I would be leaving as they reopened. Already our building was not warm enough, so the examination was scheduled for another location. I had taken on this teaching assignment without having the Peace Corps training, but the workbooks were very simple to follow. I asked two ladies in the larger community who were professional teachers to observe me, and they reported, "You've discovered most of it by yourself." I had done practice teaching in college and truly liked doing the work.

I prepared the students by suggesting topics they could choose to speak about, since this was to be an oral exam. The simplest topic for earning a passing grade would be to describe their own family. The most difficult and earning the highest grade would be to tell me something about Afghan history.

It was unfortunate, during the exam, that we were not in our familiar surroundings, and I was unprepared for the fact that I was also going to be observed during the process. The students were brought in one at a time, and it was clear most of them were terrified. When I'd done practice teaching during my senior year at the University of Maine, my principal told me that the students respected me because it was obvious I respected them. I found that to be true with the Afghan women as well. I never talked down to them.

It was clear that each one had prepared and rehearsed so that they knew by heart what they were going to say, but when I questioned them for further details, they froze and seemed not to understand me. That was not the case when we were alone together. They kept shifting their gaze toward the monitor, who sat with a stony face. To tell you the truth, she rather unnerved me as well. When our prize student, a young woman who must have been speaking English for years, came in, she gave a synopsis of Afghan history. She could have gone on as long as I wished, but she finally shrugged and stopped. Her self-assurance was outstanding in that group of mostly wives and mothers.

I wished I could have had a farewell alone with the women, but it was not possible.

The winter of 1968 brought lots of snow for skiing at the ski hill organized by the Germans. They, too, had a Peace Corps-style program, *Entwicklungsdienst*.

Moreover, the Germans had been a presence in the country since the years following World War II and operated both a marble and a woolen factory. They lived in the older Afghan-style homes — not the recent larger constructions favored by USAID. German women did their own marketing and were tough bargainers.

The ski hill was outside of town. It boasted a rope tow hooked up to an automobile motor and a small warming shed that also sold hot spiced wine. Walter loved to ski. This had been one of his acid tests for a wife. I'd taken lessons before I had the babies, but as a lover of any kind of dance, I was a graceful but a reluctant and ineffective skier. By the time we were overseas, I was content to sit in the warming shed and dole out sandwiches to the rest of the family as needed.

I had a partially unwrapped sandwich in front of me as two young Afghan men, obviously Kabul University students, came in. They were not in ski clothes but nice western suits and overcoats. I invited them to sit at the table in the only remaining empty seats in the hut. Simultaneously an Afghan girl child dressed in clothes suitable for skiing sat on my lap and began to eat the tuna-fish sandwich.

What happened next was even more interesting. A suave Russian man approached us and struck up a conversation with the young men. He barely looked in my direction. I realize now that he was observing the Afghan custom of not looking directly at their women; therefore, he must have seen us as a family group. What with my somewhat Eurasian features and dressed in my old ski pants and a bulky sweater of uncertain vintage, I did not stand out as a stylish American. It tickled me. It was truly like being a fly on the wall.

I remained silent, my arm around the child on my lap, and listened to him court these possible future leaders of their country. His final bid, delivered sotto voce, was "We want to get you fellows a radio." Of course, I thought. A radio, so they could hear the broadcasts from Moscow. The young men said very little and appeared to me to be embarrassed by his effusive attention. I've often wondered what became of them.

I had limited contact with educated Afghan men, but there was a teacher who came to visit me about once a month during my last year in country. I do not recollect who made the contact, possibly my Farsi instructor. This teacher, whom I will call Mohamed, a common name, had a whole array of Afghan stamps for sale. The oldest were so-called registration stamps on thin woven paper. They were undated, but he said they were from Amir Abdulrahman's time in 1893. They were in different colors for different places:

blue for Kabul, white for Peshawar, and also pink, lavender, and orange. Hand cut, they were meant to be glued from the paste pot in the post office. The modern ones seemed to have been printed in France, since they were labeled *La Journée de Professeur*, *La Journée des Femmes* (Teachers' Day, Women's Day). Mohamed assured me they were very valuable. Although I could check their prices in the catalogue, I had no idea to whom I would sell them, but my grandfather had collected stamps and so had I as a child.

I felt concern for this teacher, because he really needed to supplement his income to support his growing family. He was about thirty-seven, with a young wife who'd had a child each spring of their short married life. (It took years to accumulate the bride price, so a man was usually a good bit older than his bride.) One afternoon, Mohamed recounted their recent trip to Mazar-I-Sharif to see his wife's family, each of them holding a toddler on their lap during the long bus ride. He was genuinely worried they would soon run out of laps, so I suggested he consult an excellent Afghan doctor who lived in our neighborhood. After all, I had seen the young boys in the bazaars carrying trays of wrapped condoms for sale. They couldn't all be being used for balloons, even though each vendor had blown a couple up and painted stripes on them, possibly as an advertisement.

On his next visit, Mohamed reported that the doctor had instructed him that it was up to him to take responsibility for his wife's not getting pregnant every year. Now that we would be leaving a little earlier than anticipated, I wondered if I would be gone when next he came around, but sure enough he appeared once more. Smiling sheepishly, he announced that another baby was on the way. I wished him well and farewell, and I bought some more stamps. When we got home, I arranged them in a notebook, and there they remain.

When we'd left the States I'd told the reporter from the local paper, who came to do a story on us, that I felt the children would be some of our best emissaries. Sometimes they truly did amaze me, as when Kathryn reported her experience walking around the corner to Anisa's house to have her hair washed.

Kathryn loved to visit Anisa's salon and could easily go on her own. She had grown several inches, so her skirts were short on her, though not to the extent of the miniskirts favored that spring by the students at Kabul University. One instructor we knew remonstrated that he was not used to lecturing while looking at women's legs. Since we were leaving soon and winter was almost over, I thought there was really no need to lengthen Kathryn's skirt. Besides, though tall for eleven, she was still a child.

Kathryn told me later that she felt she should have changed clothes after school, but hadn't wanted to take the time. It was still cold weather, and she had on tights so no skin was showing. Still, a young man coming in the opposite direction shouted at her words she did not understand and spit in her face. "I didn't blame him," was all she said. I wondered how I would have reacted had it happened to me.

Chris had learned more Farsi than Kathryn, possibly from spending so much time in the kitchen with Anwar, but Kathryn could report to me accurately on the status of the relationship between Anwar and his nephew through quiet listening and observation. Her intuition was very developed and she picked up many nuances that I would overlook.

I was sad to be leaving Kabul when I felt I was just beginning to penetrate the culture more deeply. On the other hand, there were more indications than the length of women's skirts that Afghanistan would be more and more disrupted by western mores.

One glorious spring day during my last month as I was walking through the nearby bazaar, a red convertible with the top down roared by. Usually, there was very little vehicle traffic on our side of town, so that I never worried about the children on their bikes. The convertible was bursting with American teenagers — the girls sitting on the boys' laps, shrieking as only girls can in that situation. At home, one would just smile and say to oneself, "Spring is here."

Afghan teenagers did not even walk together in the street. Occasionally, I saw several teenage couples walking from the movie house — always maintaining a discreet distance between them: no holding of hands or arms around the waist. I learned they were from the few Jewish families who had not emigrated. One morning when I visited Anisa, there were several young girls in the shop. She indicated with a nod of her head that I should notice one in particular. "I don't know the English word," Anisa said, "but she has a star."

There was a Peace Corps saying that one returned from Latin America a revolutionary; from Africa, happier; and from Asia, patient. During a week Walter and I spent in India that January, I received a lesson in ultimate patience. I'm not sure what town it was, but we were riding in an auto-rickshaw and got caught in gridlock crossing the central square at noontime.

Humanity pressed in on every side. In Afghanistan, I was only in a crowd during the Jeshen Independence celebrations. The rest of the year, the populace fanned out over the rugged, sparsely populated landscape. I'd spent the better part of two years settling

294

into Afghanistan, becoming bonded to the land and the people who befriended me.

In India, people traveled in groups like so many flocks of noisy birds. As we stalled in the midst of the crush of people, I saw on my left, beside the road, an open-air market. A shopkeeper (his shop was a small area of ground) sat in the middle of his baskets of grain. Overhead, a flock of crows circled and waited to light on the baskets and peck at the grain. Patiently, the man would wave them away. They flew up only to return a few minutes later. As I watched this scene repeated over and over, something triggered in me. I couldn't conceive of being this resigned.

We had come to Afghanistan full of ideals and hopes of making a difference. Suddenly, I felt confronted with the immensity of humanity's problems.

"Get me back to the hotel," I sobbed. Once we were alone in the hotel room, I struggled to find the words to express what I was feeling. Finally, from some deep recess below the level of rational thought, came these words that proved prophetic: "Someday when I have ten years with nothing else to do, I'll get to know India." I did not realize it at the time, but I had just set an intention.

Fourteen years earlier, I had stood on the bank of the Charles River and vowed that I was prepared to raise my children, at least for a little while, in a Third World country. From that experience I had come to realize that such intentions are duly recorded in some cosmic ledger, but the timing of the due date is not in our hands.

I soon forgot the experience as I became engrossed in packing for our return to the States and the subsequent adjustment to our familiar — and so changed in our absence — homeland. Fourteen years later, a new cycle of life would begin.

Young boy selling wild lilies

Last family outing in the valley of the Judas trees

GOING HOME

MARCH — MAY 1968

CHAPTER SIXTEEN

Longing for Old Familiar Faces, and the Sadness of Farewell

HOME TO FAMILIAR FACES:
THE GREATEST GIFT

February 1, 1968
Kabul

Dear Richard and Malvi,

Happy Valentine's Day! The days come and go without the usual reminders from television and newspapers, so I was quite taken by surprise this morning that it is already February, time for Valentine greetings. As you know, I have been described as having an eastern concept of time.

We had a tea for the O'Bannons (leaving at the end of their tour) yesterday. It was a fine, snowy day. Helen said there should be no big party, so we took them to the International Club for dinner later that evening, while the children, who now babysit themselves (when we are on this side of town within phone range), stayed up and made valentines.

With little more than a month left, however, I began this morning to weed out books to sell. So many we brought, so many that were mailed to us, and they weigh so much. And speaking of books, I am very pleased with the article Malvi sent on the encyclopedias. I do want to digest it and go with Kathryn and Chris, when we get home, to look at the new editions to see which one they would use the most. They are definitely ripe for one, and even though the *Book of Knowledge* we use here is not the new edition, it is constantly in use. It's not for high-school use, however. Encyclopedias have changed since I was young!

We would really appreciate it if you would be able to give a set to the children this fall. I know you are always dying to do something for them, but I do feel that this is the perfect break for you to get out of the "What did you bring me?" role.

They have become so grateful out here for small things. Fifty afs (about five dollars) is an inordinate amount of money to them. They have been further brainwashed by me to believe that they are now old enough to work for the things they really want, like bikes. Three bikes is too much of an outlay for any parent all at once, and they have a certain amount of savings ready.

I told them we would finance them — like buying a car, with Daddy as the bank — so much down payment and working off the balance in weekly installments. Kathryn will be in demand from now on as a babysitter, but my intellectual Chris is the one who will have to develop some marketable talent. Anwar is teaching him to make French fries, so I may be able to pay him for that.

What I am reiterating is that I feel you would do yourself a disservice to meet them at the boat with gifts. Remember that for us, coming home to familiar faces and sights will be the greatest gift. I would hate to have anyone give them the impression that they had been missing anything. They haven't really.

They have received a great gift of two years in an environment where they saw more of their daddy, in spite of his long absences, and had the time to be children and to not know that terrific pressure of going somewhere and doing something all the time. For myself, I do wonder how long I will be able to stand the pressure in the States and not be longing to return to Asia.

Of course, my man has been hurt deeply but in a way that I felt was inevitable when we took the job and in a way that will make him, and is making him, a better and a stronger man in the long run. Peace Corps and Afghanistan are both great teachers, although considering what a leveler the latter is I feel the former could have a more humane personnel policy toward the staff. Their attitude seems to be, "We don't need you and are doing you a favor to hire you at all!"

That's all right with me, for I can see the day coming when the worm will turn. They will always need some outside talent, but the word is getting around slowly that you can be overworked and underappreciated. But I'd do it all over again if Walter felt up to it — which he doesn't.

The Afghan army officers you mentioned meeting have not rung us up and frankly speaking, in this small community of Kabul, neither they nor we would be comfortable with the relationship. They are "your" Afghans, but we cannot share them with you out here. We do keep our distance from the military, and from the point of view of protocol, they would be unlikely to take the initiative in calling on a chief of mission.

Their government also does not like them to have much social contact with foreigners here. As Asians, they would be very polite but never hint of this to you, and I suggest you do not mention it either. It would be embarrassing to us as well. I will explain it to you in detail when we are at home. We do wish to keep our noses clean, too, because we hope to come back one day.

It's difficult to always know what is appropriate. For instance, our Afghan language teacher in the States is now in Kabul but did not accept our invitation to Thanksgiving.

We certainly do not need anything to be sent at this time. The tour is over, and I am trying to get rid of things so we will not be overweight and end up paying more in freight than the cost of replacing items. I guessed within fifty pounds coming out and was fifty pounds under, but I gather that the packing materials here are heavier, so I will have a more ticklish job.

My mother's letters have certainly sounded buoyant. I wrote to my Aunt Georgia sending money for a homemaker or cleaning woman if one could be found. Georgia's and my great concern is the way in which my father does not spare himself one iota nor make concessions to himself for his age and how little Mother has ever considered him. Of course, my father always liked to play the role of a martyr, and martyrs are always difficult personalities.

Happy Valentine's Day! And best wishes for your improving health with spring approaching. We hope the accompanying photos will serve as a belated valentine greeting with love and kisses.

P.S. I saw the ambassador at the embassy lunch counter the other day, and he looks and acts so much like Richard it really made me homesick.

LOTS OF HEARTACHES

February 23, 1968
Kabul

Dear Phyllis,

I am becoming worried about you. I have not heard of you or from you since Christmastime. Karen said then that your kids had a lot of illness. Doesn't that make you want to go straight back to Canada — that, and a lot of other things about the American scene? It always seemed to me that Canada was a wee bit saner. Perhaps, indeed, that is what you are preparing for.

We have heard that we may be leaving here on March 28, but we have received no orders as yet. We think if we do, we will take the boat from Le Havre in France, landing in New York on May 15. I must talk with the teachers tomorrow about the children's missing so much school, but we do feel that we should take advantage of being over here and to take our time coming home. Also, Walter has had enough rushed journeys.

Tentatively, we will spend two weeks in Israel and the rest in Athens, Rome, Florence, Venice, possibly Vienna, and then we don't yet know where, after that. We are not very good tourists and tend to sort of wander into things.

Luckily, in the spring, it shouldn't be crowded, and we do plan to travel by train after Rome. We are running great tests on how each of us will pack a small carpetbag or a sort of local Boston bag made of camel hide. Won't we confuse people? It pays to be able to carry your own stuff, because once you leave the East, there is no one fighting to carry things for you. When I think of how we got up to Gulmarg in Kashmir on the horses, with three men scrambling up a more direct footpath with the suitcases strapped on their backs! Our dog Poopsie is coming too, but she will fly, direct!

Please don't read this letter to anyone beyond this point.

There have been a lot of heartaches in this job, Phyllis. The State Department, like other Foreign Service jobs, has a system of evaluation that can really ruin you. Often evaluators are "polishing the apple."

Ours was a young professor who has never been responsible for any number of people, but who was apparently chosen because he is married to an Iranian and had taught in Iran — very different from Afghanistan, even though it is next door.

The last evaluation was finished just as we arrived. The writer of that report is now head of the evaluation department. From reading the new evaluation, it seemed to me the writer wanted to prove the program had gone to the dogs. There was nothing the staff had done correctly or well enough, according to him. He talked only with the volunteers, of whom there are always some who love an ear for their gripes. He checked very little with the staff on their allegations, or with Afghans. It burns me up!

Walter, who has to write the rebuttal, is eagerly composing it, beginning with the Afghan proverb, "A new servant can catch a running deer," and hoping to end with the recommendation, tongue in cheek, that they make the evaluator the director to see what he can do.

All in all, I thought the evaluator's piece would make a good master's thesis for someone who had read all the books and thought up all the bright ideas, but had never lived with putting them into daily practice. Of course, young people today are quick to assume they know all the answers. We old fogies are superfluous to them — until they have a problem.

You know Walter, how he leaves not a stone unturned. For example, last Saturday morning he received a wire that a married PCV, in a distant point near the Iranian border, had lost her mother. The jet leaves here for the West on Sunday and not again until Thursday. The next plane might be the undependable Ariana Afghan Airline's prop plane on Tuesday.

So he spent the day getting word to the girl (not easy with one phone available at the hospital in Herat for all the volunteers). It meant sending someone from the hospital to find her. He instructed her and her husband to get a taxi across the desert to Kandahar during the night, then to take the morning Ariana Afghan Airline plane to Kabul. He got the American advisor of Ariana to keep radio contact with the plane and the Iran Air captain to agree to hold his jet until they arrived.

Then all the airport personnel galvanized to run the couple's passports in one door and out through the departing passport section, while Walter escorted the couple across the field into the jet, giving them their money and instructions while the ramp was being wheeled away.

The jet took off fifty minutes late. Walter's comment was, "Iran Air makes a hundred thousand dollars a year off of us." His secretary's was, "When you leave, Mr. Blass, there will be no one who knows how to galvanize half the government bureaus in Kabul to get a couple of PCVs home for a funeral." I have been told that back in the evaluator's good old days or "Early Peace Corps Afghanistan," people sat around for a week waiting to get a plane out for a parent's funeral.

I have a great deal more sympathy for politicians now that I've had a smack of it. Your man can work his balls off, and if not enough people like his personality or something else about him, it is made to sound as if he were something he isn't.

Phyllis, I do hope there is nothing seriously wrong with your health — no major problems. I can just imagine that you are ripe to get out of that little house and have some breathing space. I was hoping, for your sake, that David would find a job in Canada this summer.

Otherwise, I'm looking forward to seeing you and the children and Dave this spring.

Lots of love,

Jan

DON'T WANT TO START CONSPICUOUSLY
CONSUMING AT HOME

March 6, 1968
Kabul

Dear Malvi and Richard,

Today came the letters regarding insurance and Chris's rabbit passing away. I decided to tell Chris about Smokey in the afternoon rather than waiting for bedtime. He got up and walked out into the garden immediately. Katie explained that he felt closer to Smokey than to our dog Poopsie, who seems to be closer to Greg — although Chris does pet her a lot, as we all do.

By the way, a letter received today from Jason about what to do about Poopsie before we arrive and move into the house. He said that he never did get the dog run built; however, he has had good experience putting his dog in a kennel while in Europe. Perhaps we will let him handle that decision.

We are following the news about Malvi's neurological examinations, and I, for one, have never been clear about the symptoms. I am so glad that she will talk to the doctor about how unsatisfactory the technician's performance was. In many ways, although we do not have sophisticated equipment out here, we get better attention. Because of the personal relationship we have with a doctor who knows us, I would rather be sick out here than at home. One staff wife, who has been in the hospital for two weeks with a pulmonary embolism, said she would not want to be evacuated to Frankfort. Here, there are RNs around the clock and servants at home with her preschool children. She has been very sick, and we were all very worried. This is probably one of those 10-percent risks that come with birth-control pills. She had clots in her varicose veins in the States and should not have been on the pills.

I do not think that you need to think of getting another rabbit. It was an inevitable experience to lose a pet — something that must happen eventually and is really a necessary experience in maturing. Chris is no longer a little boy. You will have to revamp your attitudes toward your grandchildren because they are all quite a bit different from when you last saw them.

We are all looking forward to working out this idea of a cabin in Colorado. John Bing, who lives in such a cabin in Estes Park, where he works for the organization that runs our training program, has invited us to visit to test it out. He says there are lots of opportunities for teenagers to work on resorts in the summer. Christopher learned very quickly to ride a horse in Kashmir and dreams very much of owning one, or being around them. Let him work on that dream for a while. I am very much of the theory that children ought to dream for things for some time, wrestling with the problems of attaining them, rather than having parents and grandparents supply. One writer has said that today's child mentions casually in the morning that he is interested in a camera, and by supper has a Polaroid.

For heaven's sake, if you have money burning holes in your pockets, donate to the Service Committee or some organization that is working on making society a better place for your grandchildren by attacking some of its gross injustices. We have now achieved such a good foundation for them to appreciate what they have and how poor some people can be. I don't want to go home and start conspicuously consuming. In fact, I am having some pricks of conscience about what my own role will be in this "house business." So much is pushed on us in the stores and magazines and TV. It is easy to think you need a lot that you really don't.

One of the things that disappoints me the most is that

nothing I have heard from the NJ Friends seems to indicate they are doing any thinking on the crisis that from abroad seems to be in the wings for our society. The talk is still about building a meetinghouse. It makes me rather sick at heart to think of returning to a situation that has moved so little in the past two years. As a family, we have gotten along without a meetinghouse or First Day school for two years. I shall be interested in the children's observations when we return. Kathryn is a pretty shrewd observer.

She read in the guidebook for Israel about the tradition that has developed of the young people walking from Tel Aviv to Jerusalem for the Passover. I am very interested, also, in what will be her reactions to that culture. Obviously, she has an attraction to Judaism, or thinks she does.

My husband will be so ready for vacation. The ambassador is most disgruntled about his leaving. He insisted that Jack Vaughn ask his concurrence and is giving it "with reservations." But two months is nothing. We would have left the first week of June anyway. John Bing, just here from Washington, reports that the anxieties about Walter's leaving are pouring in, and volunteers he talks with here, who bitched so much a year ago, are now worried about the new regime-to-be.

Better the devil you know, than the one you know not! Now that the worst is over, I feel rather amused by it all. It's like being a politician or a movie star. One day you are up; another, your box office is down. Right now, we are very popular — maybe just because we are leaving.

By the way, we found out that we are the only persons on post without health insurance. Washington does not take care of it. According to Walter, there was no need here, what with the dispensary. He will write when he gets home from Jalalabad.

Love for now, Jan

PHYLLIS HAS KEPT US EMOTIONALLY HOOKED INTO SCOTCH PLAINS

March 11, 1968
Kabul

Dear Phyllis,

Your letter came today just as I was getting nervous and about to write Karen concerning your welfare. We're quite certain we would have remembered one of your newsy letters, but we've heard nothing since Walter got back at Christmastime. After all, we read your letters several times. You alone have served to keep us emotionally hooked into Scotch Plains.

Save the *Times* articles. We leave in sixteen days and will be packed in six. I'm a little blasé about the idea of traveling now and really look forward more to seeing our old friends. You are right, Phyllis, Walter has given his all, day and night, seven days a week. He has been responsible for the lives and safety of more than two hundred young people spread out over a very primitive country. It is interesting how young people operate. They treat us much like parents. They complained so bitterly to the evaluator that they nearly got us fired, and yet now that we're leaving, they are all filled with anxiety.

Honey, although I do love your baking and it's sweet of you to think of it, I've had good homemade flat bread, pies, cakes, and cookies every day. In fact, to a large extent, I've lived on Anwar's excellent baked goods plus fruits, nuts and vegetables. I gave up on meat. What I look forward to is a fresh fish dinner with real coleslaw or a tossed salad, and a cup of Dannon's vanilla yogurt for dessert, which is interesting — because we do get good homemade yogurt here, made from powdered milk.

I'm convinced that I've had a balanced diet, because I really don't have cravings. Life has also been so meaningful. We have been so completely used up — our whole selves being demanded every day. I shall probably have some kind of nervous collapse when everyone departs by 8:30 AM, and there I am alone!

It is coming! Yes, these children will grow up — yours as well as mine. Yes, it was great being with Walter. I actually decided I might make it for the next fourteen years, although I'm sure I'll go back to crabbing with him about money, the housework, and what he isn't doing in the flowerbeds!

By the way, I sent the second newspaper article to my hometown paper in Portland, Maine, because I referred much to being a Down Easterner in the Middle East. Besides, the *Scotch Plains Times* never wrote back, even though they published it. Either the editor has changed or he never had a mother who taught him to write thank-you notes. Maybe letter writers are born, not made, Phyllis. Some people just can't "let go" on paper.

Terrific about Ricky's mother. I always thought her problem was to get away from her mother. I really don't think Mrs. B. knows how to let go. Perhaps she just reminds me too much of my own mother. It occurs to me now, how well my mother took this assignment. Possibly it's because it's my husband's work — a government assignment and a great honor. She has not voiced to me the fears and objections she did when I went away to college or to Jamaica.

I hope the United States holds together and we don't disembark into the middle of a garbage strike or a race riot.

Love,

Jan

I'VE ASSERTED MYSELF A GOOD BIT
OVER THESE TWO YEARS

March 20, 1968
Kabul

Dear Richard and Malvi,

The household effects, weighing a total of 3,000 pounds, and 556 pounds of airfreight are all in crates and boxes. We now have nine suitcases and two duffel bags filled with sleeping bags, to accompany us as far as Rome. Then we will ship our large suitcases to the boat. Kathryn has an airline flight-type bag, made of plastic on the bazaar, and has it all rehearsed how she can travel with it, her purse, and a cloth shoulder bag from India for her books. She used to watch Cheryl, who never had to check anything but just walked on board with her meager drip-dry wardrobe in one small bag.

The boys are not so clever. They will each struggle with a small suitcase and a small shoulder pack for things they collect. If they can carry it, they can buy it, but we are not going like pack animals.

In this regard, Kathryn and I talked about Malvi's money offer and decided it should go for a cuckoo-clock replacement and a new dirndl for her. We won't discuss it with the boys now. They each have a few dollars saved in their account books. Walter will let them draw it out in local currency wherever we are.

You will find that I have asserted myself a good bit over these two years, so you might as well be forewarned. I'm terribly interested in Richard's articles. My husband brings home the bacon, fixes broken electrical appliances and cars, and seasons salads.

The children now see how much work I used to do, so I have the understanding that they will have to work for what they get from now on. Kathryn is going to be given a monthly salary that includes the cost of clothing and will do her own selection next year. One can't learn too soon to manage money. She's really quite good about it. She was a real tough bargainer in the bazaar. In fact, we all look at *things* with a jaundiced eye now. I hope it lasts.

Malvi's trouble sounds a lot like what my mother's mother had. She finally had the necessary operation. She let it go for many years without consulting a doctor because she lived on a small island off the coast of Maine where there was a Christian Science meeting and practitioner but no doctor. Luckily, Blasses always consult doctors first, even though they don't always believe their advice.

I am very unhappy today. A woman never likes the "ruined nest". I'm competent, thank God, since Walter is useless or a nuisance (and luckily again out of town) at getting organized to move, but it tears me apart emotionally. Greg and I are going to Jalalabad tomorrow with Anisa and her family. The older two want to stay near friends and with their dad. I think we are taking our world tour at the last possible time that we could travel as a family unit. The older two and Greg have had great friction this year. See you at the boat dock in six weeks' time.

Janice

Final Trip with My Afghan Friends to Jalalabad

As mentioned in my last letter to Richard and Malvi, I was invited to spend a weekend in Jalalabad with Anisa and her family. In true Afghan fashion, they were most generous and hospitable to me, and I wish I could have returned it. During the summer, Anisa even lent me the key to their garden in Paghman so that I could take Walter there on his day off; however, he was not able to let go of his cares and enjoy the simple pleasure of just relaxing in a Persian garden beside a running stream, so we only went once together. Otherwise, I went with Anisa and her family and my children.

They also owned a two-room house in Jalalabad where they could enjoy the much warmer climate, particularly in winter when Kabul, at the altitude of Denver, was buried in snow. It was now early spring, and the rivers were flush with water from the melting snows. Rashid went on ahead in their small car with their three children.

Anisa and I followed in my VW with Greg as our chaperon. Greg was now seven and a half — and quite delirious to be the only sibling to go on this trip. Anisa confided that she'd offered a prayer for our safe arrival at the outset and promised to give alms to the first beggar she met. I wondered where she would meet one. I seldom saw a beggar in Kabul.

My mother had taught me the Twenty-third Psalm before I could read. I later memorized the Ninety-first, which I called upon when I felt in danger: "For he will give his angels charge over you to guard you and keep you in all your ways. On their hands, they will bear you up, lest you dash your foot against a stone."

I had a friend who felt panic on the switchback road as it dropped precipitously down a gorge from Kabul to sea level. Our family had driven it in the Peace Corps Travelall with Walter. I'd seen the wrecks that lie at the bottom of the chasm, and felt the VW would do just fine. I believed it was small enough to squeeze through any space an Afghan driver, who believed it was written on his forehead the day he would die (thus negating any need for caution), might leave in passing us on a blind curve.

We arrived safely. Nevertheless, a challenging drive, I find, is always — to use a Shakespearean phrase — a provoker of urine. As soon as we arrived, I asked to use the facilities. It was a traditional *tashnob* built in the wall of the house, clean and well kept, emptying into the street so the farmers could access it for fertilizer. When I emerged, their oldest son, who remembered life in London, was red in the face and blurted out, "I bet you wish you were back home in your nice house in Kabul right now." I informed him that I grew up with such a toilet and said, "Not only that, we didn't have special people to clean them out. I remember when my father had to do it." I don't know whether he believed me.

We all walked over to the river. Gregory fashioned a boat out of a board and a piece of string and ran barefoot back and forth in the sandy-bottomed shallows, delighting in being "at the beach." Then we visited a fair on the outskirts of town where there were booths of food and many men doing various contests of strength. In fact, I noticed that Anisa and I were the only women until a Peace Corps volunteer showed up, and she walked back to the house with us.

The house had a small garden with a well. All compounds had a well, but Anisa instructed me to bring my own water. Since I was leaving the country within days, I felt that was most thoughtful of her and complied.

She and I had a quite humorous discussion one afternoon about the bad taste of water in some American cities. She laughed as she related her trip to Washington, D.C., with her husband. "We tried a different restaurant every night," she told me, "hoping to find one that had a well with good-tasting water." She was offended but perhaps more disillusioned, however, that the Peace Corps volunteer asked to share my water. "She's Peace Corps. She should drink our water," she complained afterward.

All the furniture needed in a typical Afghan home was carpets and *toshaks*. Toshaks are mats that double as couches in the daytime, beds at night. In the evening, a pack of cards was produced as we sat on the toshaks and attempted to discover a game we all knew. I had last played cards as a child during rainy summer afternoons on the Island — simple games we too sat on the floor to play. Anisa was obviously disappointed that I did not at least know how to play Hearts. I could follow her dance steps, which amazed her, but I was a dud at cards. Clearly, if I were returning for another tour, I would at least learn Hearts.

At bedtime, the toshaks were placed in rows. The boys slept in one room and the adults with the baby girl slept in the other. There was something so secure and comforting about sleeping with the whole family. I awakened slowly with the morning light. The street vendors calling their wares, the rattle of the horse carts keeping time with the jingling of the harness bells signaled a new day — one of my last in the Kingdom of Afghanistan. When I head Gregory's joyous laughter from the next room, I knew it was time to get up.

The family decided to return to the fair we had visited the previous afternoon, while I decided to drive around and say goodbye to Dr. Zeke, our prime volunteer, who headed a team of doctors that had started a doctor-training program. His daughter and Kathryn were good friends. Dr. Zeke was at home with one of the other doctors, but the wives and children had also gone to the fair. When Zeke saw my VW, he got a wild glint in his eye and said, "You know, Janice, a VW can go anywhere a jeep can travel." He had no access to wheels other than the local horse carts.

He harbored a secret wish to visit the nomads and offer treatment in the manner James Michener described in his novel *Caravans*. The nomads were camped for the winter on the outskirts of town a few miles away. I agreed to drive, and the two men picked up their boxes of medications at the hospital.

It took very little time to bounce over the trackless rocky ground and traverse some shallow streams to arrive at the foot of a hill, where we parked. I could not see any black goatskin tents. Perhaps, I thought, the nomads lived for the winter in more permanent structures — out of sight. We expected that the men would be at the fair but knew that, in any case, the nomad women were quite independent and did not wear the veil. Zeke informed me on the drive over how the chadri made a perfect examination tent. "When a woman wants to be examined," he said, "she just grabs my arm and pulls it right over our heads."

Right away, a lone woman appeared at the crest of the hill inspecting us as she slowly walked to the stone wall where Zeke and Bob had set down their boxes of supplies. It took very few minutes for the word to spread, and soon they were surrounded by women all demanding attention at once. When later arrivals couldn't push into the circle, they came to me where I remained leaning against the car. They pulled on my arm, all the while using that intense eye talk women in the East are so good at.

Couldn't I make a path to the doctor for them? The "clinic" was all over in less than fifteen minutes. I could always see Zeke's head, for he was six foot four; now I saw the box of meds atop his head as the doctors pushed their way back to the car. We sat inside until the disappointed women dispersed. As I turned the car back toward town, Zeke sighed, "It seemed a lot easier in *Caravans*."

On the drive back to Kabul, Anisa described the traditional spring drink she would soon be making. All their many varieties of dried fruits and nuts would be soaked together for several days, but we were due to leave before it would be ready.

Parting is always a sad time, but I like to remember the words of a song my Japanese Hawaiian friend taught me: "In order to meet, you have to part." I felt we would meet again.

In leaving Afghanistan when we did, spring followed us all the way to England. First we enjoyed the Afghan spring, when the earth was covered briefly with tender blades of grass — soon to be consumed by the many sheep and goats. Everywhere, wild tulips and lilies in shades of deep red and purple sprouted from the stony ground. Out in the countryside, little children clutched huge colorful bouquets they wanted to sell you. In the fall, they had run beside the car calling, "*Toot, toot*" — not, as I supposed, imitating the car, but announcing they had mulberries (*toot*) in their baskets.

My Farsi instructor told me that the villagers made a cake of dried mulberries and that it was sometimes the only food they had in winter. Recently, I found packaged dry mulberries in a health-food market. The blurb on the package told of their being a food that accounted for the sound health and long life of mountain people in the Caucasus. I wanted to taste them and did. At the same time I wondered why we have to take over every good thing that other people depend upon.

On our family's last outing, we passed a very small boy clutching a large colorful bouquet. Walter stopped the car and got out his camera. The child hoped to sell us the flowers, but Walter first wanted a picture. Afterward, he gave the boy the coins and told him that he could keep the flowers. "We will have the picture," he told him. We still do.

Airport farewell to American and Afghan friends

Back in New Jersey, raking fall leaves

CHAPTER SEVENTEEN

Returning Home, Reentry,
and Reconfiguration

UPSTATE NEW YORK, 2006

Departure Day: My Most Treasured Gift
of Spinach Seeds from Anwar

There is a saying that we truly only see a place upon arriving or departing. Although it is a generation or more since that spring day in 1968 when we passed through our compound gate in Kabul for the last time, those last moments are still alive in me.

Christopher, relaxed as always, was sitting in an easy chair fingering a set of Afghan prayer beads, gift of Anwar, while everyone else was running around on last-minute details. He really had the body language down pat. I should have known then he would be the only one of the three who would return to live and work in Asia.

Anwar had a son too. As is the lot of servants, Anwar probably saw more of Christopher than he did of his own child. On evenings when Walter was away, Anwar waited until Bhaktari returned from his dinner in the bazaar before coming to say good-night. One evening, Chris crossed the room and put his arms around Anwar's neck, speaking, ever so softly, "Papa." Anwar's eyes moistened.

I hoped for the best for Anwar. I reluctantly let him go early so that he could get a good job — I thought — with the new Peace Corps staff couple who lived across the river on the far side of town. They needed someone immediately. Still I was worried. The new couple was used to overseas living, and I feared they had the attitude I'd heard expressed so often by old-timers, "Too bad the British didn't conquer Afghanistan. Then someone would know how to serve."

Anwar reminded me of my father, another enormously proud yet modest man, a caretaker and a person who had more talent than many others but forced by life's circumstances to live modestly. Somehow we connected across our cultural boundaries and could treat one another with respect. I wanted to give him something, so when he asked if he could buy my pressure cooker, I gave it to him as a farewell gift. Even more valued was the chit, a letter of recommendation to add to his collection, kept in a well-worn, closely guarded envelope.

Bhaktari did not receive a letter of recommendation. Walter had fired him on the spot just days earlier.

Walter had the habit of leaving his large bunch of keys next to the telephone in the reception room, where we were all gathered. In the event he received an emergency phone call, the keys were handy and the vehicle just outside the gate. Early one morning, he received a phone call from a Marine security guard at the embassy. "Mr. Blass, I followed your houseboy driving a Peace Corp Travelall to your door early this morning." Bhaktari was summoned. He looked hung over. His eyes were bleary, his speech slurred. Walter marched him to the vehicle, pointed to a forgotten woolen scarf and the dusty footprints on the seats where his friends had squatted. "You're fired," Walter proclaimed, and left abruptly for the office.

I turned to Anwar. "He looks like someone who had too much *whiskeygin*" (Afghans run these two words together). "Don't know, Memsahib." I suspected he did know, and continued, "Back home we'd make him some strong coffee. Do whatever you have to do to wake him up."

About an hour later, a wide-awake smiling Bhaktari was outside my room asking to tell his story. Surely Mom would go to bat for him. He said that a friend had come to his room and implored him for a ride to the hospital. Later, they met some other men, and he was given what he called *charss*: hashish, evidently. Bhaktari described how the colors on the compound doors, as he drove everyone home, kept changing. I knew just enough Farsi to understand the gist of his story. He repeated, "I brought it back, the car," and pleaded to be able to stay. I tried to explain that the vehicle was not ours, but belonged to the United States government, and lectured him on how lucky he was not to have damaged it under the circumstances.

I felt it was important that someone speak to him in depth in his own language about the gravity of his act so I called Anisa, who said, "Send him to me." She also told him how lucky he was and added, "She could have you put in prison." I wanted nothing to do with the police after I'd been wrongfully identified as a hit-and-run driver, but I made it clear to Bhaktari that in this case Walter was the final authority. Bhaktari would be in deep enough trouble without a written recommendation from us, his first employers.

Anwar might have been late to his new position that morning he came to bid us farewell. He smiled weakly and said that his new place across the river was far from home. "I know," I replied. "It's the only one I could find." Then he brightened and offered me a small packet folded from a sheet of Arabic-script newspaper. I peered inside and found some bumpy seeds that looked almost like beads. "What are they?" I ask. "Spinach seeds," he replied with a knowing grin.

It was one of my most treasured gifts, even though I never got to plant them because we moved into a house in the woods. Every so often, I would open the packet and remember that other land and those I had gotten to know and love while there.

The moment came to be driven to the airport. How many times must I have driven Walter for his many trips back to the States or to regional directors' conferences. Once I'd grumbled, "Be careful what you say about what it's like to live in this country. You've really been more of a commuter."

Leaning against the wall next to our front gate was the children's little red wagon. Unbeknownst to me, while I was busy packing, the children had filled the wagon with toys and given them away on the street. "We felt like such big shots," Kathryn told me years later, "but then we knew we had other toys at home. On the other hand, my Afghan playmate, who had so little, taught me the meaning of true generosity when she slipped one of her bangles on my wrist."

Now, at the last moment, Kathryn grabbed the handle of the wagon and ran into the street looking for one of her friends, but they were all in school. The street was empty except for a toddler emerging from the compound across the street that housed an extended family. He looked, for all the world, like the one I'd overlooked the previous spring when I gave out the motora hord, the little cars. Kathryn placed the wagon handle in his hand and indicated that it was now his. He looked at her blankly for a split second and then turned and bolted with it into his compound before she might change her mind.

YOU'RE GOING OUT HIGH, WALTER,
AND THAT'S THE WAY TO GO

March 28, 1968
Teheran, Iran

Dear Malvi and Richard,

I just wanted to tell you about your son's last days as Peace Corps director and how much, in this political kind of world, one has to ride out the bad days as well as the good. As John Bing put it, "You're going out high, Walter, and that's the way to go!"

The ambassador gave a reception for the three directors: past, present and future. The relationship between Walter and the ambassador has been one of mutual esteem and affection. I bought a print for him of an Afghan horseman charging full tilt, carrying a tent-pegging lance, and Walter signed in his child's German, which gave Neumann a chance (as Walter accurately predicted) to indulge in his Richard-type teasing. "I always knew you were a talented man, but it takes real talent to make four mistakes in a five-word line."

Several groups gave dinners or farewells for him. At the farewell staff dinner, when Cedric presented the gift, a lovely marble platter and embroidered tablecloth, he spoke with genuine gratitude for Walter's friendship and leadership during the two years.

Walter's reply, with his predecessor and his successor looking on, was pure poetry, and came from his center, from a deep inspiration that comes infrequently, even in Quaker Meeting. It flowed, I believe, because of the experience we went through this winter, and the discipline and loyalty Walter maintained and kept to himself when under fire. I'm going to seal this letter rapidly because Walter can get swelled-headed, and then he is unbearable. I'm glad for all that happened: the good and the bad.

The send-off at the airport this morning was an expression of genuine sadness on the part of our many friends, American and Afghan. Even the children were sad to be leaving the experience of being part of a small community but part of an idealistic effort. Walter, in his words that night, honored the one who began and the one who will continue the effort that Kennedy set us upon. He also quoted the Talmud: "Yours is not to finish the task — neither to desist from doing it."

Richard, I shouldn't say it, but I feel your son grew just a little bit taller because you would have quit, and he didn't. He played the heavy roles when they were called for, and he played the lighter ones when the times changed. One of the girls spoke of how moved she was when he took Sheila down the aisle. "It seemed so fitting. As head of the Peace Corps, he is like our father." Fathers have to stand there: to be resented, fought against or sometimes sought for advice, and missed when they leave.

Hope Malvi has found some relief for the facial pain. My grandmother suffered from something similar almost twenty years ago. There must be more help for it today. She eventually had a facial nerve cut. We need to rest now.

With love, Janice

UPSTATE NEW YORK, 2006

The Spring That Lasted Six Weeks

Because we needed to take things slowly, to readjust and decompress, Walter and I designed a six-week trip home. I always say we followed spring in our travels from Kabul, through Israel, Italy, Austria, France and England, finally arriving in rural New Jersey where the dogwood was in bloom. The first two weeks were spent visiting Walter's relatives, first in Tel Aviv and then Jerusalem, where we participated in the first Passover after the Six-Day War. I have always loved ritual, and our children were excited to be meeting their cousins. Walter was restless and eager to move on, but then that was his style, always wondering what was over the next hill. He became agitated after a few days in Jerusalem and couldn't wait to leave. He was definitely not a candidate for living in a theocratic state.

We flew to Rome and from there rode second class on the trains until Salzburg, Austria. We were scheduled to rendezvous with Isabelle in Florence. She was on sabbatical from her college teaching and accompanied by her five children. Her husband Jason would join them after we arrived in New Jersey to occupy their house for six weeks. Before reaching Florence, our family stayed in Venice for several days. Long before we arrived in England, our last stop, we began to tire of being on the road — feeling essentially homeless.

It was while the five of us were exploring Venice on foot that Gregory broke down. We had just come to a park where some children were playing and riding bikes. We had taken to Kabul an old bike that had been Kathryn's, and Greg rode it almost every day. When we departed, we left the bicycle behind with Anisa's children. Now Greg suddenly sat down on the curb with his head in his hands, fighting back tears. We all gathered around him feeling his sadness. Finally he spoke. "I'm homesick, but I don't know whether I'm homesick for Afghanistan or New Jersey. I can't remember New

Jersey." In the silence that followed, we realized we were all feeling, "Where is home now?"

Afghanistan was still unknown territory when we came home in the spring of 1968. Our country was involved in a war in Southeast Asia, and Afghanistan would not become a subject for nightly news bulletins or talk shows until we began to bomb it.

During our first months back, unpacking our two hundred cartons from storage and creating a new home for us occupied my time and required my energy. In August, I turned on the television during the Democratic National Convention in Chicago in time to view a startling episode of the police breaking up a demonstration. Although the lighting was poor, it seemed to me that a young man being beaten was one of our returned volunteers.

A year later, the memory of that scene galvanized me to join a busload of Quakers leaving from New York City to go to Washington, D.C., for the first large peace protest against the Vietnam war. If the police were going to beat up our sons and daughters, I felt the parents needed to be there. I was not alone in that thinking, for on our bus were mostly middle-aged folks like myself. My seatmate turned out to be an old friend, whose father was a rear admiral. We'd first met in 1949, when I'd worked in New York City as a young woman.

I never got near enough to the stage to hear the speeches, but I retain some powerful memories from the event: walking across the river from Arlington National Cemetery around midnight carrying a candle and a card with the name of an American soldier who would not be coming home; calling out that name and dropping it into a large wooden coffin in front of the White House; being assigned to a school for a place to rest until morning; sleeping in the only remaining space in the chapel, which turned out to be under

332

the offering table for the mass. I awoke to see two pairs of polished black shoes next to my head and crawled out to stand in the circle for a folk mass. The two priests with whom we shared bag lunches afterward were also in town for the event. They apologized profusely, saying, "We didn't have the heart to wake you two ladies."

The whole event was a defining moment for me, even though I never again attended a large demonstration. I experienced a camaraderie so missing in suburbia but that I'd become used to in the Peace Corps, and once again, I came to realize that ordinary people were several thousand lightyears ahead of their leaders. It's a view I still hold.

As Greg first observed so long ago, our family story fits into one of two categories: Before Afghanistan or After Afghanistan. Our life in Kabul stood in between, as breathtaking and indescribable as her mountain ranges. Returning to New Jersey, like coming down from any high-altitude experience, was deflating. We did not slip easily into our Before Afghanistan grooves. It took time.

For Kathryn, reentry was challenging. "It was too hard to talk about this as I was going through it," she said later, "for we had developed a worldview that other kids couldn't understand."

"When we moved to Afghanistan with the Peace Corps," Kathryn said, looking back, "I was so excited about going to such a new and strange place that I don't remember missing home or my friends. After I had gotten over the time difference and my first attack of the Asian-style stomachache, I was ready to begin exploring my new surroundings. There were so many fascinating things going on, we never stopped exploring during the whole two years.

"I fantasized a great deal about how it would be to be an Afghan girl, and when we vacationed in Kashmir, India, and what was then Ceylon, I had the same longing to be a native girl. But one cold morning some of my illusions were shattered. I came out of a warm house all bundled up, having just had breakfast, when I saw my Afghan playmates scrounging through our garbage. They were picking out the oranges that we had squeezed and were eating the little bit of pulp that was left. A few of them had on only thin sweaters and plastic sandals. It was then that I began to realize that they might not have such an exotic life as I had imagined.

"When we came back to America, I had a painful time adjusting to a new school and making new friends. Because I was so miserable here, I was homesick for Afghanistan. Here time seemed to race by me, and I longed for the way time didn't matter in Afghanistan."

Christopher was a somewhat shy middle child in a family of intense personalities. He observed situations before jumping in and kept his own counsel. Before Afghanistan, his grandfather drove to the elementary school one day to pick him up and found him standing outside the playground fence looking in. How I wish Richard could have lived to witness Chris as a young man: choosing to work with Hmong refugees in Thailand — his first assignment in a lifetime of working for charitable organizations.

While we were in Kabul, Christopher always made his moves quietly without drawing attention to himself. Once home, Christopher seemed to adjust to life here through his music. Back in New Jersey, he lost no time in catching up with the Beatles he had been introduced to by his Egyptian friend in Kabul. He let his hair grow long and learned to play the guitar. He became quite good at it and still delights me when I request not a Beatles song but Harry Belafonte's calypso, "Women Are Smarta."

Greg was the one who talked unabashedly about his experience and love for Afghanistan. Back in New Jersey, he entered third grade in the fall and made full use of the "show and tell" period. Before we knew it, he was asking Walter to arrange a cassette of slides for him to take to school. He invited me to come and bring his sister's fancy dress, with the embroidered mirror work and the silver jewelry, our friend Anisa had given her. I arrived to find the classroom deserted. Greg was on the stage in the all-purpose room giving a talk to the assembled third grades (all three of them).

As the Christmas holidays approached, he became disconsolate. Our family celebrated both Christmas and Hanukkah, but for him something was still missing. He came down to the kitchen late one evening as I was tidying up. "I'm never going to forget that country," he sobbed. He was homesick for Kabul and most of all missed the presence of animals everywhere. "If I want to see a camel, I have to go to the zoo. I just want to walk out in the street and see a camel."

Of all of us, Greg has always been the one most in touch with his feelings. He insisted I bring his Afghan toshak, his sleeping mat with its matching bright red quilt, back with us to New Jersey, and he slept on it on the floor for over a year. His Viennese grandmother would look in on him and skeptically inquire of me, "He likes that?" Only when spring came around again did he move into a "real" bed.

Five of us went to Kabul. Six came back. In fact Poopsie, our mongrel Afghan hound street dog, preceded us. She adapted to her new surroundings with great joy. In Kabul, she lived in a walled garden. In New Jersey, she played in the streets with the children and other dogs. As you might have guessed, she soon presented us with a litter of puppies.

We kept the male pup that looked most like her and named him Max after Maxwell Smart in *Get Smart*. He was lovable, but did not have his mother's intelligence. His mother had been the connecting link for us with Afghanistan. Max became the glue in our family as the children grew — each developing a separate ego and individual lifestyle while Walter and I drifted increasingly further apart.

There had always been one constant in our lives, and that was Maine. Now besides my parents to visit in Maine, we had Josh and Heidi, a Peace Corps volunteer couple who had met each other in Kabul. When I graduated from the University of Maine in 1950, there was such an exodus of graduates leaving the state at such an alarming rate that four college presidents met to confer on how to turn the tide. In 1968 on our first trip back to Maine, I was amazed to see how many old buildings young people were renovating. Josh and Heidi participated in the renaissance occurring in my home state by purchasing and upgrading an old farm. Kathryn and Chris, before they became acculturated enough to tackle Scout camps, spent a summer there learning farm chores. Gregory always chose the Island every summer over camp. There he became the son my parents never had, the recipient of their undivided attention and Dad's sole apprentice in learning to use carpenter tools and handle boats.

The seventies, then, was the decade when our family grew up. For Kabul, it was a time of increased westernization. Young men and women were dating. There were cinemas to attend. I remembered only one cinema in Kabul but learned recently that the Taliban destroyed sixteen after they came to power in the nineties. And the Intercontinental Hilton, which had begun construction before we left, was completed so that tourists had a familiar place to rest after a strenuous, not-to-be-forgotten trip to see the world's largest standing Buddhas in Bamiyan — also later destroyed by the Taliban.

Meanwhile, on the side of a small mountain that divided the capital city, the inhabitants still carried their water uphill or purchased it from a vendor who dispensed it from a goatskin slung around his shoulders. Why is it that modernization of basic services lags behind things like cinemas?

As Kabul was becoming more westernized, we in the West were being treated to an explosion of offerings from the ancient wisdom of the East. Today even in small towns there are teachers for a variety of martial arts, acupuncturists and yoga classes, but when I began to study and later teach *tai chi chuan* in the early seventies, I was a trendsetter in my New Jersey neighborhood.

It took time for me to find my niche back home. Before we'd left for our tour, I'd been evaluated for how well I might adapt to a hardship post. Walter, on the other hand, was amazed at how he had been hired with no supervisory experience, and surmised that it was part of the mystique of early Peace Corps that they trusted to luck. Miraculously, he discovered on the job a passion for mentoring that he pursued into his senior years.

If I had not worked previously with the Friends project in Jamaica, I would have had no basis for understanding how out of sync I felt when I returned to an affluent American community. The proliferation of items in the supermarket overwhelmed me. I could not remember the children's favorite ice cream. And where had all those flavors come from? I longed for the homemade ice cream Anwar produced in our hand-crank freezer.

In contrast with the profusion of manufactured items, the produce was often tasteless. If one wanted organic produce in 1968, one needed to grow it oneself. In Afghanistan, after I learned to be cautious with raw vegetables, we ate freely of the deep orange carrots, the leeks, spinach and potatoes, the many kinds of melons, grapes, pomegranates, oranges and nuts available in season in the many small stands. Back in New Jersey, the first time I served Chris a baked potato, he stared in disbelief. "This is a potato!" he exclaimed. White potatoes in Kabul had the color of old ivory like some of the heritage potatoes now available at farmers' markets.

Having those two hundred boxes to unpack and a home to put together was my saving grace after all. While Walter commuted to a company that had not fully expected him to return and now relegated him to a windowless office, I began to make use of the many hours I had alone for introspection.

Slowly, I accepted the inevitability that, given our dreams, we had gone to a place like Afghanistan, and that our original vision there had been so sorely compromised. In the end, I came to realize it is not so easy to change the world. I had experienced a sense of failure and was now disillusioned, angry, and impatient. In fact, the world seemed dark and dreary to me. What was there left to look forward to?

When our friend Isabelle finally said that she'd had quite enough of my lamentations, I began to realize that the only thing I could possibly change was myself, but old habits don't die easily. I needed some new ones. I cannot remember now who it was that

338

suggested I study tai chi chuan, but it was someone who knew I loved to dance, and she felt I would enjoy the movements.

I learned that there was a traditional Chinese master teaching at the Cathedral of St. John the Divine in New York City. He held the classes out in the garden in good weather, otherwise in the library. From the fall of 1970 on, I began to travel every week to the city to his classes and eventually he authorized me to teach beginning classes. I had classes in three locations. As far as I know, they were the first tai chi chuan classes in New Jersey.

The hours of practice made me physically stronger and infinitely calmer. In the winter of 1973–74, I spent many hours when I had the house to myself creating a dance from the tai-chi movements while I recited lines from Kahlil Gibran's poem on Love. "As Love crowns you so shall it crucify you. As love is for your growth so is it for your pruning" are some of the lines that still come to mind.

During the summer of 1974, I attended a Quaker conference at Pendle Hill. During Quaker Meeting for Worship, one sits and waits upon Spirit before speaking. This time, I spoke the poet's words as I danced. For years afterward, I was sometimes asked if I'd ever danced again in Meeting, but I never did. For in December 1974, I met the spiritual teacher that India described as one of her national treasures, and began to study meditation with him.

When I had asked Master Liu if he could teach me to meditate, he said that it would be dangerous for him to do so, for he had never "been to the mountaintop."

Swami Muktananda, the meditation teacher I would come to choose, was someone who had been to the mountaintop.

I learned that Baba, as he was called, was living currently in an old yeshiva on New York City's West Side and that he gave small group audiences (*darshans*) every morning at nine o'clock.

As I was agonizing about going to meet Baba even before reading his book, a friend who had met him advised, "You don't have to read his book first. Just be prepared for your heart to open." Ralph's words helped. In spite of this reassurance, I felt unprepared for this meeting, wondering what was the protocol for the situation — shades of my Foreign Service experience. When Baba's translator asked me if I had any questions, I simply blurted out my friend's advice. Then I added what was much on my mind at the time. "I just wonder if I'm not too old to let my heart open again." (I was forty-nine.)

When the laughter in the room died down, Baba, who had not laughed, said, "Your friend has meditated a great deal, and when you meditate, the heart is opened." As I walked back to my seat, I believe I must have looked just like the others I had been watching during the past hour, inexplicably sparkling like a grubby, reluctant child who had finally submitted to a bath.

I felt strangely at peace during the noon chant, although I also cried, and stayed for the vegetarian lunch that followed. As I walked down Broadway to the subway, the early-December scene that had seemed drab and colorless to me on the way uptown was now infused with light. Even a blackened banana peel I'd observed in the gutter on the way uptown seemed to be glowing. And on the inside, I felt that my heart was a fountain of joy.

I began getting up before dawn to meditate and found that often I couldn't stop laughing. During breakfast Chris, whose room was directly over the living room, my chosen spot to meditate, would look at me curiously and ask, "Do you always laugh when you meditate?"

As time passed and I pursued my studies of yoga philosophy, I began to realize that the Beloved addressed in the poems of the mystics resides not on the outside but inside one's own heart. I'd been circling my Beloved all along.

Sometimes one has to make a detour to connect the dots. One of the Quaker elders asked me when I returned from Afghanistan if I had met any Sufis, and I hadn't a clue what she was talking about. Then she gently explained that they were Muslim mystics and like early Quakers sometimes had to practice in secret. In due time, I would sit on a marble floor in Baba's ashram in India and listen to a group of Sufi mystics singing their love songs to the Beloved.

When the former Peace Corps volunteers began to write of their experiences in Afghanistan, I learned that ordinary Afghans knew reams of their poets' works by heart. Bill Witt, who later became a member of the Iowa legislature, described coming upon an illiterate ten-year-old Afghan boy sitting in a tree singing works of the Persian poets — poets like Rūmī, who was born in Balkh in northern Afghanistan in 1207.

After I read Bill's piece in *Worldview* magazine, I began to wonder if the shepherd we'd heard singing on the road outside Balkh might not have been singing one of Rūmī's poems.

The decade of the eighties was one of great changes. The Peace Corps volunteers were recalled from Afghanistan in 1979 after the American ambassador there was assassinated. The Russians invaded the country in December. Greg was home alone and told me afterward of seeing footage of Russian tanks prowling the streets of Kabul. "It looked like the Green Bazaar," he said, "and I thought I saw the alley where I used to buy two-af kites from a little old man." It was the first time this mother realized how far afield her youngest had ventured alone. It has taught me to remember that the future belongs to our children, and it is their innocence and trust that will lead the way.

I truly believed that the Russians would be defeated as much by the country itself as by the fierceness of its warriors. The British had tried twice to conquer Afghanistan and failed. The Afghans retrieved the cannonballs the British fired, hammered them into shape, and fired them back.

The Russians, however, had modern high-tech weapons that rained a form of death from the skies the Afghans could not send back. However, they eventually acquired the means to down the Russian helicopters. At least in one case, using traditional ingenuity, they turned one downed helicopter into a roadside teashop. Even more deadly were explosives that looked like plastic toys, and many children picked them up. When we first arrived in Kabul, there had been no plastic items in the bazaars.

My friends Anisa and Rashid became part of the Afghan diaspora. On a trip to England with Walter in 1980, we saw them briefly. Anisa insisted on preparing a meal for us, but her heart was weeping, and she went outside to talk with a friend who had just come from Kabul with the latest news. It didn't get any better. During the eighties and nineties, there were millions of Afghans living outside their homeland. I was surprised to discover there was now even an Afghan restaurant down the block from where I grew up in Portland, Maine. We lost contact with our Afghan friends for years and rediscovered them in Arlington, Virginia, after they had become American citizens.

Dr. Zeke, whom I had driven to visit the nomad encampment outside Jalalabad just before leaving, went to Pakistan to find some of his friends in the refugee camps. He brought back a discouraging story that was not really surprising when we remembered how important tribal alliances were. A young woman told him that she always sat between her husband and her brother so they wouldn't kill one another because each one was loyal to a different chieftain — chieftains now referred to as warlords.

Greg graduated from college in 1982. When I congratulated him, he turned the tables and said, "You're the one who's graduating, Mom." Then Isabelle confided to me that it was obvious to those watching on the sidelines that the marriage had been over for some time, but that I was the one who would have to make a move.

Baba once gave me a piece of advice that serves me daily. "Don't worry. Don't decide anything until the time comes." In 1982, the last child graduated from college and my recently widowed father remarried. Walter was soon to retire from his large corner office with the view across the Hudson and was already traveling to France several times a year reconnecting with his European roots and making contacts for his next career — teaching corporate management in various far-flung locations around the world.

The time had come for me to live out my own dream, expressed in my tearful outburst in India years before. I would spend a total of two years in India, not as a tourist but as a yoga student always in the same small village following the ashram schedule of meditation, chanting, and selfless service. In this way, I came to know not so much India as my own inner landscape.

In the end, Walter was able to be at peace with my decision. He was constantly on the go making new friends and dashing over the next horizon. Early in our relationship I'd told him that I needed time for my soul to catch up with me. Walter had said, "You can stand more of your own company than anyone I know." In truth, he was easily bored. Now, after some reflection, he surprised me by saying, "I always wanted a sister, and one of the things you've become for me is a sister."

Walter felt uneasy about meditation, although he was intrigued that I would go every week to a women's maximum-security prison to teach hatha yoga and meditation. Then there were times when he surprised me, and it seemed as if he had been reading over my shoulder. That sister/brother sentiment was straight out of a story Baba told that became a favorite of mine. A teacher asks his disciples, "How can you tell when the sun has risen?" The questions a spiritual master asks are always deceptively simple, but the students could not come up with an answer. Finally, the teacher says, "When you can look into another man's eyes and see a brother, when you can look into another woman's eyes and see a sister, then the sun has truly risen."

A measure of how dark things became in Afghanistan during the nineties were the stories of how the new Taliban government was treating women. It was no longer possible even to see women's eyes, for they were required to wear the chadri, now referred to as *bourka* or *burqa*, that covered them completely so that they looked out from a small square of latticework. This garment is now familiar to most Americans, but when we were in Afghanistan, many women in Kabul, the majority of the younger generation, wore only a simple scarf to cover their hair.

When I moved to upstate New York in the nineties, I was hoping I would see more of my friend Helen. She was retiring from teaching at a community college but then was suddenly off to Africa with Oxfam. On another assignment with the American Friends Service Committee, she traveled to North Vietnam to distribute prostheses. And then, she got in touch with me to report laughingly, "I'm following you to Kabul."

I would talk with her briefly when she was on home leave. She was always anxious to get back to her post and her small room in the Kabul Hotel, now severely run down from all the wars. Unlike many NGO directors, she lived simply, wearing *salwar kameez*, breakfasting every morning with her staff on naan and green tea.

This Quaker lady seemed unfazed by the Taliban. Although they forbade her to work or even meet with Afghan women in Kabul, there were areas of the country they did not control. I finally asked her how she handled contact with Taliban officials.

She described how she dressed for official interviews: black gloves, black walking shoes, black stockings, black slacks covered by a long black coat, and over her head and around her shoulders a black cloth. Only her face showed, partly concealed by her improvised head shawl. The official in his black turban sat sidewise so that he would not do the unforgivable — look at her directly, certainly not into her eyes where he could possibly discover a sister. Once on the street, her interpreter reported that as they descended the stairway from the second floor, the official had leaned far over the banister trying to get a forbidden glimpse of her face!

I have tried to understand the insanity of the ways of the new regime and finally chalked it up to reaction to the sudden invasion of western mores and the raising of a generation of young men by poorly educated mullahs in the *madrassas* in Pakistan. Then there were those sixteen cinemas. In the West during the seventies, there was a sexual revolution we all had to integrate. That was reflected in our movie fare. Today, I feel we have greater honesty and role sharing between the sexes, but we can't deny that we, too, have experienced a backlash against women and an increase in domestic violence.

It has been very exciting to read of the number of women who are now working today in Afghanistan. Not only Afghan women but western women and former volunteers from those early days.

I get my best information on Afghanistan today from the *Christian Science Monitor*, which I read every weekday, e-mails from former Peace Corps volunteers who have returned, and, best of all, recent films made by Afghans themselves. *Kandahar* is a film based on the true story by an Afghan woman who immigrated to Canada. Disguised in a chadri, she tries to enter Afghanistan from Iran in order to rescue a friend. The woman acts in it herself along with ordinary Afghan people in place of professional actors. It is deeply moving.

Women in Afghanistan is a documentary I viewed in 2005. It was produced by two young Afghan women studying filmmaking, traveling with their teacher. It is remarkable in many ways, not the least that the father of one of the women, who speaks in the film, trusted his daughter's teacher so much that he allowed her to travel across the country without a male relative.

The young women interview a woman in Herat who lost several family members to a misdirected American cluster bomb. How does one apologize for that?

They also visit the Hazarajat. We see the holes in the cliffs left after the Taliban destroyed the ancient Buddhas. Just as devastating are the holes created in families that have left so many widows and orphans. The Taliban sent busloads of their fighters to execute the Hazara men because they are Shiites.

Today there are signs of reintegration. Under the new government, Hazaras are now recognized as full-class citizens. Finally, I feel reassurance about Anwar's fate, and that of his people.

I hear, too, that one cinema of the sixteen destroyed by the Taliban is being reconstructed in Kabul so that in the future Afghans will be able to see films created by their own people.

Many times I've faltered in my resolve to finish this book, particularly when I've allowed myself to become discouraged by my country's broken promises and the excessive use of power by all sides in Afghanistan. Then I remember a saying my Jamaican coworker taught me — which I wish I could reproduce in the lilting Jamaican dialect: "When you have the will, you have not the way.

When you have the way, you have not the will." I have come to realize that change comes not from above but from ordinary people. For instance, the Afghan widow in the Hazarajat who was caring for so many orphans and walking miles to badger the authorities for supplies to feed them. And more recently an Afghan couple, both doctors, retired from many years in the States, who made the arduous overland journey to the Hazarajat. There, in the modern, well-equipped clinics established by the Hazaras, they offer their expertise in training the new generation of health-care professionals.

Best of all, there *is* the new generation. During the college graduations of 2006, a piece in the *Monitor* reported about three young Afghan women who were receiving degrees from Roger Williams University in Rhode Island. One of them has the intention that she will become the president of Afghanistan.

Katheryn and Janice, 1979

Walter in his Manhattan corner office, 1980

Afterwords

"We had incredible experiences;
some together, some alone.
Some strengthened our bonds,
some strained our bonds."

Kathryn Blass

CHRISTOPHER REFLECTS

Dear Mom,

It's been such a gift to be able to read all those letters you wrote while we were in Afghanistan. They brought back a lot of memories and began to give me some little understanding of what the experience must have been like for you. Of course as a child, I was completely unable to comprehend that! How much energy it must have taken to schlep three kids halfway around the world in 1966, and deal with all the challenges we encountered there. It truly was the most defining and influential period of my life, and I am so grateful for your making the sacrifice to give us that experience.

One of my earliest memories of the whole adventure was when the local newspaper reporters came to our house in Scotch Plains. I seem to remember there were both a man and a woman, and I thought they were Lois Lane and Jimmy Olsen from *Superman*. I was in awe of them. Then I was totally dismayed when they had us stage that photo that appeared in the newspaper, with us "trying to cram enough for two years" into what was actually an empty suitcase with only a single shirt hanging out the front. It was one of my first memories of having my illusions shattered.

That first plane trip was so exciting. Malvi and Richard gave Greg and me the little blue "flight log" books to record all our airplane trips. And we were allowed to go up into the cockpit to have the pilots fill in the books with all the flight information. It was a measure of the different time we lived in then.

Once we got to Afghanistan, there were a lot of lessons — not only about the dangers of drinking water straight out of the tap. One of my strongest memories is of being in a small shop in Kabul and slipping a penny piece of candy into my pocket. Out in the car I said aloud, "Gee, I wish I had a piece of candy!" Then I pulled out the candy from my pocket, feigned great surprise and exclaimed, "Wow, look!" Walter slammed on the brakes, drove back to the shop, and made me give the candy back to the shopkeeper and apologize for stealing it. I was in tears and dying of shame and guilt, and the shopkeeper was smiling and saying, "No, it's fine, he can have it." But Dad was intent on me learning a lesson.

There were also lots of adventures, some you didn't know about. One day I walked a long way, maybe down the whole length of the block, on top of the walls separating the housing compounds, with my friend Peter. We looked down into people's back yards. Some smiled and waved at us and others were extremely angry.

I have so many images from that time. They're still with me as vivid sensory impressions. The naan shop down the street from our house. The mud-brick building, the deep round pit in the ground with a fire at the bottom. The bakers slapping around the dough, shaping it into thin, flat ovals, using their fingernails to make little grooves in the top and then reaching down into the pit to slap it onto the side wall to bake. The smell of the godown, our locked pantry. Shelves lined with cans of tuna. The strong flavor of fresh pomegranate juice. Anwar letting me help make it, squeezing the pomegranate seeds though a nylon stocking.

And then all the people. Sitting in fourth-grade French class, about as multinational as they come. The cute Filipino girl in the other row. The Indian teacher who wore a sari. My friend Djamshaid, son of the Iranian ambassador: riding back from his house in the limo; how good he was at drawing tanks and soldiers. My Egyptian friend Ibrahim, putting on the first Beatles album I ever heard and telling me, "This is what is happening in America right now."

The animals that were everywhere around us. The servants showing me a small rodent in a large coffee can. I thought it was a hamster, something harmless and friendly, and cute . . . the next thing I remember was lots of blood, my mother furious with the servants, and having the rodent kept in a cage in the garden and fed for ten days to make sure it didn't have rabies.

Two or three young western girls carrying a small ragged-looking puppy down the street, looking for a home for it. I said, "I'll take it." It turned out to be a she. We ended up bringing her back to the States with us (probably at great expense) where she had a litter and we kept one of her pups.

More adventures. With my prize fishing rod, brought all the way from America, determined to catch a fish, even in a roaring white-water river of freezing glacier melt . . . Then in the Travelall on the way to Pakistan, my father suddenly slamming his fist down on the dashboard and shouting, "Damnation! I forgot the registration papers! We can't take the car across the border!" What an adventure it was to walk across the border and hitch a ride in an open truck the rest of the way to Peshawar.

The realities of the lives of the people in our neighborhood. How poor the kids across the street were. No shoes, ragged clothes, yet so happy. I was stunned to hear that they had taken the orange rinds from our garbage to eat what was left in them after I'd squeezed them for orange juice. I was amazed that they could be so hungry that they would do that. It's memories like this one that have steered some of my life decisions since.

Coming back to the U.S. was more of a shock to me than going to Afghanistan. I probably *expected* Afghanistan to be very different and to feel a bit out of place, but America was supposed to be "home." I can still remember the feeling of being brought into my fifth-grade class for the final month or so before summer vacation in 1968: "Everyone, this is Chris. He just came back from two years in Afghanistan." On top of my everyday shyness, I felt so out of place, like a stranger in my own country. I didn't feel I had anything in common with the other kids in the class.

In the end, that whole experience left me with a greater openness to and interest in foreign cultures and people, and a constant awareness of how many people in the world were "less fortunate" than we in the U.S. By the time I graduated from college in 1979 I had developed a desire to do something "socially redeeming" with my life. Then it took me quite a number of years to figure out what that might be.

I went overseas again in 1983, back to India and Nepal, since Afghanistan was still occupied by the Russians. Stepping out of the airplane at 3:00 AM in New Delhi, the smell of the air brought memories rushing back. The feeling of strangeness about the place and my place in it felt familiar. I did feel a little uncomfortable standing out as much as I did. People would see me coming half a block away and start hawking their wares.

Up in Kashmir I bought myself one of the local wool cloaks so I wouldn't attract so much attention, pulled on a wool hat, and would walk at night through the back streets and market. At six foot four I was still quite recognizable as a foreigner, but I could get much closer to what was going on and actually pass unnoticed by many people. It gave me more of a feeling of being there and being an anonymous part of what was going on.

I had some interest in working overseas, but absolutely no idea where or how to find work. A very long series of "coincidences" led me to Thailand, where I was offered a job in a refugee resettlement camp training Lao and Cambodian refugees for resettlement in the U.S.

It was the first time in my life I felt I was doing something worthwhile — and it helped me develop a sense of purpose in life. The training I received and gave in cultural orientation provided an opportunity not only to see my own culture from an outsider's point of view but also to learn about many different aspects of the cultures of my students and fellow teachers.

Looking back at how it all happened, I realize how as soon as I made the decision to be open to the possibility of going overseas, everything I needed came to me. Some of it was rather spooky — like the woman I chatted with in the departure lounge at JFK who asked if I had heard of the Experiment in International Living. I hadn't. But I jotted down their address, and five months later I was working for them on the other side of the world. When I came back to the States I went to their graduate school in Vermont.

I was surprised to find how much at home I felt in such a multicultural situation. It's as if the cultural diversity became a part of who I am. I am an American, most definitely, but also aware of how much any nationality or ethnicity is just an accident of birth, the veneer on top of much more basic human characteristics that · bond us all together.

Thank you for making that experience part of my childhood. It was a gift that has continued to benefit me throughout the rest of my life.

Love, Christopher

The Istalif Chest

THE LAST WORD

When we first began to work together, Ellen asked me, "Could you sit down now, with the snow falling all around, and talk about what your time in Afghanistan meant to you? And what led you to write this book?" The letters from Kabul, of course, were written a generation ago and lay in a box in my friend Phyllis's house until world events and the relentless eye of the media focused the public's attention on that part of the world. Now the places I describe leap out at the reader and suggest a familiar landscape. The people I describe are not warlords or terrorists but real people who occupy a permanent place in my heart.

I believe it was Shakespeare who wrote, "There is a power that shapes our ends, rough hew them how we may." If the letters had not surfaced I would be writing about the grandmothers in my family and how their hopes, dreams, and tragedies influenced me. Being able to reread my letters was much like what I expect finding a grandmother's journal would feel like. The immediacy of the letters and their timelessness brought me face to face with how they accurately and truthfully describe one portion of a lifelong journey of discovery that continued after we returned.

I have also come to the realization in working on this book that the most lasting relationships in my life have been with other women. No matter what culture we come from, there is universality to our experience as women that makes it possible for us to bond. A heart bond is elastic and strong. It reaches over the miles and over the years and endures even if the parties never meet again.

Not too long ago, I was able to talk on the phone with Anisa, who now lives in the D.C. area. When I asked her if she had made any friends there, remembering how much I enjoyed her friendship in Kabul, she replied, "Oh, there are people here from all over the world, but it's not like you and me."

As I write this final episode, it is fitting that it is late winter, for I am in the winter of my life. My hair is the color of the snow that still drifts down and covers the fields that surround the pond below the house and the upland meadow that stretches to the forest beyond. The snow will remain unsullied here in the glen until the spring sun melts it into a sea of mud.

It startled me to read some of my letters, to see how I really did know what my soul longed for even when I felt trapped in trying to be the perfect wife and feeling I was failing miserably. I am able now to live simply in a small house with a few of the things I treasure from our time overseas, some family pieces, and a minimum of clutter. I have a cardinal rule that when I make a new acquisition, something of equal size and weight must be discarded.

I came first to the Catskills in the summer of 1976 on a yoga retreat and thereafter every summer until 1992, when I moved into the ashram retreat center as a full-time participant. Sharing a room while following a monastery schedule is great preparation for deciding what is important in life. The October that I turned seventy I purchased this place in a cluster of a dozen others grouped around a little pond. From the hill behind us I can look down and imagine the longhouses of Native Americans who once occupied the land.

I do miss the ocean, and return every summer to the place our family always referred to as the Island — even though there are hundreds of islands off the coast of Maine. My life is centered here now, in the mountains. The hamlet has no traffic signal — only a blinker on Main Street. I fear that will soon change. Since 9/11 we have been discovered as a place to build second homes.

Where we lived last in New Jersey, I had no view of the sky as I had in Kabul or on the island of my childhood. Here I can watch the moon from where I lie in bed as she makes her stately passage across the heavens.

When I originally saw the billboard announcing this little enclave as a retirement community, I scoffed, "Who would want to retire there?" But here I am. The market dropped suddenly, and the community was never completed, so it has the feeling of a village.

The passage of time has mellowed me and nature is reclaiming the land that had been scraped of topsoil. First came the mosses and lichens, then the grasses, and eventually the pines that can thrive in sandy soil.

I grew up with pines in Maine, the Pine Tree State, and the pines have always been with me. In Kabul, their music in the wind transported me back to my island home. Here they move in as a witness to the regenerating power of nature. I help things along by scattering wildflower seeds. Every year we have more varieties.

From the home I shared with Walter, I have brought the Istalif chest — and it is the first thing people notice when they come into my house. It stands on four legs that rise above its level top surface to form posts. The wood is colored by someone's kitchen fire and smoothed by the touch of many hands. Anwar laughed when I told him how much I'd paid for it, because it is actually a bit wobbly. There were small copies in the bazaars made for tourists to carry home. This one is full-size and obviously belonged to someone. It has an ongoing history. When we gave Christopher a jackknife for his first birthday back in New Jersey, he tried to duplicate the decorative notched edging of the chest on the hardwood maple kitchen table.

Istalif was a village that nestled into a mountain on the road north of Kabul on the Shemali Plain. It always reminded me of some of the cliff dwellings in our Southwest, with its back protected by the mountain and facing the sun. Istalif was a tourist stop, known for its handmade pottery and animal figures covered with an exquisite turquoise glaze.

Because the clay crumbled easily, it was difficult to get these pieces home intact, but I successfully brought back three: a camel, a fat-tailed sheep, and an archaic horse. The horse's arched neck, I learned, is a Greek motif, concrete evidence of Alexander's passage through Afghanistan on his way to conquer India. It is another one of the many reminders of Afghanistan's long history of being invaded and its cities and villages turned to rubble.

Since our time there, there have been decades of fighting on the Shemali Plain and the land has been heavily mined. Recently, I was privileged to read some letters written by a Peace Corps volunteer from our time who married an Afghan. They returned after many years in exile to Kabul, where her husband is presently in the government. It was some time before it was safe for her to be driven out to the countryside. When she could, she visited Istalif and was astounded by what she saw. Just as quickly as a strip of land was cleared of mines, the people were repairing the grapevines, making sun-baked bricks from the earth, and rebuilding their homes. She marveled how much they were accomplishing by their own sweat and considered how much more a man could do with fifty dollars. She concluded that if Afghanistan can somehow be sustained for five years, there is hope for all of us.

In my house, the Istalif chest sits in front of the bay window that looks out into my pocket-sized secret garden. Here amongst the flowers stands a bronze replica of the *Nataraj*, the dancing Shiva, the image of a Hindu deity purchased from Muslim entrepreneurs in the bazaar in Mumbai. His dance represents the cycles of time — time on the cosmic scale as well as time as we experience it in our own lives: creation, preservation, destruction, concealment, and revelation.

I was twenty-eight when I got married and there were twenty-eight years of marriage. Those who know some astrology will recognize the pattern. Every twenty-eight years, the planet Saturn returns to the position in our natal chart it occupied at the time of our birth. It is a time of challenge to move on gracefully or stay stuck. The third Saturn return, they say, is the time to prepare for death.

For my seventy-fifth birthday, I took a meditation Intensive. Gurumayi Chidvilasananda, the radiant woman Baba left to carry on his teachings, was leading it. Before meditation, we chanted *Om*. One thousand voices following her rich contralto rolled inside the hall like ocean waves.

When we became silent and entered meditation, I had one of those rare illumined images appear on my inner screen. On the screen, I see my three children sailing a boat out to sea behind the Island and realize they are going to scatter my ashes. That is my wish — to return to the sea, or as the Native Americans say, to Grandmother Ocean.

JUL 2 3 2008 DATE DUE		
AUG 0 1 2008		
SEP 0 3 2008		
SEP 2 7 2008		
NOV 1 2 2008		
DEC 1 0 2008		
JUL 1 7 2009		
BPC 1/13		

ISBN 142511349-4

9 781425 113490